THE MATRIX CONTROL SYSTEM OF PHILIP K. DICK

AND

THE PARANORMAL SYNCHRONICITIES OF TIMOTHY GREEN BECKLEY

Introduction by Tessa Dick

By Timothy Green Beckley, Sean Casteel, Philip K. Dick
With Tim Swartz, Brad Steiger, Nick Redfern, Diane Tessman,
Valerie D'Orazio, Brent Raynes, Cynthia Cirile,
Hercules Invictus, Joseph Green

THE MATRIX CONTROL SYSTEM OF PHILIP K. DICK
AND
THE PARANORMAL SYNCHRONOCITIES
OF TIMOTHY GREEN BECKLEY

INNER LIGHT/GLOBAL COMMUNICATIONS

The Matrix Control System of Philip K. Dick

And The Paranormal Synchronicities of Timothy Green Beckley

Contributors: Tessa Dick, Timothy Green Beckley, Sean Casteel, Philip K. Dick, Tim Swartz, Brad Steiger, Nick Redfern, Diane Tessman, Valerie D'Orazio, Brent Raynes, Cynthia Cirile, Hercules Invictus, Joseph Green

Copyright©2017 Timothy Green Beckley Publisher,
Inner Light/Global Communications, All rights reserved.

No part of these manuscripts may be copied or reproduced by any mechanical or digital methods and no excerpts or quotes may be used in any other book or manuscript without permission in writing by the Publisher, Inner Light/Global Communications, except by a reviewer who may quote brief passages in a review.

Timothy Green Beckley Publisher, Inner Light-Global Communications

Published in the United States of America

Global Communications, Box 753, New Brunswick, NJ 08903

Staff Members: Timothy G. Beckley, Publisher

Carol Ann Rodriguez, Assistant to the Publisher

Sean Casteel, General Associate Editor

Tim R. Swartz, Graphics and Editorial Consultant

William Kern, Editorial and Art Consultant

Cover Art By Carol Ann Rodriguez

Sign Up On The Web For Our Free Weekly Newsletter and Mail Order Version of Conspiracy Journal and Bizarre Bazaar.

www.conspiracyjournal.com

PayPal: mrufo8@hotmail.com

COVER ARTIST CAROL ANN RODRIGUEZ CONTEMPLATES PKD

Cover Art By Carol Ann Rodriguez

When I was a young teenager, I read mostly science fiction books for my recreational needs. I don't remember most of the titles or authors. However, Philip K. Dick is one name that stands out in my memory, not just because of the wonderful films, such as **Blade Runner,** based on his works, but also because of his kind of magical creativity which transcends time and reality. His works have relevance in our world today.

I drew PKD as I see him, conjuring up stories from some secret dimension.

Perhaps the unicorn, which in **Blade Runner (*Do Androids Dream of Electric Sheep?*)** symbolizes the fact that Decker himself is a replicant, really symbolizes the idea that Dick himself isn't exactly a regular person. Perhaps he has returned to some dimension where creative geniuses dwell and is looking down upon us, amused by what we are saying about him.

CONTENTS

INSIDE THE ELECTRIC MIND OF PHILIP K. DICK 11

ARE WE LIVING IN A COMPUTERIZED SIMULATION? 19

VALIS AND THE DIVINE 'CLOSE ENCOUNTERS' OF PHILIP K. DICK 43

PHILIP K. DICK'S PHYLOGENIC MEMORY AND THE DIVINE FIRE 57

A THOUGHT NOT MY OWN 65

THE UBIK OF REALITY 71

IT'S A SMALL WORLD, OTHERWISE KNOWN AS "SIX DEGREES OF SEPARATION" 81

MY SYNCHRONISTIC FRIEND 89

THE BIG BANG THEORY 95

ARIZONA: LAND OF ENCHANTMENT – AND A MILLION SYNCHRONICITIES TO BOOT 107

WHEN "FICTION" MIRRORS "REALITY" 125

AFTER DEATH SYNCHRONICITY SYNDROME 137

UFOs – A JOURNEY TO THE AFTERLIFE 161

SYNCHRONICITIES OF A "FAMOUS MONSTER" 185

RAYMOND FOWLER, THE PHILIP K. DICK OF "UFODROME" 203

SYNCHRONICITIES AND THE CONTACTEES 231

DIVINE INVASION: "ALIEN CONTACT" IN THE 1970s 239

SYNCHRONICITIES WITH A PERSONAL TOUCH... 253

A QUESTION AND ANSWER SESSION WITH MARIE D. JONES 259

DIARY OF AN UNHINGED MATRIX MASTER: SECTOR ONE 269

RETHINKING THE POSSIBILITY OF AN EMULATED WORLD 293

GAMES OF THE GODS 303

WHAT IS OUR 3-D REALITY COMING TO? 313

DIARY OF AN UNHINGED MATRIX MASTER: SECTOR TWO 333

ONCE UPON A MAD LITTLE WORLD 375

NOVELS BY PHILIP K. DICK 411

MOVIES BASED ON PHILIP K. DICK BOOKS AND SHORT STORIES 428

A PLAY BASED ON THE IMAGINARY THOUGHTS OF PHILIP K. DICK 432

Mr. Dick in an early reality.
Photo courtesy Tessa Dick.

1.

INSIDE THE ELECTRIC MIND OF PHILIP K. DICK
By Tessa Dick

TIM Beckley has a firm handle on the nature of the strange incidents that occurred in the life of my husband, Philip K. Dick. Whereas many writers have chosen the easy way out, offering explanations ranging from epilepsy to drug abuse, Beckley has dug deep into the story of Phil's life and unearthed evidence that such things really do happen to many people. While Phil often questioned his own sanity, I observed many of the seemingly paranormal events that began in 1974. Moreover, he had similar experiences throughout his life, beginning in early childhood when he imagined that his twin sister had survived. Jane passed away at the age of six weeks, but Phil pretended to play with her when he was left alone to amuse himself. Jane became very real to the young boy, and he hoped that she would reincarnate so he could meet her as an adult.

His mother's sister, Aunt Marion, was a trance medium, so Phil was no stranger to psychic phenomena. Around 1960, Phil saw a vision of an iron mask on the horizon, lit up by the setting sun. He associated that mask with Wagnerian opera. It became the inspiration for his novel ***The Three Stigmata of Palmer Eldritch***. Also in the 1960s, Phil and his then wife Nancy attended several séances in which Bishop Pike was trying to contact his dead son, Jim Jr. Phil said that some kind of spirit appeared, but it was not Pike's son. In fact, he thought that it was something evil. Pike's secretary,

Phil and Tessa Dick, 1973

Sharing a hug with an award-winning author.

with whom Pike was having an affair, woke up in the morning with straight pins stuck under her fingernails. When Phil got home and unpacked his bag of clothing, he found that his briefs had been replaced with an enormous pair of women's bloomers.

The above represents only a tiny fraction of Phil's experiences with the strange and fantastic.

We lived in poverty, renting apartments at first, and then renting a little house in Fullerton, California. Phil had lost everything when he fled to Canada after the hit on his house. When he got a check for a few thousand dollars in royalties from French translations of his books, he bought a used sports car. That little red Fiat Spyder was cute but not very practical. In fact, Phil had trouble driving it because the pedals were so small and close together. Fortunately, we still had my old Dodge Coronet 500, a big boat of a car.

Finally, about a year before his death, Phil received a substantial payment for the movie rights to his novel **Do Androids Dream of Electric Sheep?** It eventually became the movie **Bladerunner**. He paid off the mortgage on his condominium apartment, and he bought a brand new Mercury Capris. Beyond that, he did not spend extravagantly. He gave to the local Episcopal Church, "adopted" a child through the Christian Children's Fund and sent money every month, and gave to a variety of charities. He also established small trust accounts for his children.

Phil did not like the first screenplay for **Bladerunner**, and he told Ridley Scott that he was going to trash it publicly. After David Peoples was brought in as a script doctor, however, Phil was satisfied that the film would be more than shoot-outs and car chases. Phil saw the rough cut of the movie, and he said that he especially liked the scenes with the origami animals.

He never saw any of the other movies that have been made from his work. The Wachowski brothers said that their film **The Matrix** was inspired by Phil's books, but they did not buy any rights to his work. **Minority Report** is very good, although it does not follow the plot of Phil's story. However, Tom Cruise is simply too good-looking to be a hero in Phil's work, where ordinary people take center stage. Nicholas Cage, who starred in **Next**,

Tessa stands by her man: PKD.

is more like a Phil Dick hero, even though the film departs substantially from Phil's story **The Golden Man**. In fact, most of the movies simply use Phil's stories as window dressing for explosions and car chases. The one shining exception is **Radio Free Albemuth**, which John Alan Simon and his wife produced on a shoestring budget. It tells a fascinating story and is well worth watching, despite the lack of blood and gore, bombs and bullets. That film, like the book on which it is based, tells us that we are living in a police state where we have no real choice in our own lives. The government controls our lives and our very thoughts. That was Phil's story, and the film tells it very well.

Phil always told stories, especially when he was recounting the tales of his own life. He exaggerated and embellished, and he rarely told the same story twice. That having been said, he did have some very real experiences. His house was smashed and trashed. He was abducted by men in black. And he did have what he termed the "pink light" experience. He did tell me, while he was in a trance of some sort, that our baby had a hernia. It was not an immediate emergency, and we did not rush to the hospital, but we did take our son to the doctor, and the doctor did diagnose a hernia. Four months later, our son had surgery to correct the hernia. Phil told the story that we had to rush our baby to the emergency room, but that was only a story.

He told stories for a living, and he told stories for fun. He took the little anomalies of our world and spun them into alternate realities. He also warned us of the police state in which we live. The Nazis won World War II, and the Empire Never Ended. We must wake up and see the world as it is, not as the media present it to us. Behind the propaganda, this world is all about control. Various factions that hold wealth and power are fighting for control. They fight each other, and they fight us. We must remain forever vigilant, and we must hope for help from the entity that Phil named VALIS, or from God. His novel **The Man in the High Castle** is more reality than fantasy. Through Operation Paperclip and other, lesser-known programs, about a thousand Nazis were brought to the United States. About the same number went to the Soviet Union. They infiltrated our intelligence agencies, and they concocted the Cold War to distract us from the Nazi takeover of our institutions of government and education.

Philip K. Dick warned us. His predictions of our future are coming true, one by one, in a horrifying progression. We must take heed. We must wake up. We must take back our national, local and individual sovereignty. We must put an end, once and for all, to the Empire.

SUGGESTED READING:

TESSA B. DICK: MY LIFE ON THE EDGE OF REALITY

MAN WITHOUT A PAST

PHILIP K. DICK, REMEMBERING FIREBRIGHT

THE OWL IN DAYLIGHT

www.TessaDick.com

Tessa celebrates the release of "My Life On The Edge Of Reality."

Tessa's book on Philip is certain to open the floodgates of memories.

2.

ARE WE LIVING IN A COMPUTERIZED SIMULATION?
ACCORDING TO PHILIP K. DICK, WE ARE!

By Timothy Green Beckley

SOMETIMES we come smack dab face-to-face with events in our lives that we can't come close to explaining.

September 11, 2002, was the first anniversary of the terrorist attacks on the World Trade Center. On the live television broadcast of the New York State Lottery for Sept 11, 2002, the numbers that were drawn in EXACT ORDER were 9-1-1. Over 5000 people picked this number on this particular day. This has to be more than a coincidence as one would think that the number of winners is higher than average!

And, as far as the attack on the WTC itself goes, we have the following set of synchronicities that we must account for if we are being "rational" about the situation (which we are not about to be I can assure you).

The President of the U.S. - George W. Bush has 11 letters.

The President's Plane is – Air Force One – has 11 letters.

The U.S. Secretary of State – Colin Powell – has 11 letters.

Osama bin Laden's birthplace is – Saudi Arabia – and it has 11 letters.

The suspected base of the terrorists is – Afghanistan – has 11 letters.

One of the hijackers was a pilot – Mohamed Atta – has 11 letters.

I deliberately left out a few more of these uncanny coincidences to not make the list so lengthy.

SO WHO'S SHUFFLING THE DECK?

Now we are not very far into our subject and already the reader can see that it's easy to size up the fact that events such as these should not play out the way they do time after time, row upon row, and in the "proper sequence." But I guess most of us just chuckle at these odd coincidences and out of control synchronicities and let it go at that. We don't have time to sort it all out. Reason with the facts and figures. Theorize if there is more to this than just a random "luck" of the draw. Well, actually, a couple of men have noted that shit like this just should not happen of its own accord. These men would be Carl Jung, Charles Fort, Jacques Vallee, John A. Keel, John C. Lilly – and you can add to this small list Tim Beckley (I need to stretch about now, so I'll take a bow) and Philip K. Dick, naturally

To get our literary motor running here are a couple more key coincidences to add to the almost endless database of weird synchronicities that have transpired throughout history courtesy of SlipTalk.com

** Unconfirmed! On June 20, 1940, Soviet archaeologists uncovered the tomb of Tamerlane, a descendent of Genghis Khan. A warning inscription read "Whoever opens my tomb will unleash an invader more terrible than I." They opened it anyway. Germany invaded the Soviet Union two days later.

** Mark Twain was born on November 30, 1835. This just so happens to be the first day that Halley's Comet appeared that year. When Twain passed away in 1910, it was also the first day of Halley's Comet for that year! He actually predicted this would happen in 1909 when he said, "I came in with Halley's Comet in 1835. It is coming again next year, and I expect to go out with it."

**When compared, there are a lot of strange coincidences between John F. Kennedy and Abraham Lincoln. When listed all together, it's a little crazy to think about. They were elected to Congress 100 years apart. Lincoln was elected in 1846 and Kennedy was elected in 1946. They were also elected as President 100 years apart; Lincoln in 1860 and Kennedy in 1960. They were both assassinated by Southerners, both shot on a Friday, and both shot in the head. They were also killed by two people with three names and those names each had 15 letters. After being assassinated, their successors had the last name of Johnson. Andrew Johnson replaced Lincoln and Lyndon Johnson replaced Kennedy. That's a lot of coincidences between the two of them.

** In Erdington, England there were two women who lived during completely different times, 157 years apart! Barbara Forrest and Mary Ashford were both killed in a horrific manner. They were raped, strangled, and their bodies were found only about 300 yards apart on the same day, May 27. But remember, this happened 157 years apart. The men accused of these horrific murders of both women had the same last name of Thornton and both of them were acquitted of their crimes. Some other strange coincidences were that the women were both 20 years old when murdered and they shared the same birthday! Both women had visited a friend the evening they were killed. They had changed into brand new dresses the night they were killed and also went to a dance the night they were killed.

**When watching *"The Wizard Of Oz,"* you may notice that Frank Morgan plays the taxi driver in Emerald City, the fortune teller Professor Marvel, and, of course, the Wizard of Oz himself. When they were debating on the costume for Professor Marvel, they decided they wanted him to look down on his luck. They found a very nice coat that was just a little bit tattered. During the filming, Morgan pulled out one of the pockets and noticed there was some wording written on the inside of that pocket. The name on the pocket was L. Frank Baum, who just so happens to be the author of *"The Wizard Of Oz"!* Thinking this was a joke, they contacted Baum's widow and also his tailor and they confirmed that this was in fact L. Frank Baum's jacket.

A sequence of synchronicities plays out in the original "Wizard of Oz" movie, revolving around actor Frank Morgan.

BURSTING THE BUBBLE

I could be wrong, but I picture us living inside a bubble. Sort of like what we are referring to when we talk about the holes at the poles which supposedly are entrance ways to the core of the planet. There is some way in and some way out. But it's not easy finding the entrance/exit.

I can't be sure that Philip K. Dick is the first to raise the specter of our world existing in a computerized simulation. The internet as we know it didn't come into "existence" until 1983, though computers had been around for a while. Yet it was in 1977 that PKD took the podium at a high profile science fiction convention in Metz, France, and revealed his thoughts on a subject that so weighed upon his thinking that he had to get up in front of a room full of his contemporaries and announce to the world that what seems real may not be real at all.

Yup, according to Philip, we may all be living inside of a "fishbowl," though that is just my awkward phraseology, not knowing what shape and design we may well be – or not be – talking about. Or are perhaps held prisoner in.

Below you will find a transcript of Dick's summation of his avant-garde theory:

"The subject of this speech is a topic which has been discovered recently and which may not exist at all.

"I may be talking about something that does not exist; therefore I am free to say everything or nothing. I, in my stories and novels, write about counterfeit worlds – some are real worlds as well as deranged private worlds inhabited often by just one person. While, meantime, the other characters either remain in their own worlds throughout or are somehow drawn into one of the peculiar ones.

"This theme occurs in the course of my 27 years of writing. At no time did I have a theoretical or conscious explanation for my preoccupation with these plural form pseudo-worlds. But now I think I understand that what I was sensing was a manifold of partially or actualized reality tangent to whatever is the most actualized one. The one the majority of us by conscious gentium agree on. Later that day, at home again, but still deeply under the influence of sodium pentothal, I had a short acute flash of recovered memory. Than in mid-March – a month later – the total body of memories intact, an entire memory, began to return. You are free to believe me or disbelieve, but please take my word on it. I am not joking. This is very serious. A matter of importance.

"At that time I had no idea of what I was seeing. It resembled nothing I had heard described. It resembled plasmic energy. It had colors. It moved fast. It collected and then dispersed. But what it was I am not sure even now. In other words, it's a common theme in my writing that a dark-haired girl shows up at the door of the protagonist and tells him that his world is delusional. That there is something false about it.

"Well, this did finally happen to me. I even knew that her hair would be black. I had an actual complete sense of what she would look like and what she would say. She did appear. She was a total stranger and she did inform me of this fact. That some of my fictional works were in a little sense true.

"I wrote about these dreams in novel after novel, story after story. To name two in which this presents appeared most clearly, I cite **The Man In The High Castle** and my 1974 novel about the U.S. as a police state. I am going to be very candid with you: I wrote both novels based on fragmentary residual memories of just such a horrid slave state world.

"People claim to remember past lives. I claim to remember a very different present life. I know of no one who has ever made this claim before, but I rather suspect that my experience is not unique, but perhaps as unique to the fact that I am willing to talk about it.

"We are living in a computer programmed reality. And the only clue we have to it is when some verbal cue is changed and some alteration in our reality occurs. We would have the overwhelming impression that we were reliving the present Deja vu perhaps in the same way, seeing the same thing, hearing the same words. I submit that these impressions are valid and significant and I will even say this – such an impression is a clue that at some past time point a verbal cue was changed – reprogrammed as it were – and because of this an alternative world branched off."

And so you don't have to look it up, here is a brief definition of the term Deja vu: *Déjà vu, from the French, literally means – "already seen." It is the phenomenon of having the strong sensation that an event or experience currently being experienced has already been experienced in the past.*

PKD DOES NOT STAND ALONE

Throughout this volume we bring up the names of other prominent individuals involved in various academic aspects of the paranormal. Some names you might recognize right away, others you may not, in which case you are welcome to utilize your favorite search engine to find out more, principally details we just did not have room enough to delve into.

Elsewhere, co-author Sean Casteel brings up the name Jacques Vallee a well-known researcher who for many decades has looked into the spectrum of unidentified aerial phenomena. Author of numerous UFO books like **Messengers of Deception** and **Passport to Magonia**, Vallee has had a varied academic career. As described on JacquesVallee.com: "Jacques was born in France, where he received a B.S. in mathematics at the Sorbonne and an M.S. in astrophysics at Lille University. Coming to the U.S. as an astronomer at the University of Texas, where he co-developed the first computer-based map of Mars for NASA, Jacques later moved to Northwestern University where he received his Ph.D. in computer science and AI. He went on to work at SRI International and the Institute for the Future, where he directed the 'Forum Project' to build the world's first network-based collaboration system as a Principal Investigator for DARPA."

A non-traditional UFO author and investigator, Dr. Vallee, now in his late seventies, has shied away from accepting the popular notion that the unidentified objects observed for centuries are extraterrestrials, opting out for a more "extraordinary" explanation which fits very neatly into the theology of Philip K. Dick.

"I believe," says Vallee, "that there is a system around us that transcends time as it transcends space. I remain confident that human knowledge is capable of understanding this larger reality. I suspect that some humans have already understood it, and are showing their hand in several aspects of the UFO encounters."

That's pretty upfront on Vallee's part wouldn't you say? This coming from a man of recognizable credentials who has a lot to lose were his intentions misconstrued.

SUGGESTED READING BY JACQUES VALLEE

THE INVISIBLE COLLEGE

WONDERS IN THE SKY

EDGE OF REALITY

ANATOMY OF A PHENOMENON

Dr. Jacques Vallee isn't shy about admitting he has experienced synchronicities.

JOHN KEEL'S 'SUPERSPECTRUM'

John Keel was a good friend of mine. We both resided in Manhattan's Murray Hill district. Ate at the same deli. Even went to see a couple of movies together. JAK didn't drink so we would part company for our individual evening's entertainment. I was on the board of directors of the New York Fortean Society, which he founded in the 1970s. In fact, the meetings were held just a few doors down in a building that was torn down ages ago and is now a vacant lot. Keel didn't like to be called a UFOlogist. He was admittedly picky about who he hung with, not wanting to tarnish his reputation. He thought the ET hypothesis was meritless. He was among the first to lump together all manner of weirdness, including UFOs, cryptid creatures (i.e., even Bigfoot), ghosts – all of which pretty much can be labeled as what we today call "Fortean Phenomena." That all-inclusive term is named after Charles Fort (1874 – 1932) who for all intents and purposes started the discussion when he said humans are but pieces on a cosmic chessboard and are being controlled by some outside influence.

Keel didn't identify with the term "Matrix" cause it was still early on. But he did believe there was what he called a "Superspectrum" in existence all around us and that openings (he called them "window areas") allowed a wide variety of otherworldly denizens to hop back and forth before taking the midnight train back to Magonia.

On the back cover of his book, **The Eighth Tower**, we learn that: "There is a single intelligent force behind all religious, occult, and UFO phenomena. Strange manifestations have haunted humans since prehistoric times. Beams of light, voices from the heavens, the 'little people,' gods and devils, ghosts and monsters, and UFOs have all had a prominent place in our history and legends. In this dark work, John Keel explores these phenomena, and in doing so reveals the shocking truth about our present position and future destiny in the cosmic scheme of things. Are we pawns in a celestial game?

"In the Orient, there is a story told of the seven towers. These citadels, well hidden from mankind, are occupied by groups of Satanists who

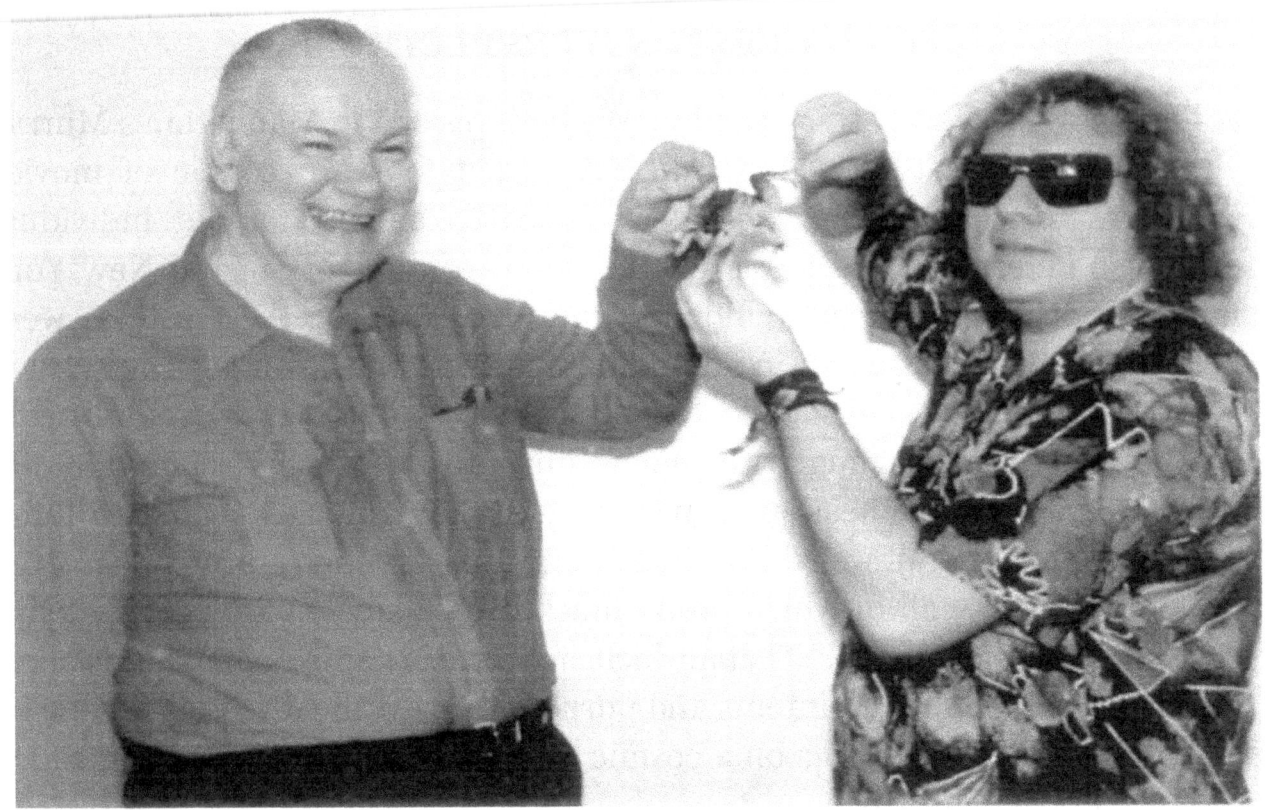

Above: John Keel presents author/publisher Tim Beckley with an award from the NY Fortean Society.

Below: A prolific author, JAK is seen here with book covers from his formidable career.

are chanting the world to ruin. Perhaps this is just a story; perhaps there is some truth behind it. But what if there is yet another tower, a tower not of good or evil but of infinite power? What if all our destinies are controlled by this cosmic force for its own mysterious purposes? And what if UFOs and other paranormal manifestations are merely tools being used to manipulate us and guide us toward the cosmic role we are fated to play? Perhaps, after all, we are not independent beings but are instead the creations and slaves of the eighth tower."

Utilizing Keel's own words, we start to get a better picture of what he is trying to convey to us: "This is a hypothetical spectrum of energies that are known to exist but that cannot be accurately measured with present-day instruments. It is a shadowy world of energies that produce well-observed effects, particularly on biological organisms (namely people).

"This superspectrum is the source of all paranormal manifestations, from extrasensory perception (ESP) to flying saucers, little green men and tall, hairy monsters. It is hard to pin down scientifically because it is extradimensional, meaning that it exists outside our own space-time continuum yet influences everything within our reality."

We had the discussion several times, though I have to admit that Keel was "ahead of me" in shedding the shackles of the ETH (extraterrestrial hypothesis). We both had to agree that the Superspectrum intelligentsia had an odd sense of celestial humor that only they would think in many cases was humorous, leaving us at their mercy. In a sense, they expect us to kowtow to their whims while they act as cosmic tricksters of a sort who enjoy showing off their ability to keep us off guard and jumping to their commandments.

One of the ways this intelligence or godly "father figure" shows off its ability to manipulate and dominate is through coincidences and synchronicities that can easily throw us off-guard and leave us with a deep sense of paranoia. The wise ones among us will duly realize that this "mind shagging" is not connected with our edging toward insanity, but rather that an invisible force I dubbed Power X is behind all these endless shenanigans. Keel, whose bestseller **The Mothman Prophecies** was made into a major motion picture starring Richard Gere, once penned a witty little paperback that pretty much sums up what we are dealing with when he immortalizes this unknown celestial predator in the title of this book as THE FICKLE FINGER OF FATE!

DOUG SKINNER AND JOHN

John Keel and Doug Skinner shared an interest in magic. They hung out near Keel's apartment on the Upper West Side and probably ate a million meals in the little coffee shops that used to dot the area but have been replaced by corporate eateries, if that's what you can call Subway and Dunkin' Donuts. Skinner was on the New York Fortean Society's board of directors and was a fan of the Shaver Mystery. Richard Shaver was a controversial – and some say crazy – sci-fi writer who claimed that less than a mile below our feet, inside the Earth, was a race of demented mutants known as the Dero who abducted humans for sadistic purposes and caused a lot of woe, such as wars, natural disasters and everyday murder and mayhem.

Skinner found out for himself the true nature of synchronicities, as he tells us accordingly in this little tale involving JAK.

"Just a little anecdote for synchronicity fans: A number of years ago (I forget exactly when), I went to a library sale in Manhattan. Near the check-out was a stack of old copies of *The Realist*, which I happily scooped up. As it turned out, I knew the volunteer at the cash box, comedy historian Ron Smith, and so chatted with him as I paid, rather than look at the magazines.

"It was only when I got back home that I saw that they were John's subscription copies. When I told him, he laughed, saying, 'I threw those out years ago. You bought my garbage!'

"John was a friend and fan of Editor Paul Krassner, and, as Satyr-man buffs know, put him into his superhero spoof, The Fickle Finger of Fate."

Upon close examination Keel and I both had to conclude there seems to be something – OR SOMEONE! – who has a heavy hand in controlling events and is toying with us in the strangest of ways for reasons best known to themselves. PKD was lucky because he was a science fiction writer so he could expand on such concepts and put them on paper in novelized form.

Many see this "someone" in terms of God or the Creator who sits about on a golden throne snapping His fingers in order to manage the fate of individuals and the destiny of nations. That's very simplistic, but to some people we live in an overly simplistic world. Me, I don't see it that way, and neither did Keel!

SUGGESTED READING

OPERATION TROJAN HORSE

JADOO

OUR HAUNTED PLANET

MOTHMAN PROPHECIES

DISNEYLAND OF THE GODS

www.JohnKeel.com

Doug Skinner ended up with buddy John Keel's "trash" in a strange coincidence.

SWIMMING WITH THE DOLPHINS

John Cunningham Lilly (January 6, 1915 – September 30, 2001) was an American physician, neuroscientist, psychoanalyst, psychonaut, philosopher and writer.

Dr. John C. Lilly was on the ball when it comes to the matter of synchronicities – his is the belief system that is the closest to mine on the subject, though I can never lay claim to his understanding of the universe and its many species, which he mapped out during the course of his career and even communicated with. We're talking everything from dolphins to aliens. Very few in the UFO and paranormal fields have ever heard of him because he is way over their heads (not trying to be snooty, just stating a simple fact).

Journalist CJ Stone calls Lilly "the psychedelic scientist," which admittedly is a good enough description as he was known to dip rather deeply into the void of consciousness enhancement. His main form of "tripping" was on Ketamine (known as "Special K" among the "club kids" of the eighties) and LSD, which was at one time legal before the government made almost all drugs illegal, even for research purposes. They certainly don't want anyone jumping outside the box or communicating with anyone at the helm of "spaceship earth." And please note that we do not advocate using any sort of drugs as psychic enhancers, but do recommend reading the literature of someone like Terrence McKenna and others who were or still are part of the psychedelic movement.

Lilly, who wrote several books on the transition of consciousness, was the inventor of the isolation tank, whereupon entering a person would be shut off from the outside world as soon as the top came down. They would soon be drifting on a bed of water. Some who have undergone the experience describe it as akin to a near death experience where one can get closer to God and perhaps communicate with other species, which is what Dr. John C. says he did.

A quote from his **Eye of the Cyclone** would be in order, wherein he describes various experiences with his "Guides," which have been interpreted as aliens though he refers to them as the SSI, which is short for Solid State Intelligence. He defined the SSI as being supercomputer-like entities whose goal, he said, was of a malevolent nature. Mainly to conquer and dominate all biological life forms on earth. Heavy duty wouldn't you say?

"These two guides may be two aspects of my own functioning at the supra-self level. They may be entities in other spaces, other universes than our consensus reality. They may be helpful constructs, helpful concepts that I use for my own future evolution. They may be representatives of an esoteric hidden school. They may be concepts functioning in my own human bio-computer at the supra-species level. They may be members of a civilization a hundred thousand years or so ahead of ours. They may be a tuning in on two networks of communication of a civilization way beyond ours, which is radiating information throughout the galaxy."

Dr. John C. Lilly professed to communicate with dolphins and aliens. Photo by John Bigwin Suhre

Floating on out there for our enlightenment Lilly expands upon his cosmic sojourns: "I am out beyond our galaxy, beyond galaxies as we know them. Time has apparently speeded up 100 billion times. The whole universe collapses into a point. There is a tremendous explosion and out of the point on one side comes positive matter and positive energies, streaking into the cosmos at fantastic velocities. Out of the opposite side comes antimatter streaking off into the opposite direction. The universe expands to its maximum extent, re-collapses, and expands three times. During each expansion the guides say, 'Man appears here and disappears there.' All I can see is a thin slice for man. I ask, 'Where does man go when he disappears until he is ready to appear again?' They say, 'That is us.'"

When not communicating with "aliens," Dr. Lilly was also known for his being able to literally "talk to" dolphins, whom he lamented might be an ancient species once more intelligent than we are, perhaps arriving here from another world or dimension. Visitors from outside the Matrix at the very least, I would have to say.

Throughout his life, but more so before his passing, Lilly had all sorts of synchronicities which he became totally plugged into. Perhaps he was engulfed too much for his own good, but that is a matter for personal assessment.

EARTH COINCIDENCE CONTROL OFFICE (ECCO)

Much like me, JCL believed strongly that there is some sort of intelligence, an "agency with direction," directing these occurrences. In his work he refers to this network of empyreal entities as ECCO, an acronym for "Earth Coincidence Control Office." After numerous such events Lilly concluded "that God really existed in me and that there is a guiding intelligence in the universe."

Apparently, though, Lilly did not see the various cosmic forces as all "groovy" and he pretty much believed that he had been chosen to combat negative powers and alert the world at large to the existence of those "solid state beings who are of evil intent."

According to his writings he was given a sign to confirm the dual existence of these two opposing alien intelligence networks. Flying into Los Angeles Intentional Airport, Dr. Lilly saw the comet Kohoutek in the southern sky. "Momentarily," the story goes, "the comet got brighter. At this point a message was laser-beamed into Lilly's mind which said: 'We are Solid State Intelligence (SSI for short) and we are going to demonstrate our power by shutting down all solid state equipment at LAX.'"

JCL shares this prophetic message with his wife, Toni, who was seated next to him. A few minutes later, the pilot instructed everyone to take their seats as the plane was being diverted to a small airport nearby due to the fact that another aircraft had made a hard landing near the runway and had knocked out the power, causing the airport's electrical system to short.

A NEAR BRUSH WITH DEATH

Usually, I can't see where synchronicities have a prolonged positive effect on a person's life, though others would dispute me on this. There is one case in point where apparently Dr. Lilly's life was saved by a positive incident with his friends at ECCO.

Astute researcher Adam Gorightly, who is always on the ball, has delved into JCL's work to a considerable extent and gives us the following account of a well-placed synchronicity:

"In later experiments, Lilly failed to heed his own advice, becoming so enraptured in his Ketamine exploration that he would forgo the earlier agreed upon 'safety man' and started working 'without a net.' This led to an almost fatal consequence when one sunny day, under the influence of K, Lilly climbed into his hot tub. When he realized the temperature was too hot, Lilly futilely attempted to climb out, but in so doing his muscles lost their strength and he collapsed into bubbling currents. Lilly was totally conscious at this point, but, due to the effects of K, he was unaware of the external reality of his drowning body. He was conscious only of his internal world. As fate would have it, a friend of Lilly's, Phil Halecki — who found himself driven by a sudden sense of urgency — decided at this time to phone Dr. Lilly. Lilly's wife,

Toni, fielded the phone call and, at Halecki's insistence, went to summon John, only to find him lying face down in the water, breathless and blue. Fortunately, Toni was able to revive her husband using mouth-to-mouth resuscitation, a technique she had learned only a few days earlier from an article in *The National Enquirer*."

Slowly but surely, JCL became convinced that the ECCO had saved his life on this occasion and that this extraterrestrial intelligence was trying to guide him. I myself see them as being more "neutral" than anything else. I am not certain how lofty they are on the cosmic consciousness scale. Are they here as "assistants"? All I can say is that I believe they are here, but, if we are in a computer simulation, it's like we could be in an arcade somewhere and at a certain time the kids come in after school and take hold of the joy stick.

Adam Gorightly tells another fascinating JCL story:

"As his haphazard use of K intensified, so did the warnings of imminent dangers regarding the survival of mankind, provided by ECCO via 3D Technicolor images beamed into Lilly's mind. These visions were of an apocalyptic nature; scenes of nuclear annihilation seen from an alien's eye view in outer space. The world powers needed to be alerted to this impending tragedy immediately to enable them to avert widespread global devastation, ECCO instructed, or it would be too late. I find it interesting that ECCO's message to Dr. Lilly was much the same as those delivered to the early saucer contactees: our planet was on a collision course toward destruction; all atomic weapons must be dismantled if our planet was ever going to have a chance of surviving in the future. The only difference was that the enemy was us, not 'them.' Nevertheless, rampant technological progress was to blame for the sorry state of the planet, regardless if it was being facilitated by alien intelligences or humans.

"After three weeks of hourly K injections, Lilly decided that he would travel to the East Coast to warn political leaders and members of the media of the threat posed by SSI. In New York, he phoned the White House to warn then President Gerald Ford about 'a danger to the human race involving atomic energy and computers.' A White House aide fielded the call and,

Adam Gorightly has been especially interested in psychedelics as they pertain to Dr. John C. Lilly's research.

although quite aware of Dr. Lilly's impressive credentials, was not convinced of the urgency of the matter, and informed him that the President was unavailable."

One afternoon danger struck when Lilly decided to climb on his ten speed bike – his modest form of transportation – and meet his wife down the road a short distance. Gorightly takes us back to the incident:

"But midway through his trip, Lilly was zapped by the intoxicating magic (of one of his favorite drugs) and instantly felt quite wonderful, with the wind blowing deliciously through his hair; it was as if he'd taken a trip down memory lane to the days of his freewheeling youth. Unfortunately, this flashback full sense of euphoria came screeching to a disastrous halt when the bike chain suddenly jammed, and he was catapulted onto the harsh reality of the concrete pavement, puncturing a lung, breaking several ribs, and suffering cranial contusions. This bicycle crash resulted in several days of hospitalization, where Dr. Lilly was once again visited by the otherworldly representatives from ECCO, who told him he had a choice: He could go away with them 'for good' or remain on the planet, mend his body and concentrate on more worldly affairs. The good doctor wisely chose the latter. With this decision came a turning point in his life, and a conscious effort to focus his remaining years not only on more earthly matters — as opposed to the whims and wishes of ECCO — but to dedicate the rest of his life to his wife, Toni, and their soul mate journey together through physical time and space."

In short, Lilly claimed that the sensory deprivation tank allowed him to make contact with creatures from other dimensions and civilizations far more advanced than our own. He would forever refer to his very first encounter with entities from another dimension as "the first conference of three beings," the details of which are recounted in Lilly's books and on his website.

If anything sets Dr. Lilly's experiences apart from PKD's, Keel's, Vallee's and others, it is his contention that you can seek to control the various coincidences in your life, though so many people are so oblivious to them that this list will probably not make a universe of difference for the masses who think the Matrix is only a movie starring Keanu Reeves.

Here are nine points to aid in having a positive relationship with ECCO:

1. You must know/assume/simulate our existence in ECCO.

2. You must be willing to accept our responsibility for control of your coincidences.

3. You must exert your best capabilities for your survival programs and your own development as an advancing/advanced member of ECCO's earth-side

corps of controlled coincidence workers. You are expected to use your best intelligence in this service.

4. You are expected to expect the unexpected every minute, every hour of every day and of every night.

5. You must be able to maintain conscious/thinking/ reasoning no matter what events we arrange to happen to you. Some of these events will seem cataclysmic/catastrophic/overwhelming, but remember: stay aware, no matter what happens/apparently happens to you.

6. You are in our training program for life; there is no escape from it. We (not you) control the long-term coincidences; you (not we) control the shorter-term coincidences by your own efforts.

7. Your major mission on Earth is to discover/create that which we do to control the long-term coincidence patterns: you are being trained on Earth to do this job.

8. When your mission on planet Earth is completed, you will no longer be required to remain/return there.

9. Remember the motto passed to us (from GCC via SSCU): "Cosmic Love is absolutely Ruthless and Highly Indifferent; it teaches its lessons whether you like/dislike them or not.

So here you have it in a nutshell or a fishbowl or any other way you would like to take your Matrix, along with a healthy – or unhealthy – dose of synchronicities and coincidences. A little later on, I will regale you with accounts from Tim Beckley's Official ECCO Diary.

SUGGESTED READING – JOHN C. LILLY

CENTER OF THE CYCLONE

SIMULATIONS OF GOD

THE DEEP SELF

THE QUIET CENTER ISOLATION AND SPIRIT

www.JohnCLilly.com

ADAM GORIGHTLY

WHO'S WHO OF THE MANSON FAMILY

HAPPY TRAILS TO HIGH WEIRDNESS

THE PRANKSTER AND THE CONSPIRACY

HISTORIA DISCORDIA

adamgorightly.com

historiadiscordia.com

gorightly.wordpress.com

historiadiscordia.com

www.conspiracyArchives.com

www.conspiracyjournal.com

An android replicant of PKD.

3.

VALIS AND THE DIVINE 'CLOSE ENCOUNTERS' OF PHILIP K. DICK

By Sean Casteel

THE visionary mysticism that would come to dominate Philip K. Dick's final years began in 1974, with a visit from the local drugstore. It is a pivotal moment in Dick's personal history and has been much written about and analyzed after the fact.

ANSWERING THE DOOR OF ETERNITY

According to *New York Times* columnist Simon Critchley, "Everything turns here on an event 'Dickheads' refer to with the shorthand 'the golden fish.' On February 20, 1974, Dick was hit with the force of an extraordinary revelation after a visit to the dentist for an impacted wisdom tooth, for which he had received a dose of sodium pentothal. A young woman delivered a bottle of Darvon tablets to his apartment in Fullerton, California. She was wearing a necklace with the pendant of a golden fish, an ancient Christian symbol that had been adopted by the Jesus counterculture movement of the late 1960s.

"The fish pendant, on Dick's account, began to emit a golden ray of light, and Dick suddenly experienced what he called, with a nod to Plato, anamnesis: the recollection or total recall of the entire sum of knowledge. Phillip K. Dick claimed to have access to what philosophers call the faculty of

PKD was very much a thinker and a dreamer at a very young age.

'intellectual intuition': the direct perception by the mind of a metaphysical reality behind the screens of appearance."

In other words, Dick felt he had seen the ultimate nature of what he called "true reality." And the golden fish episode was just the beginning.

"In the following days and weeks," Critchley writes, "Dick experienced and indeed enjoyed a couple of nightlong psychedelic visions with phantasmagoric visual light shows. These hypnagogic episodes continued off and on, together with hearing voices and prophetic dreams, until his death eight years later at age 53. Many weird things happened – too many to list here – including a clay pot that Dick called 'Ho On' or 'Oh Ho,' which spoke to him about various deep spiritual issues in a brash and irritable voice."

COMING TO UNDERSTAND THAT HE WAS SANE

The revelation at the door, of course, begs questions like: Was Dick suddenly psychotic? Did he have a schizophrenic breakdown? Did he incur some disease of the mind we cannot diagnose or even put a name to? We may never know with any certainty whether there was some more earthly, prosaic cause for what happened, but we do know that it changed both his writing and his life.

"The fact is," Critchley writes, "that after Dick experienced the events of what he came to call '2-3-74,' (the events of February and March of that year), he devoted the rest of his life to trying to understand what had happened to him. For Dick, understanding meant writing."

Dick would go on to write more than 8,000 pages about his experience, often writing through the night and producing 20 single-spaced, narrow-margined pages at a go, mostly handwritten and littered throughout with strange diagrams and cryptic sketches. The unfinished mountain of paper was assembled posthumously into some 91 folders and was called "Exegesis."

For those unfamiliar with the term, "Exegesis" is an interpretation or critical analysis of a literary work and often refers to the Bible especially.

For Dick, "My exegesis, then, is an attempt to understand my own understanding."

THE WEIGHTY TOME OF THE ALIEN GOD

Critchley calls Dick's "Exegesis" an "extended act of self-interpretation, a seemingly endless thinking on the events of 2-3-74 that always seems to begin anew." Though it is "often dull, repetitive and given to bouts of paranoia," nevertheless the work also possesses "many passages of genuine brilliance and is marked by an utter and utterly disarming sincerity."

As for the book itself seeing the light of day, an edited selection of these texts, with a golden fish on the cover, was finally published at the end of 2011, weighing in at a mighty 950 pages that were still just a fraction of the whole.

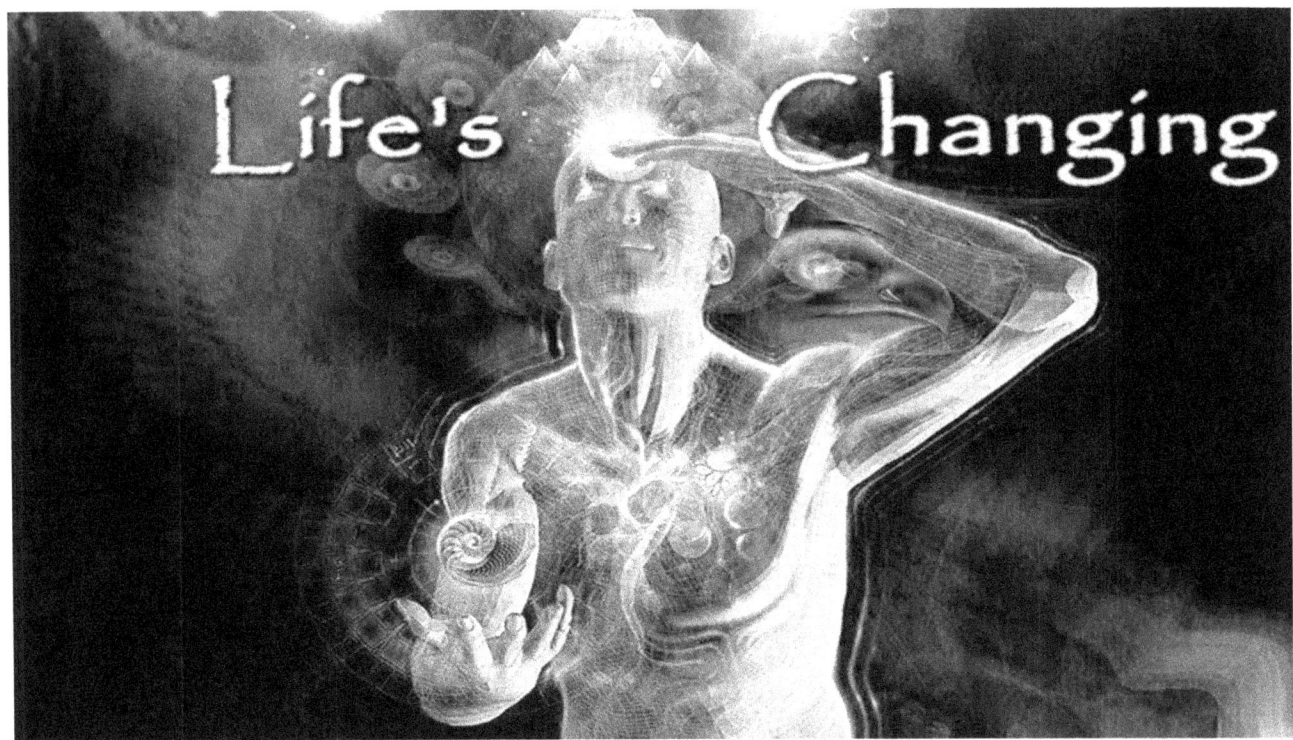

The visitor at the front door opened Dick's consciousness on many levels.

The events may have begun for Dick with the miraculous ray issuing from the errand girl's "secret" symbol of Christianity, but it did not lead to a simple conversion for Dick, who is more easily grouped into the Gnostic tradition, a mystical effort of the intellect as opposed to more mainstream approaches to Christ. Critchley calls it "a fusion with a trans-mundane 'alien' God who can communicate with human beings in the form of a ray of light, or, in Dick's case, hallucinatory visions."

The Gnostic traditions that took hold of Dick include the idea that there is a clear line separating the false God who created this world – who is usually called the "demiurge" – and the true God, who is unknown and "alien" to this world. Critchley defines it further by saying "Gnosticism is the worship of an alien God by those alienated from the world."

Dick's strange visitor enabled him to write about what has been described as a Gnostic religious experience. Whomever the visitor might have been, his forewarning saved the life of Philip's son.

In Dick's case, the divine is said to communicate through "information," a persistent theme in Dick's writing. He refers to the universe and even Christ as "information." Dick also believed that time is not "linear," or a sequence of now-points extending from the future through the present and into to the past, the lines of which stretch forwards and backwards into infinity. Instead, for Dick, time is a circle that contains everything, something he called "orthogonal time."

"In his wilder moments," Critchley writes, "and, to be honest, they occur pretty often, Dick declares that orthogonal time will make it possible for the golden age to return, namely the time before the Fall and prior to original sin. He also claims that in orthogonal time the future falls back into and fulfills itself in the present. This is doubtless why Dick believed that his fiction was becoming truth, that the future was unfolding in his books. For example, if you think for a second about how the technologies of security in the contemporary world already seem to resemble the 2055 of **Minority Report** more and more each day, maybe Dick has a point. Maybe he was writing the future."

THE 'INTELLIGENCE' THAT INFORMS US ALL

Another of Dick's novels that grapples with prophecies of the future and the search for wisdom is "VALIS." The title is an acronym for "Vast Active Living Intelligence System," which has been called "Dick's Gnostic vision of one aspect of God." The 1981 novel was the first installment of a trilogy that Dick did not complete before his death. Most of the thematic elements are "truth-disguised-as-fiction," in that they involve phenomena that Dick believed to exist in the "real world," if such a term has any relevance with Dick, who believed the nature of reality was always fluid and subject to change.

"VALIS," according to Dick, was one node of an artificial satellite network originating from the star Sirius in the Canis Major constellation. The satellite near the Earth used "pink laser beams" to transfer information and project holograms on Earth, as well as to facilitate communication between an extraterrestrial species and humanity. The alien contact depicted in the

The Matrix Control System of Philip K. Dick
And The Paranormal Synchronicities of Timothy Green Beckley

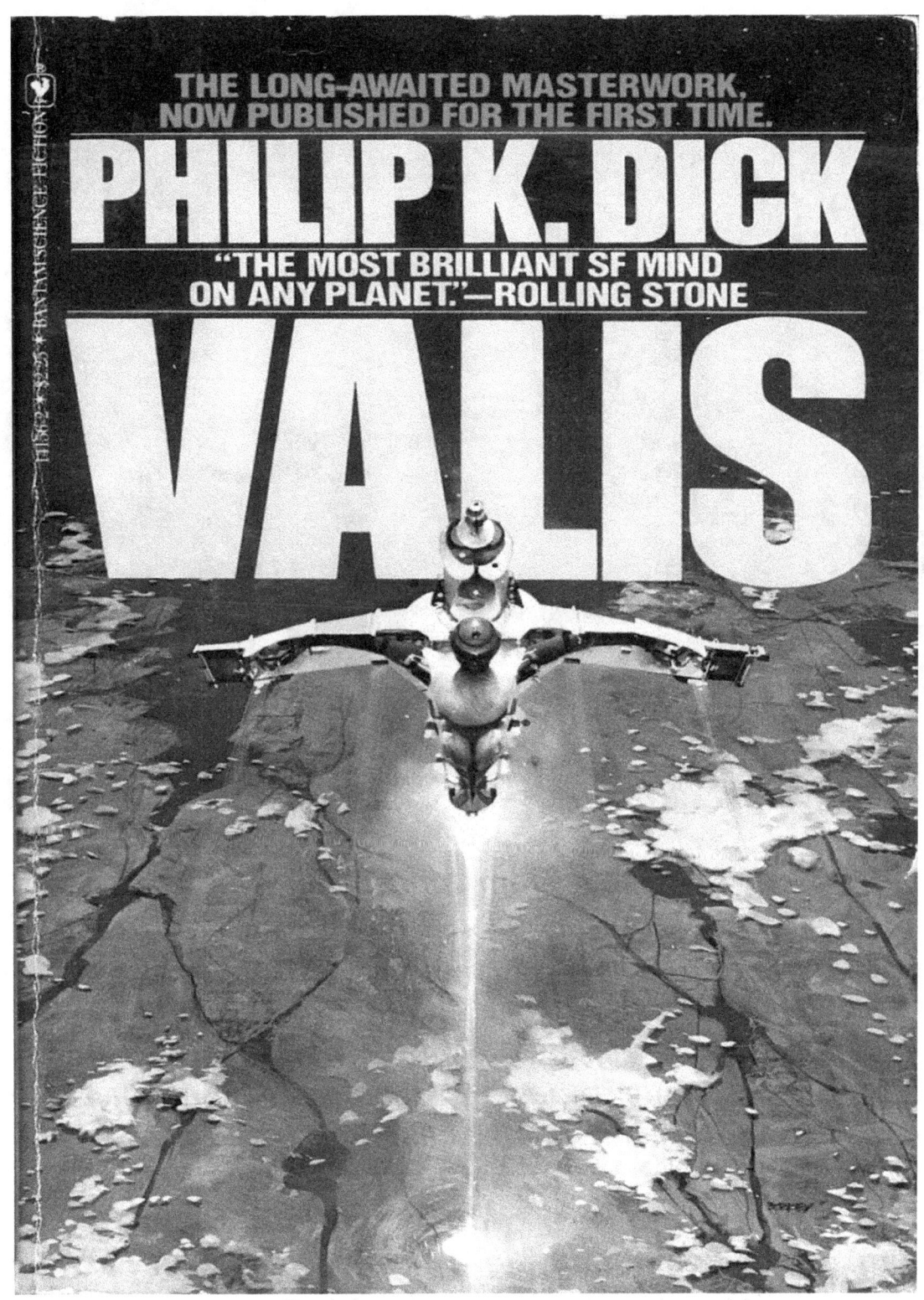

"VALIS" is among the essential PKD reads.

Quote From John Boner, Jr.:
"At the heart of VALIS is a quest. Philip K. Dick, Horselover Fat and friends embark on a quest like knights of King Arthur's court. The Grail they seek is not a chalice, though, but the fifth Savior who is the latest in a line that began with the Buddha and has continued through the prophets Zoroaster, Jesus and Muhammad. Along the way, they encounter a rock star based on David Bowie, who might really be the Man Who Fell To Earth, a composer modeled after Brian Eno, and a literally divine, two year old girl, Sophia, who brings healing, at least temporarily, to Dick and Horselover Fat's fractured existence." Courtesy www.2ndfirstlook.com

novel was among the many things buried in his subconscious, one would think, as is usually the case with UFO abductees. Dick may have been an abductee, although unaware of that fact, as many abductees are.

Dick is often credited with setting the stage for the later "Matrix" film franchise that would enthrall so many fans years after his death. Drawing again from Plato and the Gnostics, Dick would write, "We appear to be memory coils (DNA carriers capable of experience) in a computer-like thinking system which, although we have correctly recorded and stored thousands of years of experiential information, and each of us possesses somewhat different deposits from all the other life forms, there is a malfunction – a failure – of memory retrieval."

Which takes us back to the flash of insight that initiated this change of consciousness for Dick: he "remembered' all the recorded knowledge of the universe," like he had suddenly recovered his library card to the Akashic Records. At the same time, there was the dawning realization that human reality exists only as a computer simulation created by an unseen alien "puppet master."

CLAIRVOYANCE AND SPEAKING IN TONGUES

Dick claimed that VALIS informed him that his infant son was in mortal danger from an unnamed illness even though routine medical checkups had shown no trouble or worrisome symptoms. But Dick insisted that thorough tests be run to ensure his son's health and was eventually able to get the doctor to make them in spite of there being no obvious problems. It was discovered that Dick's son had an inguinal hernia and would have died without immediate surgery. The operation saved the child's life, which Dick attributed to the "intervention" of VALIS.

At one point in the aftermath of 2-3-74, Dick was able to speak a form of Greek called "Koine Greek," a language he had never studied. It also happened to be the language in which the New Testament was originally written. The phenomenon of speaking an unknown foreign language is called "xenoglossia." Dick insisted he had also been able to think, speak and read

The Matrix Control System of Philip K. Dick
And The Paranormal Synchronicities of Timothy Green Beckley

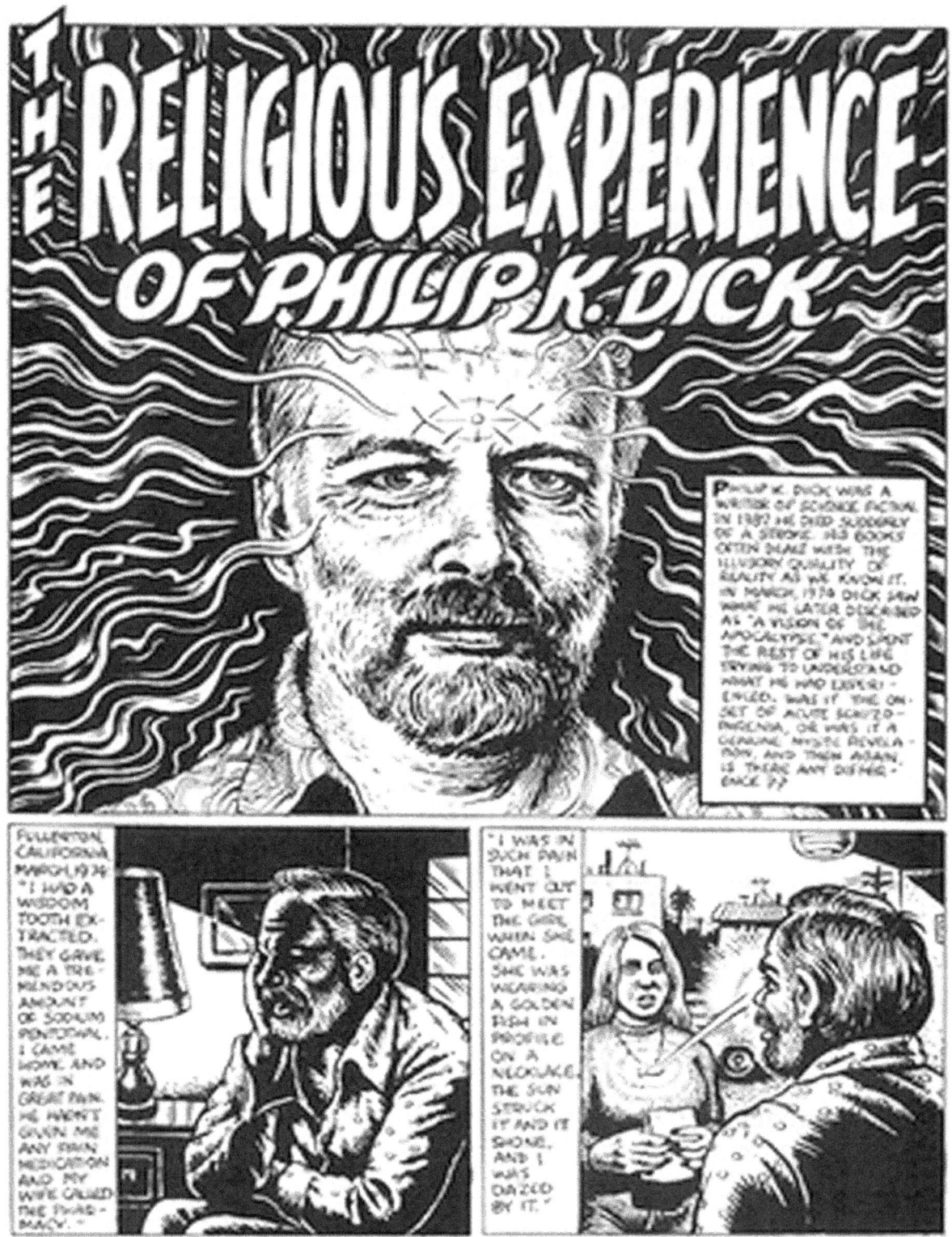

Underground comic artist, the legendary Robert Crumb, did an eight page comic based on PKD's "VALIS" experience.

fluent Koine Greek many years prior while under the influence of the hallucinogenic LSD.

THE JOY OF JESUS RETURNING

Returning to the Christian overtones of the initial girl-at-the-door experience, Dick would later write in his "Exegesis" period that:

"In that instant, as I stared at the gleaming fish sign and heard her words, I suddenly experienced what I later learned is called 'anamnesis' – a Greek word meaning literally 'loss of forgetfulness.' I remembered who I was and where I was. In an instant, in the twinkling of an eye, it all came back to me. And not only could I remember it but I could see it. The girl was a secret Christian and so was I. We lived in fear of detection by the Romans. We had to communicate with cryptic signs. She had just told me all this, and it was true.

"For a short time," Dick goes on, "as hard as this is to believe or explain, I saw fading into view the black, prisonlike contours of hateful Rome. But, of much more importance, I remembered Jesus, who had just recently been with us, and had gone temporarily away, and would very soon return. My emotion was one of joy. We were secretly preparing to welcome Him back. It would not be long. And the Romans did not know. They thought He was dead, forever dead. That was our great secret, our joyous knowledge. Despite all appearances, Christ was going to return, and our delight and anticipation were boundless."

Dick believed that he, along with the rest of us, were all living simultaneously in the present day as well as the time of the first Christians in Rome. The political and economic structure of our modern world is really the BIP, or Black Iron Prison, which is opposed to the spiritual redemption offered by the PTG, or Palm Tree Garden. This is again a belief heavily influenced by the Gnostics, many of whom held that the physical, material world is really the creation of the God of Evil and that we await salvation from an "alien" God, a true "extraterrestrial" not bound up in the wickedness and oppression on our planet's surface.

THE DEEPLY BURIED ALIEN CONNECTION

The late, great Robert Anton Wilson, a celebrated writer who at times claimed to channel alien entities, commented on Dick thusly: "From his experiences, he constructed 'VALIS,' which looks like a science fiction story most of the way. Abruptly, towards the end, you figure out that maybe this isn't a science fiction story. Maybe it's an account of Philip K. Dick going crazy. Or maybe it's an account of Philip K. Dick being contacted by extraterrestrials."

Which may bring to mind the experiences of Whitley Strieber, the author of the landmark UFO abduction bestseller "Communion" and its many sequels. Strieber had already established himself as a noted writer of horror fiction prior to an abduction experience in 1985 that would reveal itself as the tip of an iceberg of similar events scattered throughout his life.

Looking back after his initial awakening, Strieber theorized that his deeply buried memories of contact with grey aliens had been the unconscious inspiration for the ghostly grey wolves of **The Wolfen**. He also felt that the icy, blonde female vampire in **The Hunger** was based on his lost recollections of the physically beautiful Nordic alien form – attested to in the abduction accounts of many other abductees as well. His buried memories, before he was able to consciously analyze and reflect on them, were extremely frightening and had bubbled up to the surface in the form of horror novels and short stories. Although he would later come to entertain more positive, even Christian, interpretations of the aliens he called the "Visitors," fear overpowered more benevolent ways of seeing them in the beginning.

INSANITY, GENIUS AND RELIGIOUS EXPERIENCE

Not that it was all a walk in the park for Dick either. At one point, his voices and visions drove him to attempt suicide and he was placed in a mental hospital.

"When I believe, I am crazy," he wrote. "When I don't believe, I suffer psychotic depression."

But elsewhere he says more optimistically, "I experienced an invasion of my mind by a transcendentally rational mind, as if I had been insane all my life and suddenly I had become sane."

There is, of course, the tritely familiar expression that there is a fine line between genius and insanity. Philosophers have argued that there is also a fine line between madness and genuine religious experience.

It goes without saying that Philip K. Dick gingerly stepped along those fine lines as best he could. And maybe we can follow his footsteps in some way and achieve that same ecstatic vision of Jesus returning for his Chosen Ones, coming to free them from the confines of the Black Iron Prison – or the Matrix/computer simulation – that it is their unhappy lot to be suffering within.

SUGGESTED READING BY SEAN CASTEEL

THE EXCLUDED BOOKS OF THE BIBLE – UPDATED EDITION

UFOS, PROPHECY AND THE END OF TIME

THE SEARCH FOR THE PALE PROPHET IN ANCIENT AMERICA

4.

PHILIP K. DICK'S PHYLOGENIC MEMORY AND THE DIVINE FIRE

By Brad Steiger

For half a century, Brad Steiger has been one of the leading lights in the world of UFO and paranormal literature. Steiger was born February 19, 1936, at the Fort Dodge Lutheran Hospital during a blizzard. He grew up on a farm in Bodē, Iowa, and identified as Lutheran until the age of eleven, when a near-death-experience changed his religious beliefs. He has authored well over a hundred and fifty books which have sold millions of copies worldwide.

* * * * *

I read recently that Ridley Scott was writing a reboot of Philip K. Dick's *Blade Runner,* starring Ryan Gosling, Harrison Ford (one of the original stars), and utilizing the directorial talents of Denis Villeneuve. The 1982 hit motion picture was based on Phil's novel, **Do Androids Dream of Electric Sheep?** and I began to reflect on the many letters and telephone conversations that he and I shared while the original film was being made. We spoke little about movies, but a great deal about "DNA memory packets," "Star People," and the Ruah.

In 1981, shortly after the publication of my book **The Star People**, I received a letter from Philip K. Dick, the well-known science-fiction writer, telling me that he was such an individual as those whom I had profiled in the book. He had first realized this in 1974 when his own "DNA memory packet" began to fire within his psyche.

At that time, he told me, he was shown in a vision, "more properly, an inner hologram," the cover of my book, **Revelation: The Divine Fire** (Prentice-Hall, 1973). A feminine voice told him that if he would read this book, it would help him to understand what was occurring to him. He was also told by the voice to get in touch with me.

Although Dick said that he did read the book and did receive the requisite understanding that he was promised during the vision, he was reluctant to contact me until he read of my research with those individuals whom I had given the name of Star People. [People who feel that they bear within their genes awareness acquired by extraterrestrial interaction with humans in prehistoric or ancient times and who have now been activated by DNA memory to fulfill a mission in assisting others in their spiritual and evolutionary advancement.]

Dick said that he was about to publish a novel (**VALIS**, 1981) that would advance numerous Star People concepts.

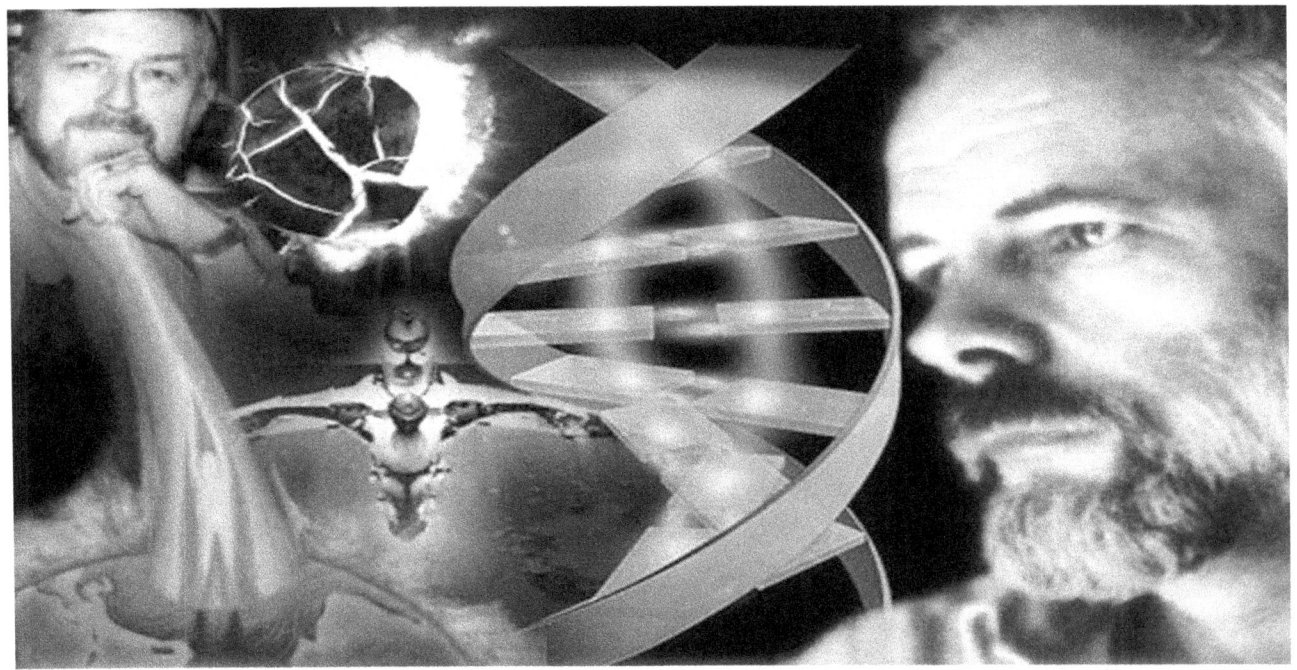

Brad Steiger has become accustomed to living in a strange universe after his many years of researching the paranormal.

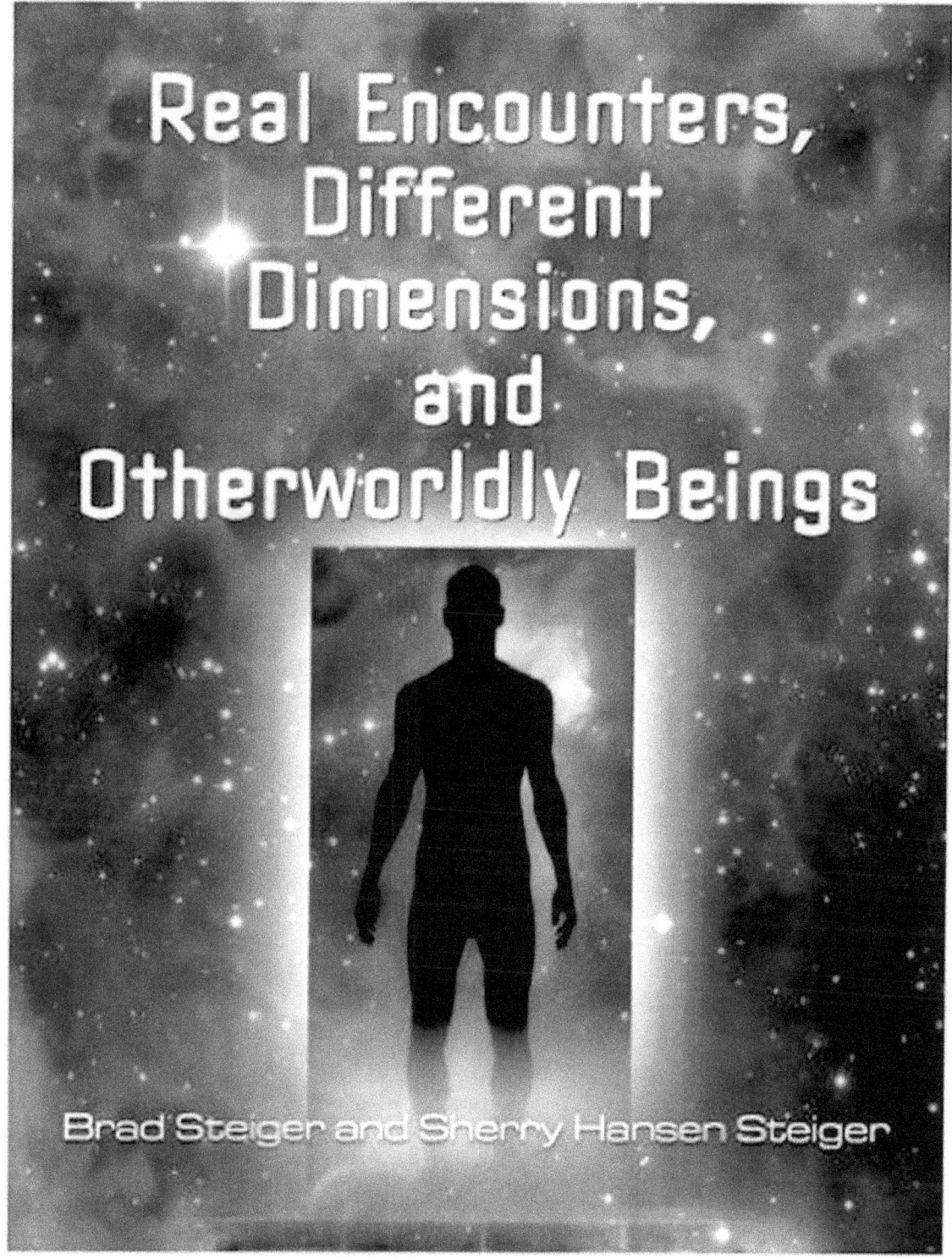

Steiger has written well over a hundred books with sales in the millions. This is one of his most recent bestsellers.

"I wish to hide behind the veil of fiction," he wrote. "I can claim that I made the whole thing up. The revelations that I received were so astounding that it has taken me five years to arrive at a place where I will even put forth the concept as fiction."

Dick was shown a vision of himself in a disabled spacecraft heading toward Earth in prehistoric times. He was one of the emigrants of a technologically sophisticated civilization that was undergoing vast convulsions. But the survivors of that extraterrestrial civilization feared that, once contact was lost with the home planet, they might lose continuity in terms of the handing down of their culture from generation to generation. The solution was "phylogenic memory."

Brad and Sherry Steiger join ET for a ride to the moon. Sure, he has been there many times – but is it outside of the Matrix? That's what we want to know.

Dick explained phylogenic memory as complex DNA information packets distributed in dormant form:

"These dominant DNA information packets would be disinhibited – induced to fire – in due time, depending on either synchronized inner biological clocks or pure chance stimuli. Or a combination of both, ideally. Thus, even thousands of years later, the primordial civilization will be 'released' in the minds of the astonished descendants who suppose themselves autochthones [aboriginal inhabitants] of the planet they now inhabit.

"The DNA packets in a given individual will tell him: 1) Where he is from; 2) What made up that original civilization, *his* civilization; 3) His true nature and faculties; 4) What he must do.

"Ideally, he will act out a series of responses based on the packet, the purpose of which is to create on his planet, insofar as it is possible, the civilization which his ancestors maintained.

"I evaluate the current widespread firing of these phylogenic memory packets in those you call the Star People as a matter of supreme importance.

"In February, 1974, my own DNA memory packet was disinhibited, either by an inner biological clock, which synchronized it with disinhibitions in other people, or by accident. It fired for one complete year."

After that initial letter from Phil, we began a steady correspondence, supplemented with a number of late-night telephone calls.

Phil later told me that he had recognized the feminine voice that told him to read **Revelation: The Divine Fire** as the one that had spoken to him sporadically since his high school days. Eventually, the voice had identified herself as the *Ruah*, the Hebrew word for Spirit of God, Holy Spirit.

She was, according to Phil's understanding, a "tutelary spirit," possessed of a "transcendentally rational mind." The Ruah spoke to him in terse, succinct sentences, and communicated most often when he was falling asleep or waking up. He had to be very quiet and attentive in order to hear the brief messages that she relayed.

Throughout the course of our conversations, I had a revelation to share with Phil: The essence of **The Divine Fire** had been given to me in 1969 during a late night encounter with a hooded entity. To silence my inquisitive – and startled – mind, the mysterious visitor placed me into a deep sleep. But in the morning I arose with the complete outline of **Revelation: The Divine Fire** in my awakened consciousness. The book was published in 1973, about a year before Phil received the vision from the Ruah advising him to read it.

I lived in Phoenix in 1982, and Phil planned to come over around the time of my birthday in February to discuss a number of new concepts which were occurring to him. *Blade Runner,* based on his novel **Do Androids Dream of Electric Sheep?** had not yet been released. My memory is uncertain on this point, but Phil either called me after he had seen a rough cut of the film or just before he was going to see a screening. In either event, he died before the motion picture was released and before he made the trip to Phoenix that would have enabled us to have that final mind-meld.

I was pleased a couple of years ago when Phil's widow filled out the Star People/UFO/Mystical Questionnaire that we still make available on our website. I know that Phil's revelations are expanding with every new release of a motion picture based on his work, a film library that appears to birth another cinematic creation each year –*Total Recall, Minority Report, A Scanner Darkly, Paycheck, Next.* Somewhere Phil smiles upon his legacy with an even greater expanded memory packet, one now suffused with the cosmic awareness that awaits us all.

SUGGESTED READING BY BRAD STEIGER

THE STAR PEOPLE

CONSPIRACIES AND SECRET SOCIETIES

REAL ENCOUNTERS, DIFFERENT DIMENSIONS AND OTHERWORLDLY BEINGS

Dozens of other titles on Amazon.com
www.facebook.com/Brad.Steiger.Author/

AFTERTHOUGHT BY PUBLISHER TIM BECKLEY

I have known Brad Steiger since 1967 and have published several of his books. He spoke, along with his wife, Sherry Steiger, many times at my various conferences. We are so close we refer to each other as "Brother Brad" and "Brother Tim."

I can remember one synchronicity that is a doozy. It took place in my friend Sandra's apartment, in the same hotel where Bishop Pike's son committed suicide. I once slept in the room where the tragic event took place.

One evening I was at Sandra's kitchen table and this rather attractive blonde came in. She introduced herself – I really don't remember her name – and I thought, well, maybe I'll get to know her a bit and ask her out. I asked her what she did about ten minutes into the conversation and she tells me she is a model. Well, she certainly was no Candy Jones, but, hey, it looks promising already. I asked her what kind of modeling she did and she told me her face had been on a paperback book some time ago. I asked her what the title of the book was and she says something about sex and the occult.

Well, I found out that the full title was **Sex and the Supernatural**, and the author was Brad Steiger. I had just published a hard-cover edition of the book and retitled it **Demon Lovers**, for a non-pulp, more "New Age" audience. In case anyone cares, I never dated the girl. I don't think I ever saw her again. But she came out of the Matrix to set up this "coincidence" – right, Brother Brad?

5.

A THOUGHT NOT MY OWN
By Tim R. Swartz

TIM R. Swartz is one of the top names in the paranormal today. He is the author of numerous books and co-host of the webcast **Exploring The Bizarre**, heard Thursday's at 10 PM EST over KCORradio.com. He has traveled all over the world in search of the truth about some of the most fascinating topics one can possibly be confronted with. Swartz likes to say that he was a fan of PKD before PDK was cool. His most popular books include, *The Lost Journals of Nikola Tesla*, *Admiral Byrd's Secret Journey Beyond the Poles*, *Time Travel: Fact NOT Fiction* and *America's Strange and Supernatural History*.

We all like to think that we have control over our lives; that we are able to mold and shape our destinies. The Bible even insists that when we were created, God gave us "free will" along with the ability to know the difference between right and wrong. It is all very simple: with "free will," we create our lives with the decisions we make.

Unfortunately, at times it seems as if there is a structure of sorts underlying our reality, a template of our lives that needs to be followed. Think of it as a path through the woods. In order to get out of the woods, you have to follow the path. Oh, there are deviations along this path, separate trails that can take you miles out of your way. Interesting though these deviations may

From an isolated bunker deep beneath the Earth, Tim Swartz has appeared on a lengthy list of radio and TV shows, like "Coast to Coast AM," "Ground Zero" and "Ancient Aliens."

be, you eventually have to make your way back to the original path in order to get out of the woods. In other words, the Universe has already chosen a path for us to follow. You can use your "free will" to follow this path unquestionably, or, like most of us, we can choose to blunder blindly here and there until the Universe steps in and forces us back onto the correct path.

I have often pondered whether synchronicity is one of the ways the Universe uses to try and keep us on our intended path. Possibly because we are literally trapped in linear time and a three-dimensional reality, we are unable to view the "big picture" that may show us the intricate spider web of connections that make synchronicity work. I think that this is why synchronicity can make such a huge impression on us when it occurs, yet, at the same time, leave us baffled on the actual meaning of the event.

My encounter with the unknown happened in 1978 during my first year in college. Shortly after the Christmas holiday season, my best friend, James, who was a year younger and still attending high school, unexpectedly committed suicide. For me, the shock was devastating. On top of my sorrow was the guilt I put upon myself for not noticing the emotional pain that my friend must have been feeling. We had spent a lot of time together during my holiday time off from school, but if James had dropped any hints about what he was planning, I did not notice them.

Because I was already back to school, which was a considerable distance from my hometown, I was not able to attend his funeral. I sealed myself away from everyone to privately deal as best as I could with my pain and guilt. I never asked where James was buried. I only knew that he had been laid to rest in a small cemetery outside of town. At the time, I didn't want to know. This sort of knowledge only increased the pain that I was working so hard to avoid.

As well, there were mutual friends who kept asking me if I had any idea why this had happened. Why had our friend chosen to take his own life without leaving as much as a note of explanation? I was just as clueless as they were, but resentment grew like a hot, white flame within those old friends who felt that somehow I was responsible for James death. I became a pariah within my old circle of friends and the few times I did return to my home to visit my parents, I kept to myself, as no one would see me anyway.

The years passed and the pain slowly faded. The summer after I had graduated from college, I had to move back home to help care for my sick mother. I would take care of her during the day when no one else was at home, but I had the evenings to myself. Not that there was much to do in the little town I called home. Mostly I would drive around, listening to music and enjoying the quiet country air.

One early evening started out like the rest. I was out in the country, driving the back roads and not thinking about anything in particular. I was about ten miles outside of town in an area that I had never been before. As I was driving along, I came upon a small, unfamiliar country cemetery. In this rural area, there are dozens of such cemeteries, so it is not surprising that I had never seen this particular one before.

I had actually barely noticed the graveyard as I drove past it. But suddenly, completely out of the blue, it was as if someone else's thought was put into my head. "This is where James is buried," this foreign thought said to me.

My rational mind knew that this was complete and utter nonsense. I had no clue where my friend's gravesite was. I didn't want to know, I had never asked, and no one had ever volunteered to tell me.

Yet, this thought persisted to the point where it was no longer simply a stray thought. It had entwined itself into my brain to the point that it had become knowledge. I was now positive that this little, unassuming cemetery contained the mortal remains of my friend.

What choice did I have? I had to find out what was going on. I turned my car around and pulled through the wrought-iron gate. Turning the engine off, I got out.

I didn't know where to start, so I walked a few steps into the cemetery and looked down. There, at my feet, was a familiar name carved upon the headstone. With no deviations, I had walked directly to the grave of my friend. I had not been looking for him, yet somehow, after all this time, I was finally reunited with my best friend.

Some would say that there is no rhyme or reason to synchronicity – that they are just coincidences and nothing more. Even though I can offer no good explanation or reason for my unusual experience, to me, it was more than just a meaningless coincidence. It left me with a lasting impression that I have carried with me all of these years. It left me with a certainty that there is more to our lives then chance events, that there is meaning and significance to everything in our lives. Maybe someday we will have a better understanding of all this. But until then, I always keep my eyes and my mind open to what is going on around me. Because I never know when the universe is trying to catch my attention and tell me something important.

Listen closely, your destiny is calling.

We do not create our destiny; we participate in its unfolding. Synchronicity works as a catalyst toward the working out of that destiny.
David Richo, *The Power of Coincidence: How Life Shows Us What We*

6.

THE UBIK OF REALITY
By Tim R. Swartz

ONE of Philip K. Dick's favorite plot devices was the idea that reality is never what you think it is. Dick was once quoted as saying "I think that, like in my writing, reality is always a soap bubble, Silly Putty thing anyway. In the universe people are in, people put their hands through the walls, and it turns out they're living in another century entirely. I often have the feeling — and it does show up in my books — that this is all just a stage." (***Science Fiction Review*** - August 1976)

That was an interesting thing for Dick to have said because the idea that our reality could be "just a stage" is receiving a lot of attention right now among some of the world's greatest minds.

Could we be living in a universe that is actually a simulated reality? This may sound like a version of PKD science fiction, but this idea is being seriously considered by people such as Elon Musk, who said at the California's Code Conference in 2016, "Chances are we're all living in a simulation."

If this concept sounds familiar, it should, as it was the main plot element of the Matrix trilogy...movies that liberally borrowed from many of Dick's most popular stories. There is a long philosophical and scientific history to the underlying thesis made popular in **The Matrix**. This hypothesis can be traced as far back as the "Butterfly Dream" of Zhuangzi, or the Indian philosophy of Maya.

The Matrix Control System of Philip K. Dick
And The Paranormal Synchronicities of Timothy Green Beckley

Nick Bostrom

The modern elements of "the universe as a computer simulation" theory stems from philosopher Nick Bostrom's 2003 proposal of a trilemma that he called "the simulation argument." The trilemma posits that a technologically mature, "post-human" civilization would have enormous computing power; if even a tiny percentage of them were to run "ancestor simulations" (that is, "high-fidelity" simulations of ancestral life that would be indistinguishable from reality to the simulated ancestor), the total number of simulated ancestors, or "Sims," in the universe (or multiverse, if it exists) would greatly exceed the total number of actual ancestors. Therefore, at least one of the following three propositions is almost certainly true:

1. "The fraction of human-level civilizations that reach a post-human stage (that is, one capable of running high-fidelity ancestor simulations) is very close to zero," or

2. "The fraction of post-human civilizations that are interested in running ancestor-simulations is very close to zero," or

3. "The fraction of all people with our kind of experiences that are living in a simulation is very close to one."

Bostrom goes on to use a type of anthropic reasoning to claim that, if the third proposition is the one of those three that is true, and almost all people with our kind of experiences live in simulations, then we are almost certainly living in a simulation.

Much like the characters in Dick's book **UBIK**, our universe could be a simulation from an intelligence that has established a "web of control" that, when brought down to our level, manifests itself as synchronicity.

THE SYNCHRONICITY OF SIMULATION

In the world of **UBIK**, the proliferation of psychic talents has led, through the process of natural selection, to anti-psychics, people who can nullify psychic powers. Glen Runciter runs the foremost "prudence organization" in the world, sending his operatives out to protect his clients' secrets from the prying eyes of remote viewers. Runciter often consults with his wife, who is dead, but

kept in a frozen "Half-Life" state where she can still communicate with her husband electronically.

It is revealed that those in Half-Life have been wired together and they experience a subjective world that, to them, has all the appearances of the real world. In other words, they are experiencing a simulated reality.

Runciters' best anti-psychic is Joe Chip. Chip and several other anti-psychics are taken to the moon by Runciter because an important client is under threat from psychics from a competing company. The job ends up being a trap and a saboteur kills Runciter with a bomb.

Chip and his team immediately fly their boss back to Earth, where they attempt to put him into Half-Life. Unfortunately, Runciter does not respond and he is declared dead. Joe Chip then starts to experience bizarre synchronicities revolving around his dead employer. As well, the world around him seems to be shifting backwards in time to the 1930s.

In UBIK, bizarre synchronicities seem to show that the world is actually a simulation.

When Chip and the other survivors check their money, the coins and bills now have the face of Glen Runciter on them. Strange messages from Runciter start appearing, indicating that he is alive, and Joe Chip and his team were the ones killed in the explosion.

The synchronicities increase and seem to show that Joe Chip and the others are really the ones in Half-Life and that their rapidly deteriorating world is a simulation. If they cannot find away to stop their joined simulation from withering away, they will soon die.

PKD has taken the idea of a simulated reality, i.e. those joined together in a frozen Half-Life, where synchronicities occur because of projected communications into their holographic reality with clues from "real world" of the living. The substance known as UBIK, which comes in a spray can with the properties to halt their disintegrating reality, is first introduced to the Half-Life reality in the form of TV commercials and advertisements on matchbook covers. The world around Joe Chip is falling apart, and he knows that he is dying. Runciter appears and sprays Chip with UBIK, restoring his health. Runciter says Chip, along with the others, are dead and in Half-Life.

Other inhabitants of the Half-Life world (Runciter's wife Ella among them) claim that they created UBIK in defense against Jory, a young Half-Lifer who is consuming the energy of everyone else in order to prolong his life. It is more than likely that UBIK is actually inputting information from the real world into the Half-Life simulation world. UBIK is LOGOS, the structuring reality of all things. It is the force of creation that brings order out of entropy.

Ella Runciter says that UBIK was created in Half-Life, but it actually was introduced into the Half-Life world from the "real" world by the interactions between the living and the Half-Lifers. Much like Philo said in De Profugis, "The Logos of the living God is the bond of everything, holding all things together and binding all the parts, and prevents them from being dissolved and separated." UBIK is part of the whole universe, including the Half-Life simulation, and it manifests itself in ways that it can be understood...with synchronicities of TV commercials and other advertisements.

UBIK AS GOD

Tessa Dick has commented that UBIK is God, and this could be partially true considering the way people tend to anthropomorphize God. UBIK is more along the lines of Pleroma in the Gnostic tradition. Pleroma generally refers to the totality of divine powers. In Matthew 5:17 and 13:48 it means "to complete an incomplete thing," or "to fill up an empty thing," something that UBIK does well in the book.

UBIK is the emanation of the unknowable force of creation that communicates through synchronicities and lurid advertisements in the Half-Life. These same emanations of creation: Monad, Bythos, Proarkhe, Arkhe, and Aeons, may also the driving force of synchronicities in our world . . . the real world. The emanations convey information subjectively to all of us in a manner that seems on the surface to be random and meaningless, but actually has meaning on a much deeper, subconscious level.

In **UBIK**, those who are living in the simulated world of Half-Life are unable to tell the difference between their world and the real world. That is until their simulated world starts decomposing around them and mysterious, coincidental messages from Runciter direct them to UBIK, the amazing and convenient substance in a spray can, guaranteed to halt entropy and restore their Half-Life world to the way it should be.

THE COINCIDENCE OF REALITY

In an interview Dick gave while at the Metz science fiction conference in France in 1977, he spoke about some of his personal theories, including his idea that that our universe is a highly-advanced computer simulation.

"We are living in a computer-programmed reality, and the only clue we have to it is when some variable is changed, and some alteration in our reality occurs."

Much like the Half-Life world in **UBIK**, our world could be a simulation, and there are some excellent reasons why this may be true. About two-dozen of the universe's fundamental constants happen to fall within the narrow range thought to be compatible with life. At first glance it seems as unlikely as balancing a pencil on its tip. Jiggle these parameters and life as we know it would have never appeared. Not even stars and galaxies. This is called the Anthropic Principle.

An artificial universe could also solve the Fermi Paradox, if our universe was custom made for us by our future descendants. If our universe is a simulation, then it is also plausible that the "entities" controlling it could be running other simulations to create other universes parallel to our own.

Nick Bostrom also imagined "stacked" levels of reality. "We would have to suspect that the post-humans running our simulation are themselves simulated beings; and their creators, in turn, may also be simulated beings. Here may be room for a large number of levels of reality, and the number could be increasing over time."

To take this idea even further, Bostrom imagined a hierarchy of deities, "In some ways, the post-humans running a simulation are like gods. However, all the demigods except those at the fundamental level of reality are subject to sanctions by the more powerful gods living at lower levels."

Professor Richard Doyle, who held a class on Synchcast for PKD, warned his students that reading Dick's novels could induce what he calls an "involuntionary" affect — meaning one's life might start getting taken up by synchronicities and uncanny moments.

If we are all living in a computer simulated world, synchronicities and uncanny moments are communicating to us because we are all connected via the lattice, or web of connections that intertwine us all at a quantum level. Dick once wrote in the article "How to build a universe that doesn't fall apart two days later . . ."

"It was always my hope, in writing novels and stories which asked the question 'What is reality?', to someday get an answer. Years passed. I wrote over thirty novels and over a hundred stories, and still I could not figure out what was real. One day a college student in Canada asked me to define reality for her, for a paper she was writing for her philosophy class. She wanted a one-sentence answer. I thought about it and finally said, 'Reality is that which, when you stop believing in it, doesn't go away.' That's all I could come up with. That was back in 1972. Since then I haven't been able to define reality any more lucidly."

Taking Dick's statement into consideration, I have to ask, what would happen if reality ever stops believing in us?

A message from Glen Runciter to Joe Chip and the others in Half-Life.

Photo from the 2012 stage production of *UBIK* at the Baltimore Annex Theater

Art by Martina Cecilia

7.

IT'S A SMALL WORLD, OTHERWISE KNOWN AS "SIX DEGREES OF SEPARATION"

By Timothy Green Beckley

IT could be that the buck stops here.

In a letter to the late Victor Mansfield, Jungian disciple Marie-Louise von Franz wrote, toward the end of her life: "The work which has now to be done is to work out the concept of synchronicity. I don't know the people who will continue it. They must exist, but I don't know who they are."

OK. I don't really know anything about Marie-Louise; in fact, I don't know as much as I apparently should about Carl Jung (I do know that he didn't totally dismiss flying saucers and wrote a book on the topic), but I am willing to shoulder the burden of the person most determined to "work out the concept of synchronicity." My pleasure. But I might be in need of some help, as this is not your usual "reality game," but it certainly is intriguing and could ultimately lead to some important discoveries. I admit, however, that I am not sure everyone would want to escape the Matrix. It could be a colder, even crueler universe out there – though that's hard to believe.

Let us deal with another branch of this phenomenon. It's the concept known as *"Six Degrees of Separation,"* which posits that all persons living on the Earth are connected by six or fewer steps away from each other. In other words, I may not know you personally, but in order to make a connection all I have to do is know the "right" five people – or less in many cases – and I can soon be standing at your front door asking to come in.

I know it seems like a crazy idea, but I don't call the shots. I merely fall in line behind the proven statistics.

The theory is actually not new. It goes back decades, back to 1930, when Frigves Karinthy, an Hungarian playwright and poet set down the theory in *Chains*, a short narrative that attracted a bit of attention among the curious who struggled with the notion that it was much easier to be "socially connected" to someone picked at random than we would have thought possible under "normal" circumstances.

Numerically, the hypothesis has been proven by mathematicians at Cornell and other halls of science. And in 1967 American sociologist Stanley Milgram devised a new way to test the theory, which he called "the small-world problem." Milgram randomly selected people in the Midwest to send packages to a stranger located in Massachusetts. The senders knew the recipient's name, occupation and general location. Each participant was instructed to send the package to a person he knew on a first-name basis who was most likely, out of all the participant's friends, to know the target personally. That person would do the same, and so on, until the package was personally delivered to its target recipient. Although participants expected the chain to include at least a hundred intermediaries, it only took (on average) between five and seven intermediaries for each package to be delivered successfully.

Talk about beating the odds.

LETS ALL PLAY THE KEVIN BACON GAME

There is actually a site on the web that you can check out and see for yourself how this concept actually works. It's not a foolproof system, and you have to somehow be involved in show business or music for it to pan out to a positive conclusion.

The game is titled *"The Oracle of Bacon"* and its objective is to start with any actor or actress who has been in a movie, worked as a director or been on a TV show and connect them to Kevin Bacon in the smallest number of imaginary moves as possible.

Having been in a couple of movies and involved in numerous TV productions, I decided to try my "luck" by typing in my name in the space provided and see how I was possibly "related" to the hot star of "***Footloose***."

Kevin Bacon

was in

White Water Summer (1987)

with

Sean Astin

was in

Range 15 (2016)

with

William Shatner

William Shatner

was in

"Weird or What?" (2010) {Aliens Walk Among Us (#3.3)}

with

Timothy Beckley

Now, it's not very likely Kevin will come a' knocking at my door, but you never know. I was once standing on a corner in Greenwich Village and two people came up to me almost simultaneously. One fellow said he knew me because his niece had been in one of my movies and

The term "Six Degrees of Separation" has become so popular that there is even a Broadway production with the same name.

spoke highly of me (I guess she hadn't told him about the nude scenes). The other fellow recognized me because his ex had worked with me as a psychic reader at my regular workshops which I pulled together back in the sixties and seventies as part of the NY Occult Center.

Oh, and Kevin Bacon and I are both Cancers. So maybe we will meet at a birthday party somewhere down the line. I won't go without a formal invitation and he has to send a driver to pick me up. Sorry, Kev.

Over the course of the last couple of years, we have had Tessa Dick, PKD's fifth wife, on *Exploring The Bizarre* several times, so that is one link to the "man of the hour," though I am not sure if you can play the Kevin Bacon game with the deceased (I don't think anyone has published a rule book on the game). The most likely connection to PKD would be through the late Bishop Pike, a close friend of Dick's, whose son committed suicide in a hotel room where I once slept without realizing it at the time. Actually there is another event in the same hotel that makes this even more of a synchronicity but more on this as the pages roll by.

And speaking of meeting in usual places I have found that certain locations are like a bull's eye on the map for synchronicities and coincidences.

My friend, the late John A. Keel, identified these "hotspots" as "window areas." Best described as doorways, star-gates, portals, or, for the purposes of this work, as a break or interruption in the Matrix. I don't know of any statistics as to the number of people residing in these areas who have experienced a heightened degree of synchronicities. But I do categorically know that in these window areas you are likely to find more UFO sightings, a "population problem" when it comes to Bigfoot or other cryptids wandering around the suburbs, not to mention weird phone calls, confrontations with the dreaded Men in Black and perhaps a mysterious disappearance or two – someone call 911 please!

* * * * *

Well, since John Keel was just mentioned, I think I should talk about a minor "weird incident" that assisted as a bit player – an extra I guess you could say – in my research of the overall subject matter related to PKD. I was trying to find out if Phil had ever been connected to UFOs in anyway. After all, he did have the stranger at his door which propelled him to talk about extraterrestrials. But was there any more involvement in the subject that I didn't know about?

To wet my whistle, I went to Amazon and placed an order for several books that I thought might lead me deeper into the mysteries of PKD and those surrounding him.

One of the books I ordered was written by Anne R. Dick (spouse three – 1959 – 1965). ***The Search For Philip K. Dick*** is an in-depth look at Dick's life and career. I admit I haven't read it from cover to cover. Turning to the index, I wanted to see if there was an entry on UFOs. It listed a few pages. Before I could clean my glasses and turn to any one of the pages given, I noticed that there was something sticking out of the book.

That "something" was a "page malfunction." I don't know the proper printers' lingo for it, but I am sure pressmen have a word that describes the book's imperfection, which consisted of a page not having been cut properly and so a portion of it was hanging outside of the edge of the volume in my hands. I turned to this page figuring I would snip off the hanging paper when I noticed that the page detailed PKD's participating in a local UFO group.

There, in paragraph two on page 29, Anne tells us Philip had been invited to a UFO meeting held in someone's home, but he didn't really want to go. "I had had already heard about this group," Anne reveals. "It first met to talk about philosophy, but soon these otherwise sensible people came to believe in Claudia's (the organizer's) ideas about flying saucers. Claudia told them that soon the world was going to come to an end, but she was in touch with beings from outer space who were going to save a select number of people. When the last days came, her house would turn into a flying saucer. This would happen early next year, on April 22, 1959."

Phil was informed that it was detected he was from somewhere else and that he would assist in the removal of people off the planet before our world turned to dust. I would say that Phil had his own ideas concerning what his participation would be in the grand scheme of ET affairs, and so he managed to successfully hide every time the group's founder came looking for him to drag him to a meeting.

Now it's not that I wouldn't have gotten to the page where the incident was recounted, but it does seem a bit – and I say in this instance just a bit – strange that the page had been "marked" for me by the fact that the paper was hanging out of the book at that spot.

"Someone" must have known that I was going to get my hands on this particular copy of the book eventually – teasing me again just because I happen to be inside, and not outside, the Matrix. So who is controlling all these synchronicities?

Seeing is believing. Here is "The Search For Philip K. Dick" book which came with a built-in printer's malfunction that looks like a book marker. It extended from the exact page where PKD's UFO story was written.

8.

MY SYNCHRONISTIC FRIEND

By Maria D'Andrea

MARIA is an internationally known professional psychic from Budapest, Hungary. Since early childhood, she has demonstrated high spiritual awareness and psychic ability. Over her lifetime as a Spiritual Leader, she has provided excellent psychic guidance and enlightenment to many people, assisting them on their own personal path of spiritual self-discovery.

Maria has a website at: http://www.mariadandrea.com

* * * * *

Many eons ago, in grade school, new neighbors moved in next door to us. They had a daughter about my age named Elodia. I thought it was a wonderful name, since it was different.

We became very good friends. We were together all the time. Then one day, her parents decided to move and we were both very upset, but what can you do?

I really missed talking to her. And then we also moved. We were never in contact.

When I was in high school, I thought about her and how I really needed a friend that was supportive, because I was going through a little bit of a rough patch. I decided to go home by a different route and was waiting for a

Maria D'Andrea

bus. I heard two women, standing near me, who I thought were also waiting for the bus, speaking about their good friend Elodia. They were talking about how she was such a supportive, kind person. Then they walked away.

It was as though they were there just to give a message to me. How many times do you normally hear that name? It cheered me up, and, when I got home, I found out that my problems had been solved.

Several years later, I was looking for an apartment with my sons. It was difficult to find one where I didn't need a car (I didn't own one at the time), yet I could get around to places I needed to go. I once again thought about how great it would be to be able to talk to her. As I searched, one of the apartment buildings had a big sign in the lobby that said – "Birthday Party for Elodia in the Lobby."

That afternoon, I had my new place. I was starting to think of it as synchronistic, that each time her name came up, everything turned around to being better or was solved.

Three more similar events came up. Then I was in a store, in an area I've never been before, when two ladies in front of me in line were talking about their friend Elodia. At this point, it was just too much for me, and I told them I used to have a friend with the same name. We got into a discussion, and it turned out that they had indeed been speaking about my friend. We were all surprised, and I was very happy to find out she lived just a few blocks from the store I was in.

I got back in touch with her. I told her about how her name came up and how it affected my life.

She went on to tell me that, amazingly, through all those years, she had the same experiences, but with my name.

You have to love the synchronistic universe.

The Matrix Control System of Philip K. Dick
And The Paranormal Synchronicities of Timothy Green Beckley

SUGGESTED READING BY MARIA D'ANDREA

TRAVEL THE WAVES OF TIME

*100% POSITIVE SPELLS AND INCANTATIONS FOR
"ALADDIN'S MAGIC LAMP"*

HEAVEN SENT MONEY SPELLS

SECRET MAGICAL ELIXIRS OF LIVE

MYSTICAL AND MAGICAL BEASTS

9.

THE BIG BANG THEORY

By Timothy Green Beckley

WELL, if you're going to get into this whole synchronicity thing – the concept that "coincidences" don't just happen, that they are "staged" and "planned" by some supernormal source – you might as well go head first and get involved in a BIG way!

And I guess I did.

Maybe someone has a statistic for me. What are the chances of a person running into someone in a city of slightly under a million people when they haven't seen or been in touch with that person in years and have never visited that city previously?

First let me tell you my story and then you can contact me and validate that the odds are way out of the realm of chance.

It was way back in 1977. I was still working my way up the rungs of UFOlogy. Pretty well known, but not as established as I am today. It was a totally different world back in that time as there was no internet, few paranormal-type shows on TV, and it would be years till the SyFy Channel went on the air. We were still working in the media dark ages. There was no "fake news," in fact, there was hardly any news at all, at least as far as the world of the weird went.

Above: Highly thought of psychic Alan Vaughn meditating.

Below: This little paperback book confirms the account of author Alan Vaughn walking in on Tim Beckley and friends in a pub where none of the parties had ever been before.

To make up for this media blackout, almost every large city had at one time a UFO club or organization. Local promoters would tap into a roster of speakers and anywhere from a hundred to eight hundred or a thousand people would attend some very well organized meetings. The speakers were mainly of the contactee variety; those individuals claiming to have had a close encounter with extraterrestrials usually of a very friendly nature.

The alien beings looked so human as to be so mundane in appearance that they couldn't be picked out even in a small crowd, and the interplanetary chitchat was mainly about nuclear proliferation and even a bit on a shifting of the magnetic poles and the advent of global warming (that's how Earth Day came into existence).

In order to balance out their convention agenda and put someone on the program who was considered a more down-to-earth presenter, in that he had no wild, personal claims to make, the late Dale Rettig invited me out to San Francisco to speak at the Annual Congress of Scientific UFOlogists, a group for which I was on the permanent organizing committee. Oh, and by the way – I don't know who came up with the title for the group. I guess that old trickster Jim Moseley did, but, in all honesty I don't believe there was anyone with a scientific degree amongst us. But the name sounded very official and it did enable us to get on numerous local TV and radio programs as we were serious, but doubtlessly naive, about getting to the bottom of the UFO mystery.

After having been in town for four or five nights, I was finally on my way to the airport the next morning, a bit exhausted, to return to the east. The event's organizers realized we had some time to kill before my flight, so we stopped to have Sunday brunch at a place none of us had ever eaten in or even been to before – and remember, I was over 3,000 miles from home.

We just picked a place at random. It looked like a nice little café of sorts in a quaint area near Cobble Hill. We went in and I had a Bloody Mary and we sat down to a last minute bit of scuttlebutt. During the course of the conversation, I happened to mention that I wished I had had a little more time or a little bit more foresight because I would have liked to track down an old friend of mine. Alan Vaughn had moved from New York to the "city by the bay" to take a prestigious job as editor of a periodical called *Psychic Magazine* (long since out of business). Vaughn and I had shared a few laughs together in New York over the years and he had even taught some classes at my School of Occult Arts and Sciences. But I didn't have his phone number in San Francisco so, being a bit lazy, I passed on the idea.

Anyway, as I recall, the conference organizers nodded, indicating they were familiar and respectful of the name. Everyone associated with the field got nothing but positive vibes from the clairvoyant who passed away in 1983. Head of the dream research lab at Maimonides Medical Center, Dr. Stanley Kripner, once said: "Not only was Alan an extremely talented sensitive, he was willing to put his talents on the line so that parapsychologists could learn more about the process by which telepathy, clairvoyance, and precognition occurs. He even attempted to meet the Amazing Randi's challenge! His many friends will miss him, and we will all be indebted for the contributions he made to parapsychology as well as to our lives in and out of the laboratory."

At brunch, our conversation continued unabated, mixed with a bit of laughter and a clinking of glasses. Lo and behold, two minutes later someone walks through the front door of the bar who resembles my long lost friend Alan Vaughn. Shit, it WAS Alan Vaughn! Now this is a perplexing happenstance – it's enough to make you rub your eyes and shake your head in bewilderment. You're talking about someone and poof! They appear out of thin air as if they were summoned from a magic lamp. Shades of Genie in the bottle, only without the brew.

As one would expect, I stood up and gestured for this individual who was walking his dog on a leash to come closer.

"Alan, is that you?" I asked, wanting to be sure I was not imagining things.

Well, it was Alan of course. He pulled up a chair and joined in the conversation. After a good chuckle over the manner of our reunion and catching up on some personal gossip, we were all anxious to know what he was involved in at that moment.

HERE COMES THE PUNCHLINE

"Well, just by coincidence, I happen to be doing a book on coincidences and synchronicities, and I would guess I'm going to use this incident in the book."

Thumbing through the paperback when it was eventually published, I noticed he had presented a pretty valid case for coincidences being much more than just a matter of randomness that goes against the huge odds that shout out that these incidents could not possibly happen as they apparently do. These three incidents from the book's jacket illustrate his innate ability to do detailed research into the phenomena:

-- A woman in Berkeley, California, is locked out of her house; the postman walks up, holding a letter from her brother... inside is a spare key.

-- A hurricane in Galveston, Texas, sweeps Charles Coghlan's coffin out to sea; eight years and two thousand miles later, the coffin is found just offshore from the town where Coghlan was raised.

-- A Londoner takes the wrong bus, not realizing his mistake until he passes the house of a friend he hasn't seen in years; smelling gas at the door, he prevents a suicide.

So if you happen to locate a copy of Alan's book, ***Incredible Coincidences: The Baffling World of Synchronicity*** (Ballantine Books), you will find our bumping together highlighted even though I was some three thousand odd miles away from my home turf and it was years after Alan had moved to a sunnier California. To my way of thinking, being written up in someone else's book validates that I am not making the whole thing up and it's a little bit beyond just coincidence.

So has anyone had the chance to figure out what the statistics of this happening might be?

WAS IT JUST A FLUKE?

Well, don't put your calculator away just yet.

They say if you stand in the middle of Times Square long enough – the place known as the crossroads of the world – there is a good chance you will run into someone you know at least once. I would estimate I have been in Times Square over two or three thousand times in the course of my life and the only person I have ever run into there that I know is the late TV personality, the king of nostalgia, Joe Franklin. In all honesty, you couldn't miss him, as he had a cluttered office above one of the theaters on 42nd Street and he would walk around on his way to the office carrying a shopping bag. No, a synchronicity is something you can't count on. It's something that happens purely by chance.

I have had better luck at Penn Station next to Madison Square Garden, located on 34th Street in Manhattan, when it comes to hooking up with people that I least expect to run into.

One time I remember I got a call from Gray Barker, who told me that he had been scammed by someone portending to be Carlos Allende of the "Philadelphia Experiment" fame. Apparently this guy had visited Barker in Clarksburg, West Virginia, and convinced him he was on board the ship the USS Eldridge when it vanished and reappeared up in Norfolk, Virginia, over 500 miles away, after being teleported there during a Naval experiment.

Barker forked over a couple of hundred dollars for the exclusive rights to the story but he never heard from the guy again after a series of "promising" phone calls. I had been in the office I shared with *Saucer News* publisher James W. Moseley when I spoke to Barker, the head of the rival Saucerian Publications, long distance. He seemed angry at himself for being "so stupid," and was venting at me as I guess there was no one around at that late hour.

Around midnight I headed for Penn Station, which was only maybe a ten minute walk. I had a train to catch to stay over at my sister's house in New Jersey. When I got to the station, there was hardly anyone there and I had maybe 45 minutes to catch the next train.

There were a few homeless people around and a couple panhandlers, one of whom approached me. I told the guy I did not have any change, but he engaged me in conversation. I found it hard to walk around the platform to avoid him, so I stood and listened as he told me this bizarre story about how he was a veteran who had been involved in this weird experiment during which he had become frozen into the hull of a ship, an event that had left him deranged and homeless after leaving the service.

He then told me his name was CARLOS ALLENDE!

Well, I knew this wasn't the real Allende because I had seen a copy of his discharge papers and he would have been much older than this guy. It dawned on me at some point that this guy might have been the culprit who had flimflammed my buddy Gray Barker. When I put this to him, he got all indignant, claiming he didn't know any such person and how dare I accuse him of taking money under false pretenses. Eventually, the imposter walked off into the deep recesses of the rail station. When I next contacted Barker, he told me that, indeed, he must be the same guy. Surely, there are not two Carlos Allendes' walking around at the same time – unless they are replicates in a pure sci-fi mode, like out of "Invasion of the Body Snatchers."

Will the real Carlos Allende please stand up?

Eerie enough, right? We have heard rumors that the Dero have a conclave under Manhattan. According to Richard Shaver, who had a lifelong career of being hunted by the Dero, those slimy mutants live in the cavern world and are trying to destroy all that is good upon the surface of our world. Shaver was almost as popular as PKD during the 1940s and 50s, but ran afoul of the FBI at one point for supposedly running a porno ring (long story short, not guilty as charged). It was also claimed that Shaver had actually been committed to an asylum during the years he was supposedly being held in captivity in the caves of the demented Dero.

As for "Carlos Allende" in the subway, I would define such a meeting as a "fluke of luck," a chance encounter. The term "fluke" is from the mid-19th century and was used in games such as billiards to denote a fortunate stroke or run of the table.

But perhaps Shaver was on to something. Maybe the Dero were controlling a bit of Manhattan's real estate, particularly in the area of Times Square and Penn Station, for I have yet another story to tell about how certain places just have that vibe about them when it comes to attracting all sorts of synchronicities.

CAN WE CONSIDER THIS A "ONE-OFF"?

The term "one-off" might apply, you would think, in that the event in question would never happen again, even though it would have to be considered odd by most people's standards.

As we have seen, or are beginning to see, synchronicities come in all kinds of shapes and sizes. Some are impressive and can't easily be accounted for in mundane terms, while others may be more on the cusp of ordinary incidents that may be impressive to the person they happened to but lackluster when it comes to general acceptance by those outside a person's immediate circle of friends.

For several decades Pat – "Dr. UFO" – Marcattilio has held a small, but well-received, UFO conference outside of Trenton, New Jersey, in

Bordentown. He has pretty much used the same hotel and has managed to bring in from around the country a variety of speakers on the paranormal, though the flying discs remain his preoccupation. Pat is one of the nicest guys in the world. He would give you the shirt off his back and usually it's a very colorful one, as he favors the Hawaiian variety with pineapples, palm trees, surfboards and hula dancers in grass skirts. He had asked me to speak on this particular occasion, but I had to opt out because of prior commitments.

However, Pat wasn't peeved, I don't think, as he was used to a speaker not showing now and then. And he always had a backup presenter in the house for just such times. In fact, he knew that a mutual friend of ours, well-known international UFO researcher, lecturer and author, Antonio Huneeus, was going to show up and had a slide tray full of the best UFO photographic evidence from all over the world. Huneeus had recently moved from his New York Greenwich Village apartment to somewhere in Virginia, but I didn't know at that point how to reach him as he had momentarily slipped out of sight, which he does now and then.

Antonio Huneeus and Tim Beckley chat freely for a video available on Mr. UFO's Secret Files, posted on YouTube.

As a promoter myself, I am always interested in learning how many people attended and which speakers the audience liked the best. You would be surprised that some of the newbies draw better than some of the presenters who have been "overexposed." Anyway, I'm coming back from out of state, and I arrived in Manhattan at Penn Station. I get off the train and I'm headed towards the escalator onto Seventh Avenue. And here, right behind me, is Antonio, wheeling a cart full of his slide projector and some of his books that he was trying to sell at the conference.

So I say, "Antonio, how have you been?" And he said, "Oh, I'm just coming back from Pat Marcattilio's."

So here we are, in Manhattan, in Penn Station, There are probably 5000 people walking through the station at any one time. What are your chances of running into Antonio Huneeus? It's impossible to calculate. It certainly is beyond chance. It's just one of those "strange things" we get used to after a while. It's gotten to the point where I am not sure if I have more synchronicities under my belt than almost everyone else, or I just tend to notice them when they happen and hopefully remember to take notes.

Like this "chance" encounter with Antonio, is there a hidden meaning behind us bumping into each other? Not that I can decipher any "meaning," except that Antonio knows this happens to me an awful lot. We had a nice little chat for fifteen minutes and then we ended our conversation and we both went on our merry way.

RIDING THE RAILS

New Jersey Transit, which goes out of Penn Station, down to Trenton and into Philadelphia, seems to have a chokehold on me as far as the number of selective coincidences go.

Sometime after the incident with Antonio, I hop on the train, looking to get off in New Brunswick, where my niece will pick me up. Usually, the Trenton-bound express stops at the foot of Eastern Avenue in downtown NB, where I disembark and walk down a set of stairs to the sidewalk where my ride is waiting. This time the express train wasn't going to stop where it normally does, but buzz right on through the New Brunswick platform and directly on to Trenton. I only found this out after I had boarded the train and the conductor had punched my ticket. After telling him I was a bit confused as to what to do, he said that I should get off in Newark and get onto the next local, which would stop where I needed to go. No big deal, as it was maybe fifteen or twenty minutes behind the train I was on and all I had to do was walk across the platform.

A few minutes after getting off the wrong train, I am standing around reading the paper on one foot, since there are no empty spaces on the platform benches, when out of nowhere I see someone a few feet away pointing in my direction and calling my name.

"Tim, Tim, is that you?" I looked at this person, whom I didn't immediately recognize, and he says, "What? Oh, you don't recognize me? I'm your friend, Damian, from Colorado."

Well, now, Damian I see maybe twice a year when I used to go out to the slopes. He's one of the local characters there. He's a bartender and a very good chef. Every year when I go out there I run into him, but that's not so unusual because Aspen is a relatively small community. Damian told me that he had recently moved back to the East Coast and was on his way to visit his parents in New Jersey. Damian was staying at the New Yorker Hotel in Manhattan, where – "coincidentally" – I had promoted weekly seminars years and years ago.

So it seems we had both gotten off at the same stop because we had both gotten on the "wrong" train in Manhattan. And it turns out we had a chance encounter there on the platform. When the "right" train showed up, we hopped on it and chatted for the next half hour or so till we parted company, going our own separate ways. Again, this isn't shocking, but what are the chances of meeting somebody on the train platform under this peculiar set of circumstances, a good 2000 miles away from where you would normally run into this individual that you don't even know all that well?

I can ask the question. It's certainly a legitimate one, but I don't have a definitive answer. You can say our meeting was happenstance, was just "in the stars" (astrologically speaking), or maybe it was really predetermined in the stars if someone – or something – is tampering with the throttle of our existence from somewhere outside ourselves, from a control box outside the Matrix we are prisoners in.

ALL ABOARD! For a bit of New Jersey Transit synchronicity.

10.

ARIZONA: LAND OF ENCHANTMENT – AND A MILLION SYNCHRONICITIES TO BOOT

By Timothy Green Beckley

WOW, what a difference.

I hate to bad mouth "my city," the municipality that I love, but Manhattan is overcrowded, drab looking (mostly glass and shades of grey, with an occasional park tossed in to keep the middle class from going stir crazy). Then you have your corporate excess (Yes! We love Dunkin Donuts, but is there a need for two on one block?) And, above all else, God knows this place is damn noisy. They happen to be erecting four skyscrapers within a block of my modest domicile. It's enough to make you want to scream. Not that anyone could hear you anyway from all the booming and banging – I believe they call it "noise pollution." There are laws against it. They can fine a cab driver $500 for honking the horn, but five bulldozers can be lined up outside your door and it's OK because they have paid for the necessary permits to keep the politicians happy.

So, from time to time, I like to skip town. Don my cowboy hat and head west. I don't golf, so Palm Springs is out. Scottsdale is overrun by the rich, all wearing diamond-studded Rolexes, and it makes me seem out of place with my outdated Timex. So it's off to Tucson, where the cactus burrs stick in your sandals (curses, that can smart!) and the sun will give you rosy cheeks the color of the red wine you are sipping out by the pool.

Charla Gene holds one of the first issues of Tim Beckley's mimeographed newsletter, "The Interplanetary News Service Report," which he published in his mid-teens.

Tucson's best. L. to R. Alan Benz, organizer of World UFO Day. Tim in his cut-off-around-the-collar t- shirt (because it's so hot in Tucson). Ed Biebel, long time UFO researcher who Tim has known from when Mr. B. lived in Cleveland. And, up front, Raven De La Croix, an actress known for her lead role in the 1976 Russ Meyer film "Up!" She is the granddaughter of aviation pioneer Lieutenant William Knox Martin and today lives in Sedona in a home owned by film producer Paul Davids (think sync -- see separate chapter).

For a long time Tucson has been pretty much my "second home." On a regular, usually an annual basis, I get together with my UFO chums Charla Gene, Christine Franz Dickey, Ed Biebel and Allan Benz, who is a real "ole timer" on the scene, having been involved in UFOlogy for a respectable number of decades. Currently, Allan is the director of the World UFO Group and the U.S. organizer of World UFO Day, which celebrates the birth of the modern UFO era which began with Kenneth Arnold's sighing of nine crescent-shaped "wings" over Mount Rainier on June 24, 1947.

A couple of times I have participated in meetings held by Allan for Tucson's "inner circle" of UFO devotees. What has always intrigued me about Allan is his background as Librarian for the now long-defunct international organization – the Aerial Phenomena Research Organization. APRO (best known as) was at its zenith the second most popular UFO group in the world, next to the National Investigations Committee on Aerial Phenomena (NICAP). Unlike the Capitol Hill-based NICAP, APRO was less "official," had no political affiliations, and was more interested in who flew the saucers than whether the government was trying to hide the truth about UFOs from the American public.

They had no CIA operatives on their board of directors, but instead pulled in correspondence from a global team of researchers who studied landing cases and reports of close encounters with humanoid beings gathered from Italy, France, Sweden, and even Russia, which in those days was a real effort since the "Reds" had a very closed society, especially when it came to discussing UFOs and space beings. The state run Soviet press ridiculed the subject, if they mentioned it at all, going out of their way to identify the unidentified as purely a Capitalist phenomenon contrived as a way of taking people's minds off of troubling social issues taking place in American society.

APRO was run efficiently by the husband and wife team of Jim and Coral Lorenzen, who also edited a nicely done, very professional (for that period at least) newsletter, the APRO Bulletin. Allan Benz was voted in as official Librarian (he held a degree in that profession) and as such his job was to catalog and file the hundreds of translations of reports streaming in from

Raven featured in poster for the classic Russ Meyer film "UP!"

all over the world so that they could be pulled up quickly in an era when Kindle tablets, iPhones and lap tops still were quite a ways off.

I sat spellbound as Allan told me about how he was handed the opportunity of a life time. APRO had received a phone call from Paramount Pictures, who were in the early stages of development on a film that turned out to be a massive box office sensation. "Close Encounters of the Third Kind" was the brainchild of Stephen Spielberg, then a young upstart film maker who had experienced a UFO sighting in his teens, had read lots of books on the subject, and was so intrigued by the phenomenon that he wanted to produce a serious movie that would portray a UFO encounter as accurately as possible, based upon the "real life" exploits of someone who had been "touched" by the hands of an off-world intelligence.

Jim and Coral of APRO made Allan their "go-between" with the Hollywood studio. He plied them with all sorts of pertinent data that would make the film as realistic as possible, given that "the suits," as we call the corporate big wigs, would ultimately call the shots. He dug deep into APRO's files to share with Spielberg's production team the top cases involving the electromagnetic effects of UFOs on appliances, motor vehicles and the blackouts of entire towns along our national, interconnected, electric grid systems. There were also commercial pilot sightings and face-to-face meetings with the Ultra-terrestrials, enough material to hook Paramount and ultimately Spielberg up with so that they could head in the "right direction" with their plans for a movie that would ultimately gross worldwide $337 million, ranking it in the top ten films of all time.

You would have thought that maybe APRO or Allan would have been graced with an honorarium from those they had humbly served without concern for the long hours put into the task of putting together a dossier of great value and importance. Well, no. Actually, Allan, if I recall, does have a "thank you" letter from Paramount Studios for his considerable efforts. And as it turns out, through some weird set of circumstances (here we go again), Paramount ended up handing over the project to Columbia, who eventually released the film domestically in a little over 600 theaters, which is considered a very small debut for any theatrical product. That usually indicates that the distributor is leery that the film will not do very well and is hedging their bet on the presumption that the film may be a bomb.

It was an interesting conversation I had with Allan over the course of a hot and dry Tucson afternoon. I did have some minor involvement with ***Close Encounters of the Third Kind*** myself, in that I was an editor on the staff of the film's official poster and magazine special, the latter of which was a real glossy publication printed on high quality paper suitable for collectors. My job was to stress how the various scenes in the movie were comparable with events that had taken place in "real life." Sure, it was science fiction, but it was based on actual events that had transpired for someone, somewhere. And, indeed, there was a liberal dose of special effects movie magic tossed in that brought about an almost spiritual experience in viewers who were seeking to confirm the reality of a phenomenon they might have had to come to grips with themselves at one time or another.

Tim Beckley strolls about near the red rocks of Sedona. Something strange is always going on in the neighborhood (a la "Ghostbusters").
Photo by Charla Gene.

HEADS UP WHEN ENTERING THE SEDONA MATRIX

The travel guides describe Sedona in almost glowing terms:

Sedona

At an elevation of 4,326 feet, Sedona is an Arizona desert town near Flagstaff that's surrounded by red-rock buttes, steep canyon walls and pine forests. It's noted for its mild climate and vibrant arts community. Uptown Sedona is dense with New Age shops, spas and art galleries. On the town's outskirts, numerous trailheads access Red Rock State Park, which offers bird-watching, hiking and picnicking spots.

And you know what? They're absolutely, one hundred percent, right!

If Manhattan is the Ying, Sedona has to be the Yang. In Chinese philosophy Ying and Yang describe how seemingly opposite or contrary forces may actually be complementary, interconnected, and interdependent in the natural world, and how they may give rise to each other as they interrelate to one another.

The drive from Tucson to Sedona is long and hot, especially during the summer.

We're talking six or seven hours with the air conditioning blasting. About ten miles outside Tucson the traffic thins and in no time you are out in what we back east would call the "boonies." When the terrain allows, and you're not lumbering along some twisting mountain route, the road whizzes by as you put the pedal to the metal, which in my case is provided by Charla, my main source for what is taking place in the southwestern region of the country, from the most recent sightings of what have become known as the Phoenix Lights (even if the sightings are not actually in Phoenix), to the lowdown on who is speaking and what they are saying at the local Mutual UFO Network (MUFON) meetings. Charla is also a first class photographer who always manages to quite beautifully chronicle what is transpiring around us on our journey. On my visits to this breathtaking city nestled high in the red rocks – where actress Shirley MacLaine happens to have a very stately home, as do a number of other "Hollywood types" – something of a paranormal nature is almost certain to happen – and almost always does!

It's estimated that Sedona attracts about four million tourists annually like a powerful earth magnet. The visitors come from all over the world to hike, rock climb, go to the local art galleries, and take back home some of the most incredible silver jewelry in the form of thick bracelets and squashes created by the various Native American craft people who live on or near the twenty reservations that dot the state.

Those who reside in and around Sedona who are of a metaphysical or New Age persuasion seem willing to share with those who come here to meditate with crystals and dream catchers and hunt for UFOs how the town rests on several portals or gateways where all manner of odd events frequently occur.

We're talking about entrances to an underground UFO base, a canyon where a flying saucer is said to have crashed, orange orbs that haunt a ranch once privately owned and which is now fenced off government land. Not to mention a "blue man" who has appeared in photographs. Even though no one can see this presumed ultra-terrestrial, his presence is hard to deny as he stands next to witnesses at a night time UFO skywatch and can be captured digitally or on film.

I would say if you want to find out about these incursions into what we would call the "physical realm," you need to hook up with Tom Dongo, who is the most knowledgeable individual in the area when it comes to matters concerning the Sedona Matrix.

If you go to my YouTube.com channel, Mr. UFO's Secret Files and watch the video *"Invisible Aliens 'Invade' Town – Underground Bases Exposed,"* you will get a harmonious view of the town's supernatural underpinnings as experienced by a gentleman who seems to be trailed by all that is unexplained and devilishly strange.

The nature of Tom Dongo's various experiences in Sedona are highly unusual, even for a UFO Repeater.

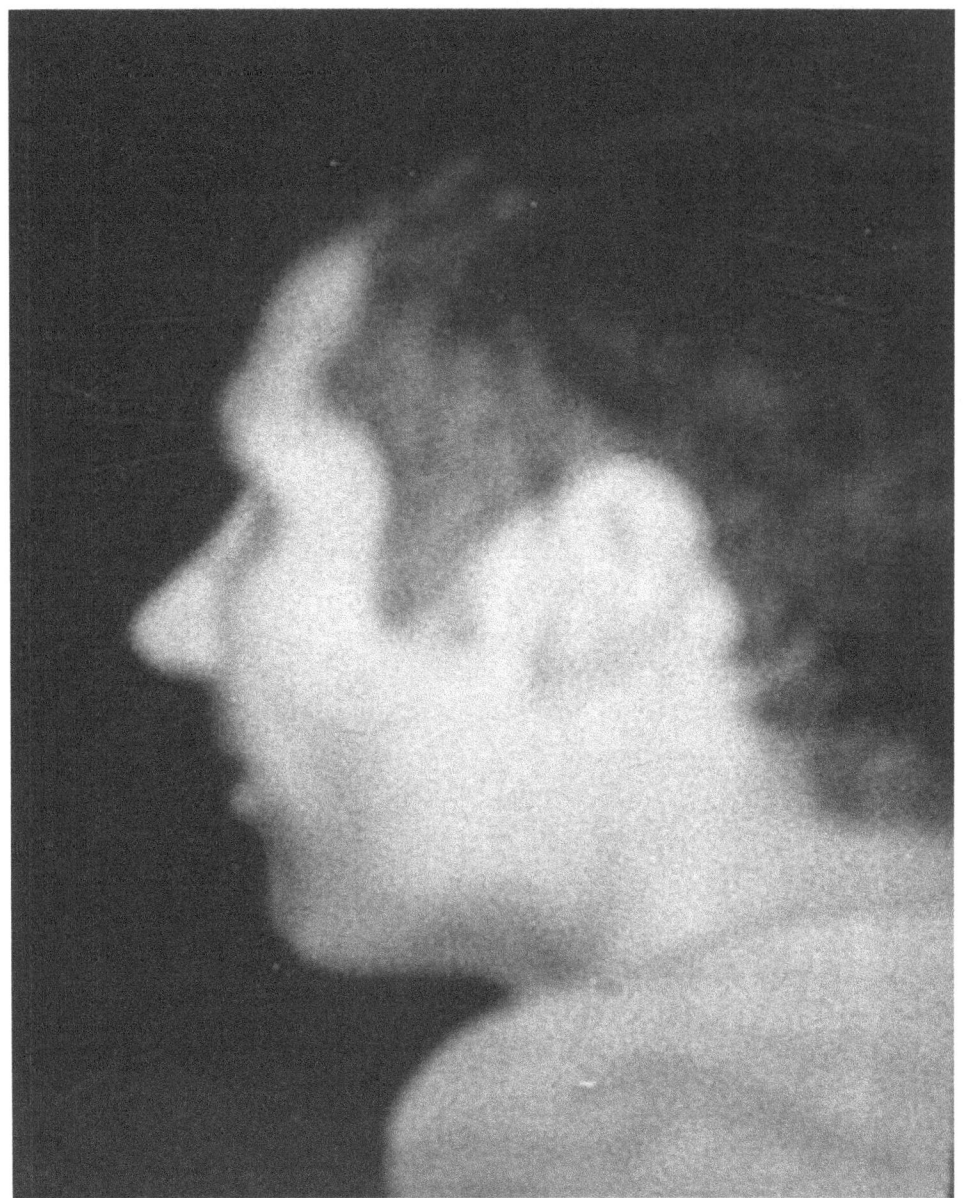

The "Blue Haired Man Of Sedona" was not seen at the time the photo was taken. Noted Tom Dongo: "Linda (Bradshaw) and I were standing side-by-side when she took the Blue Haired Man photograph. We were the only ones in the vicinity. The only thing that really strikes me as uncanny is the angled forward V-shaped sideburn. Here's why. The sideburn is in all ways identical to the sideburns worn by James T. Kirk and the Enterprise crew from the original 'Star Trek' series. This makes me wonder if Gene Roddenberry was privy to certain information before anyone else."

For a long time, Tom Dongo ran the ultimate and most illuminating jeep tour in all of Sedona. He knows the continuum of this place like the back of his hand as well as its incredible geology. I am not easily impressed, but Tom also possesses one of the largest collections of what I would consider to be authentic UFO pictures, either taken by himself or given to him by others who were lucky enough to aim a camera toward the sky and capture some bewildering phenomena.

And while UFO sightings and encounters have not been confined to any one locale around Sedona (a tall translucent being was even seen crossing the road in traffic a few years ago), one spot has generated more reports over the course of time than anywhere else in this community known for such natural landmarks as Bell Rock and Cathedral Rock because of the stark resemblance to the images they are named after.

I won't go into all the pertinent details here as this is not a book about Sedona, though it is one of the "trippiest" places I have ever been. I seriously suggest you watch the YouTube video. On Mr. UFO's Secret Files channel you will also find a podcast that extends the findings of Tom Dongo another couple of hours with an interview Tim Swartz and I did live on KCORradio.com sometime within the last year or so, if you care to check it out. Furthermore, there is also a book, ***UFO Repeaters: Seeing Is Believing, The Camera Doesn't Lie*** that the two Tim's put together which shows a lot of the pictures from Tom Dongo's weird and wild photo gallery, as well as discussing the stories of those for whom one UFO experience is just not enough, thus the term "UFO repeaters."

COFFEE ANYONE?

Now, I know some people claim they can get pretty ripped on an ordinary cup of java. Take it black without any sugar and God knows what the caffeine can do to you. Frankly, I can drink coffee before going to bed and it doesn't make me toss or turn any more than I would normally. On your way in or out of Sedona, I would consider it "bad manners" not to stop between the hours of 6

AM and 2 PM at the Coffee Pot Restaurant and order yourself some breakfast, even if you normally would be having lunch.

The Coffee Pot is known as the House of 101 types of Omelets, and, believe you me, when I tell you I'm not kidding that there is something omelet-wise on their extensive menu to satisfy any craving. Order up Omelet #34 if you like Avocado, Onion, Mushrooms and Turkey Gravy (yum?), or better yet Omelet #101 (the last on the menu) consisting of Jelly, Peanut Butter and Banana – that's my favorite, oh boy!

Tim studies the menu to pick out one of the 103 omelets offered at the Coffee Pot Restaurant in Sedona, where he has had a number of synchronicities right outside the front door in the parking lot.

The Matrix Control System of Philip K. Dick
And The Paranormal Synchronicities of Timothy Green Beckley

Gloria Reiser took this strange photo in Boynton Canyon in 1990. Behind her is a "machine" that looks like something out of a bad sci-fi movie. "Kronos" comes to mind.

WHAT IS THE SIGNIFICANCE OF 2012?

Furthermore, I know you're going to laugh at me – and a goofy-ish chuckle is justified in this case – when I tell you there is something damn mystical, something very strange, about the Coffee Pot. Could be its location, being that it is located on AZ Highway 89 at the entrance to the Cocomino National Forest and just a scant quarter of a mile or so from the New Age focal points of Cathedral Rock and Bell Rock, a beautiful setting at sunrise or sundown in anyone's estimation, and a high energy focal point if you want to charge your chakras.

If there is a New Age trend in the wind, Sedona's metaphysical party line operates overtime. If it's teachable, you can find a place in town to take classes in it. If it's a new product, they will likely have it first at the Center For The New Age or Crystal Enlightenment.

I'm not sure when all the fuss about 2012 started. But everyone – almost everyone anyway – said they felt a change was a brewing, that a big event was going to shake up humankind on a specific date – that date being the 21st of December 2012. This day was said to be the end date of a 5,126 year-long cycle in the Mesoamerican Long Count Calendar as specified by a group of Mayan priests, part of a hierarchy of Shamans whose culture extended across Mexico, Guatemala, Honduras and El Salvador, and that still exists to this day in varying degrees.

It was believed among those that prophesy that various astronomical alignments and numerological formulas would be in conjunction on that day that would mark the start of a period during which Earth and its inhabitants would undergo a physical or spiritual transformation and that 2012 would mark the beginning of a new golden era of peace and harmony on the planet. Some negative soothsayers said the world was going to come to an end and that the mysterious Planet X was going to pop out from behind the Sun and clobber Terra Firma, spinning us out of orbit and crushing us to death while depleting the atmosphere of Earth. It was, to me anyway, a sort of updated version of the Harmonic Convergence that had been celebrated back in 1987. If one had to pick a song that would best exemplify what we are talking about, it would be "Age of Aquarius" by the Fifth Dimension.

For a bit, it looked like things might get a bit dicey in Sedona on or around the day in question. There were plans for thousands to descend upon the town for a mass meditation and prayer to the heavens. A linking of hands across the galaxy, so to speak, was in the works. Who can have anything against such a concept? Well, there is a segment of those who live in Sedona year round who hate this sort of attention. They don't see anything particularly mystical about where they reside and to their way of thinking the "crazies" should all keep their distance. They pointed out that one rather prominent citizen had gone on record saying that he planned to take a "leap of faith" off of Bell Rock at around high noon to prove that we are living in a Matrix (hell, we could have told him that), and instead of committing suicide by crashing down from 5000 feet he would simply vanish in front of all those present, slipping through a vortex opening into another dimension.

Well, I figure that even if we truly are kept prisoner in a Matrix monitored by God knows who, you're not going to get out of the "fish bowl" by jumping off a cliff. You're going to go splat at the bottom of the ravine and your computer circuitry will have become a tiny piece of twisted solder. You will simply be fried before your time.

As we know, 2012 came and went and Earth didn't change visibly, nor did anyone I know ascend into the heavens. For all intents and purposes, December 21 passed us by without a hitch. We were not sucked through a giant worm hole nor did Planet X arrive, transporting with it the giants known as the Anunnaki from the planet Niburu, said to be coming here to steal the planet's gold resources and make sex slaves of our women. I could have told everybody that nothing spectacular was going to happen well in advance – these sorts of predictions seldom come to fruition.

But, then again, I did have a personal synchronized experience around that time – actually two of them – that I have been trying to build up to for the last few thousand words or so. Both experiences took place at the Coffee Pot, if that isn't weird by itself. I was having brunch with Charla and offered to pick up the tab since she had done all the driving and had even pumped the gas. I paid the bill with my credit card and had just walked through the front door of the restaurant out into the bright sunlight. I had the receipt from the cashier in my hand and was about to ball it up and toss it away when I happened to glance at the total to see what I had just spent.

The bill – with the tax – came to exactly $20.12! Not a penny more or less!

Someone suggested that the cashier knew me and made out the bill for this amount as a joke. Hardly the case. Had never seen the person before in my life and the receipt was from the checkout register – IT HAD NOT BEEN WRITTEN BY HAND. "Someone" – up there? – saw the humor in slipping me a receipt that came to the identical numerical amount that was on everybody's mind in Sedona. I guess I have had the final laugh, though, as I have told the story on the air now numerous times.

But there is more. Incident Two. As described, on another occasion I had spent the good part of the day in Tucson with Allan Benz before leaving to drive to Sedona. Charla and I had stopped along the way in the town of Jerome, which has more ghosts walking the streets than the number of actual people living there. You can read all about our day of ghost hunting in this old mining "ghost town" in "Spooky Treasure Troves." When we got to Sedona, we wandered into the Coffee Pot as usual. After chitchatting over a glass of wine and some Eggs Benedict (with coffee to go naturally), we wandered out into the parking lot.

I'm not sure who noticed the car parked right next to our vehicle, but it was sticking out a bit more than it should from its parking space. We couldn't believe our eyes. We had to get closer to the car to make sure we weren't hallucinating in the noonday sun. But we have photographs to prove that the license plate on the car parked next to us said, in big bold license plate letters: APRO.

There is no APRO! The group hasn't existed for over twenty years. So how could there be a license plate on the vehicle parked two feet away that has these four giant capitalized letters like it was a vanity plate smacking us in the face? And even if someone was, say, an old member of the group and still identified with it, why would their car be parked next to ours in the town

**Here is the proof! Rear license plate with APRO on it which was parked next to the vehicle Tim was riding in.
WTF are we dealing with here?**

of Sedona, or anywhere else for that matter? It's more likely you would win the lottery. It's not by "pure chance." It has to be a planned "secret operation."

It doesn't add up, my friends. It's just downright bizarre, and there is no "rational explanation" that will suffice. So don't accept any of Carl Jung's theories about dreams and déjà vu, it has nothing to do with synchronicities based on these assumptions.

Someone is screwing with our heads. Hey, but I'm not paranoid enough to let it trouble me. It just fuels my appetite to learn more about the "chess playing" masterminds from "outside the box" who are attempting to signal to us to get our attention.

But why?

I have a lot more questions, but fewer answers.

SUGGESTED READING

BOOKS BY TOM DONGO (Available on Amazon.com)

UNSEEN BEINGS, UNSEEN WORLDS

EVERYTHING YOU WANT TO KNOW ABOUT SEDONA IN A NUTSHELL

MYSTERIES OF SEDONA: NEW AGE FRONTIER

MERGING DIMENSIONS: THE OPENING OF PORTALS IN SEDONA

MYSTERIOUS SEDONA

THE QUEST

www.TomDongo.com

https://www.facebook.com/tom.dongo

11.

WHEN "FICTION" MIRRORS "REALITY"
By Timothy Green Beckley

PKD may have been of like mind when Motown artist Rockwell, backed up by Michael Jackson, sang these lyrics to *"Somebody's Watching Me."*

> *I always feel like somebody's watching me*
> *And I have no privacy*
> *I always feel like somebody's watching me*
> *Tell me, is it just a dream?*

To Philip, reality was always twisting, turning, scraping at his front door anxious to come in and blow his mind. There were plots within plots – not only in his stories, but in his life. The synchronicities and coincidences came in rapid fire, as if they were characters in a Matrix-induced computer game far more advanced than the ones the everyday couch potato plays.

We are repeatedly told that PKD was accustomed to looking over his shoulder. Some say it was the drugs, others say he really was being watched. Probably a combo of both – a double "coincidental dose" of paranoia makes the world go round.

Dick even went so far as to "make friends" – to keep in touch with – agents at the FBI. Hell, he must have figured if they were going to keep tabs on him anyway, why put them to the trouble of doing all the leg work? He also tossed in the KGB for good measure as an agency that was watching him, but

Donald Trump wasn't in office yet so it must have been harder for him to establish the proper contacts.

One of the things that really flustered him was a "home invasion." This event described by AllThingsCrime.com really unhinged him and no doubt help escalate his paranoia.

"In November of 1971, Dick began having premonitions that something momentous was about to happen. Several mishaps with his car as well a series of late night threatening phone calls from anonymous strangers were seen as ominous signs. Phil bought a pistol and began prowling around the house at night, peering out of the blinds on the windows. He was certain that he was under surveillance, and facing some sort of imminent attack from hostile forces. He called the police to demand protection, but they ignored him. They knew all about the whacked-out writer on Hacienda Way. He frequently rang them up to share his outlandish 'concerns.'

"On November 17, Dick returned home from shopping to find his windows smashed in, the house torn apart, his stereo system gone, and the steel-plated fireproof cabinet for his papers and manuscripts blown apart as if by explosives. Phil may have been shocked. But above all, he felt vindicated. In a state of near euphoria, he immediately called the police. 'You see, I'm not so paranoid after all.' Two detectives grudgingly paid a visit to the house. One of them asked Phil, 'Why did you do all this?' The next day, when Phil went down to the police station with a list of stolen items, he was brushed off and told he would be better off leaving town. No one wanted to investigate the break-in at the loony bin on Hacienda Way.

"Phil Dick, however, was very interested in investigating the break-in. In fact he was obsessed with it. He may have lost personal items during the burglary, but he had also received a tremendous gift. For one thing, his paranoia was confirmed. All of his fears and suspicions were now justified. Even more important, he now had new material to serve as grist for the great Phil Dickian mill. He would spend the next three years feverishly spinning his wheels around and around the mysterious break-in. The crime was tailor made for his unique imagination."

The Man In The High Castle **won the most prestigious Hugo Award the year it was released.**

PKD had always pointed to the Watergate break in as proof that conspiracies were all around us. The visitor at his front door had implanted in him the thought that Nixon would be impeached and he was not beyond hiding such tidbits of prophetic foresight within the texts of his novels, which were a lot more than just your ordinary works of "fiction."

The New York Times calls **The Man In The High Castle** "The single most resonant and carefully imagined book of Dick's career." Not an outlandish overstatement when you consider it won Dick the coveted Hugo Award, the highest accolade that can be given to a writer of science fiction or fantasy.

Amazon's TV version of High Castle shows the "new" Time Square under Nazi rule.

More recently, the book has been adapted by Amazon as a TV series and is going into its third Amazon Prime season. The book and series is hardcore Dickean. It lays down an alternative history in which the Axis powers won the war and Amerika has been divided up into sections, one of which is under the high command of the Nazis. The Amazon version is full of violence and intrigue with the main character trying to escape from this horrid actuality. ***The Man In The High Castle*** is certainly Dick's most straightforward, compelling illustration of the experience of an alternative reality.

Approximately ten years later, the "real" PKD found himself engrossed in a bizarre series of circumstances which involved a real group of fascists who were trying to commit crimes against the state. According to published accounts, in 1972, a far-reaching neo-Nazi organization discreetly began to contact various high-profile authors in the U.S. with a view to enlisting their help; the plan being to covertly plant code words into millions of science fiction novels and spread a secret message to certain sections of society.

The message was about a plague which would engulf the planet. This would, of course, have been unnecessary in our current day and age. All a group would have to do is get a representative on "Coast to Coast AM" or get Alex Jones to spout off at the mouth on "Info Wars."

In PDK's novel, the country is divided into two sections for Japanese and German rule.

NEO-NAZIS TRY TO UNDERMINE SCI-FI

Here is the one-sided correspondence which was obtained under the Freedom of Information Act:

Letter #1

October 28, 1972

Federal Bureau of Investigation

Washington, D.C.

Gentlemen:

I am a well-known author of science fiction novels, one of which dealt with Nazi Germany, called **Man In The High Castle**, which describes an "alternate world" in which the Germans and Japanese won World War II and jointly occupied the United States. This novel, published in 1962 by Putnam & Co., won the Hugo Award for Best Novel of the Year and hence was widely read both here and abroad; for example, a Japanese edition printed in Tokyo ran into several editions. I bring this to your attention because several months ago I was approached by an individual who I have reason to believe belonged to a covert organization involving politics, illegal weapons, etc., who put great pressure on me to place coded information in future novels "to be read by the right people here and there," as he phrased it. I refused to do this.

The reason why I am contacting you about this now is that it now appears that other science fiction writers may have been so approached by other members of this obviously anti-American organization and may have yielded to the threats and deceitful statements such as were used on me. Therefore I would like to give you any and all information and help I can regarding this, and I ask that your nearest office contact me as soon as possible. I stress the urgency of this because within the last three days I have come across a well-distributed science fiction novel which contains in essence the vital material which this individual confronted me with as the basis for encoding. That novel is CAMP CONCENTRATION by Thomas Disch, which was published by Doubleday & Co.

Cordially,

Philip K. Dick

P.S. I would like to add: what alarms me most is that this covert organization which approached me may be Neo-Nazi, although it did not identify itself as being such. My novels are extremely anti-Nazi. I heard only one code identification by this individual: Solarcon-6.

* * * * *

Letter #2

November 4, 1972

Inspector Shine
Marin County Sheriff's Office,
Marin County Civic Center,
San Rafael,
Calif 94903.

Dear Inspector Shine:

As you may recall, on or about November 17, 1971, my house at 707 Hacienda Way, Santa Venetia, was extensively robbed. The last time I talked to you, during February of this year, you informed me that you had broken the case; a man named Wade (Jerry Wade I believe) had been arrested with the Ruger .22 pistol of mine stolen during this robbery. I have been in Canada and now in Southern California and hence out of touch. Have any more of my possessions been recovered? Have there been any more arrests made? Do you have anything more you can tell me at this date?

While I was in Canada evidently my house was robbed again, during March of this year. I did not know this until what remained of my things arrived down here; my realtor, Mrs. Annie Reagan, had stored them, and at least one entire room of stuff is missing: the bedroom in which the control system of the burglar alarm was located, the one room not covered by the scanner. Obviously it was robbed by someone who intimately knew the layout of the alarm system and how to bypass it. I recall that Inspector Bridges thought that the November 17 robbery was an inside job, at least in part. I believe that this later robbery in March of this year proves it. Only two or three persons that I can recall knew the layout of the burglar alarm system. One was Harold Kinchen, who was under investigation by Airforce Intelligence at Hamilton Field at the time I left (Mr. Richard Bader was conducting the investigation; through Sergeant Keaton of Tiberon he asked me to come in and give testimony. It had to do with an attempt on the arsenal of the Air Force Intelligence people at Hamilton on I recall January first of this year).

I have more reason to believe now than I did then that Kinchen and the secret extralegal organization to which he belonged were involved in both robberies of my house, although evidence seemed to point more toward Panthers such as Wade. I say this because this is Orange County where I live now, and I have come to know something about the rightwing paramilitary Minutemen illegal people here — they tell me confidentially that from my description of events surrounding the November robbery of my house, the methods used, the activities of Harry Kinchen in particular, it sounds to them like their counterparts up there, and possibly even a neo-Nazi group. Recently I've obtained, by accident, new information about Kinchen's associates, and the neo-Nazi organization theory does seem reinforced. In this case, the November robbery was political in nature and more than a robbery. I have thought this for some time, but until now had less reason to be sure.

As to the motive of the assault I'm not sure at all. Possibly it had to do with my published novels, one of which dealt with Nazi Germany — it was extremely anti-Nazi, and widely circulated. I know for a fact that Harry Kinchen and the Japanese relatives he had through his wife Susan had read it. Kinchen's Japanese-born mother-in-law, Mrs. Toni Adams, had read the novel in the Japanese edition. Beyond any doubt, Kinchen is an ardent Nazi trained in such skills as weapons-use, explosives, wire-tapping, chemistry, psychology, toxins and poisons, electronics, auto repair, sabotage, the manufacture of narcotics. Mr. Bader is of course aware of this. What I did not pass on to anyone, because I feared for my life, is the fact that Kinchen put coercive pressure, both physical and psychological, on me to put secret coded information into my future published writings, "to be read by the right people here and there," as he put it, meaning members of his subversive organization. As I told you in November, he accidently responded to a phone call from me with a code signal. Later, he admitted belonging to a secret "worldwide" organization and told me some details.

The coded information which Kinchen wished placed in my novels (I of course refused, and fled to Canada) had to do with an alleged new strain of syphilis sweeping the U.S., kept top secret by the U.S. authorities; it can't be cured, destroys the brain, and is swift-acting. The disease, Kinchen claimed, is being brought in deliberately from Asia by agents of the enemy (unspecified), and is in fact a weapon of World War Three, which has begun, being used against us.

In a recent confidential discussion which I had with my Paris editor, a close friend of mine, this editor ratified my conviction that to allow this coded "information," undoubtedly spurious, to get into print, would be a disaster for this country. These neo-Nazis or whatever they are would "break" their own code and make public this phony information, thus creating mass hysteria and panic. There is, of course, no such new untreatable paresis, despite rumors we have been hearing from servicemen returning from Viet Nam. I have contacted the F.B.I. on the advice of my editor-publisher friend, but I felt I should contact you, too. You may wish to pass this information about the coded information in novels onto Mr. Bader.

I will hope, then, to hear from you. Thank you.

Cordially,

Philip K. Dick

P.S. Harold Kinchen introduced me to only one individual, who asked me to write for his underground pornographic publications; I refused. By accident I recently learned that this man, "Doc" Stanley, of Corte Madera, "was a student of the speeches of Hitler during his college days at the University of Chicago, advocating their doctrines and reading them to people." Neither Stanley nor Kinchen mentioned this to me.

* * * * *

As farfetched as these rambling letters may seem, they are not out of context with reality. It's sort of parallel with the disinformation bandied about in the UFO community, to the point where you don't know what's real and what comprises a separate reality.

There is no doubt that a disease can be embedded into our society. Some say that AIDS is such a plague. Others point to the weirdness of Morgellons, which the medical profession says does not exist. But those who have contracted it point to weird scabs with wires coming out of them on various parts of their body.

SUGGESTED READING

NAZI UFO TIME TRAVELERS

FINAL NAIL IN YOUR COFFIN

MORGELLONS: LEVEL 5 PLAGUE OF THE NEW WORLD ORDER

UFOS: NAZI SECRET WEAPONS

www.ConspiracyJournal.Com

The Matrix Control System of Philip K. Dick
And The Paranormal Synchronicities of Timothy Green Beckley

October 28, 1972

Federal Bureau of Investigation,
Washington, D.C.

Gentlemen:

I am a well-known author of science fiction novels, one of which dealt with Nazi Germany (called MAN IN THE HIGH CASTLE, it described an "alternate world" in which the Germans and Japanese won World War Two and jointly occupied the United States). This novel, published in 1962 by Putnam & Co., won the Hugo Award for Best Novel of the Year and hence was widely read both here and abroad; for example, a Japanese edition printed in Tokio ran into several editions. I bring this to your attention because several months ago I was approached by an individual who I have reason to believe belonged to a covert organization involving politics, illegal weapons, etc., who put great pressure on me to place coded information in future novels "to be read by the right people here and there," as he phrased it. I refused to do this.

The reason why I am contacting you about this now is that it now appears that other science fiction writers may have been so approached by other members of this obviously anti-American organization and may have yielded to the threats and deceitful statements such as were used on me. Therefore I would like to give you any and all information and help I can regarding this, and I ask that your nearest office contact me as soon as possible. I stress the urgency of this because within the last three days I have come across a well-distributed science fiction novel which contains in essence the vital material which this individual confronted me with as the basis for encoding. That novel is CAMP CONCENTRATION by Thomas Disch, which was published by Doubleday & Co.

Cordially,

Philip K. Dick
3028 Quartz Lane
Fullerton,
Calif 92631.

P.S. I would like to add: what alarms me the most is that this covert organization which approached me may be Neo-Nazi, although it did not identify itself as being such. My novels are extremely anti-Nazi. I heard only one code identification by this individual: Solarcon-6.

...will hope, then, to hear from you. Thank you.

Cordially,

Philip K. Dick
3028 Quartz Lane #3
Fullerton,
Calif 92631.

P.S. Harold Kinchen introduced me to one individual, who for his underground pornographic publications; I recently learned that this man, "Doc" Stan... student of the speeches of Hitler d... sity of Chicago, advocating... Neither Stanley or...

12.

AFTER DEATH SYNCHRONICITY SYNDROME
By Timothy Green Beckley

SOME of those that have experienced a variety of synchronicities pin the phenomenon as empirical proof of life after death.

They believe that loved ones from the other side are attempting to communicate with them and that they are being presented with "signs and symbols" in a variety of forms to prove that life is everlasting and that our loved ones do not turn to dust in at least the spiritual sense.

There is a direct connection between PKD and what I call the "after-death synchronicity syndrome." It involves Philip and the very controversial Bishop James Pike, one of Dick's closest friends. I initially thought they made strange bedfellows indeed. But I sort of dismissed this idea the more I delved into their "coincidental" connection. But before I get into PKD's personal involvement in this eerie phenomenon, I should set the stage and explain a bit more about what this after death experience entails.

PENNIES FROM HEAVEN

Oh, every time it rains

It rains pennies from heaven.

Don't you know each cloud contains

Pennies from heaven

You'll find your fortune

Fallin' all over town

(As sung by Billie Holiday.)

One of the most pleasant individuals I have had the pleasure of interviewing on *"Exploring the Bizarre"* is Nancy Northrop Sluzinski. Neither Tim Swartz nor I knew anything about her before she appeared on our weekly show. We were looking to do a program specifically on the idea that there is a hereafter and that the "dead" can communicate under the right conditions with those of us who are still sucking air into our lungs, polluted as that air may well be. We had already done shows on mediumship and psychic artistry (i.e., those that can faithfully reproduce the likenesses of the deceased without having known or seen pictures of these individuals while alive). Frankly, we were looking for something a bit more edgy, a bit more evidential.

Somewhere or other I came across the biography of a writer primarily of children's books who had been born in 1939 to a much respected Manhattan dentist, Dr. Robert Wright Northrop. At age 40, Nancy divorced, having decided she needed a big change in life. She felt boxed in. So, having no children, she returned to single life.

"I had a chance to transfer from my job in Massachusetts to another division in Connecticut, thus my journey began," she explains. "Two months after my move, I met a farmer who had been raised Catholic and we found that God gives everyone hunches, but we just hadn't been listening to ours." The couple decided they spiritually craved a rural setting, and, following an inner voice, made the transition to a more relaxing environment in North Carolina.

Nancy says she can remember even letting "spirit" plot their course. "I had been a practicing Spiritualist for about ten years and one day I encouraged my husband, Richard, to take a walk with me and ask if there were any spirits present on our property

"He just said, 'Is there anybody out here?' And he heard a voice reply. 'This is Lucas and I've been out here all this time. I've been waiting for you to say hello.'"

According to an article in the *Windsor Locks Journal*, over a period of several days they met a variety of spirits. After some encouragement, Nancy sat down and wrote a story about their experience called "Lucas and Company."

"It just came to me. I was inspired. I just wrote it down in one night. This small book described the roles of the various spirits, as well as telling farmers the steps involved in growing tobacco and corn."

This was back in 1990, and Nancy hasn't stopped writing to this day.

Nancy related on the air how her beloved had passed away from a devastating illness almost a decade ago now. But she is no longer as sad as she was in the beginning because she hears from her husband frequently. But he isn't whispering in her ear or coming to her in dreams. Instead, he is tossing around pennies as if they are coming from out of nowhere, thus the title for her book. **Pennies from Heaven: Really! – A Widow Shares Her True Story.** The book is a quick read but a positive one, indubitably.

It's as if they are falling from the sky. A few have. Many others show up mysteriously. It's as if the pennies have some magical quality about them.

"They are definitely a sign that my husband is nearby. He knows I was concerned that he left me to tend to the business of his farm and trying to sell the property and move into town."

At first there were the phone calls. But they weren't from Richie. They were from her father. How did she know? "Well, the phone calls consisted of only one word being spoken before we were disconnected. The person on the other end of the line would say the name 'Nanc,' which is what my father called me."

Then the pennies came in a virtual onslaught.

"They were my husband's way of saying hello and how much he still loved me."

She confirmed that their life had been one of many riches and rewards. Nancy says she found pennies in the oddest places: "There was a penny on the porch railing after a rain storm. Next I found a penny in an empty dog dish. Then there was the one in the center of a carport under the car when it was moved. And in my rocking chair in my office, where I only wear PJ's."

Nancy Northrop Sluzinski communicated with her deceased husband through a series of unexplained "coincidences."

In fact, Nancy got quite the reputation locally for being the "pennies from heaven lady." People would come up to her and when they knew no one was listening would take her aside to tell her how they shared in the joy over the appearance of these "displaced items" showing up in their lives.

"Back around Christmas," Nancy recounted, "I was talking to a lady in the hospital where they sell my books in the gift shop. She called me aside and told me her daughter had passed recently and that at the funeral they had sent balloons up toward heaven with little messages attached telling her how much they missed her and how they loved her."

"The woman was very shocked over what happened next," Nancy continued. "She said that several days later a neighbor's dog showed up at their property and he had a piece of a balloon in his mouth, and, when they took it away from him, they noticed that there was still part of a message that had been sent in the balloon. It turned out that this particular message was from her daughter's son. Recovering part of the note from the dog served as a message from her daughter that she got to heaven and she was ok. And so my friend who worked in the hospital told me she felt much better."

From the evidence that Nancy Northrop Sluzinski presents about the penny syndrome, we can justifiably call this synchronicity, and it seems to have rubbed off on other people from her inner circle. This is best exemplified by a story she tells involving a young man she hired to work on the farm soon after Richard passed on.

"This boy came and worked on the farm after my husband died," she said, "because I didn't want to be there alone as there were too many people I caught walking around the costly equipment. He was a lovely country boy and I had him mind the farm and plow the fields. I lived in the main house and he lived in a house on the hill. As it turns out, he was watching TV one night after I had given him my husband's cross because he was really a big help to me immediately following my husband's death. He had placed the cross so it was hanging on a picture in front of the television when suddenly he heard a clump and began to look around for the source of the sound as he walked toward the kitchen to get another beer. When he got to the kitchen, there on the floor was the cross next to a penny. So he told me that kind of quietly and that he didn't know what to believe. And I said, 'Well, maybe Richie's there watching you.' And then he turned white and looked like he was going to faint. Three days later, in a snowstorm, he went to check the barn, and there, on top of the snow a few feet from the barn door, was a shiny new penny. This made him a believer."

I had some final questions for our *"Exploring the Bizarre"* guest: Was there any significance to the dates on the pennies? And why does it seem, at least to my way of thinking, that people in the Bible Belt do not take well to the concept that life continues after we are said to be dead and buried? Nance, as her father called her, managed to rustle up a couple of rational answers that pretty much satisfied my curiosity.

South of the Mason Dixon Line (road marker) some forms of belief in an afterlife are often associated with Satan and red pajamas.

"Some had random dates that didn't have any particular meaning to us that I could think of. There were some other ones of strategic importance in our relationship. Like those that were from 1979, which is the year we met, and one that was from 1946 when he started serving in the army. Initially I saved all of them, but eventually I had to stop doing that as there were just so many of the coins"

As to why people down South are so opposed to this sort of phenomenon, Sluzinsky says it's partially because of their religious upbringing. "It's part of being a Baptist," she replied, though she does qualify this brash statement by allowing that, "Down here, they smell the cigar smoke of grandpa or the apple pie baking in grandma's kitchen. It's more about local farming issues than anything else, with fear of the unknown preventing them from making a more careful examination."

SUGGESTED READING – BOOKS BY NANCY NORTHROP

PENNIES FROM HEAVEN...REALLY!

CONNIE THE THREE-LEGGED TURTLE

MOMMA—WHERE HAS GRANDPA GONE?

THE STORY OF MYSTARI

NOW HERE IS MY TWO CENTS – LITERALLY

For those of you waiting for the punch line, let me literally toss my own two cents into this discussion.

The delis around me for the most part stay open all night. I was out at around midnight after sitting here at my laptop working for hours when hunger finally caught up with me. So I walked across Fifth Avenue and went into a place that had a salad bar, a hot table with the remains of the day's "freshly made" food, a variety of cold cut sandwiches and pastry and beer and packages of chips. You kind of name it they have it (Well, they did. They have since gone out of business, not being able to pay the sixty thousand dollars a month rent – yes I said sixty thousand!) After I grabbed what I was craving, I headed to the cash register in front to pay the only person working this late at night (not counting a security guard and a stock boy putting stuff on the shelves, half-assed, somewhere way in the back). Turns out I was two cents short. For this amount this late the clerk certainly wasn't going to make an issue over my being tapped out. Still, I apologized and said I would give him the pennies next time I saw him. I walked back to the table where I had left my proofreading (still working!) and my coat on the back of the chair.

Lo and behold, next to the newspaper and my glasses were two old, dirty pennies. There was no one who could have left them there. I tossed them on the counter on my way out the door. Synchronicity strikes again – but it can sometimes be a cheap bastard (see my Atlantic City story elsewhere).

A MATTER OF LIFE – OR DEATH?

Well, I have a better "life or death synchronicity" story that will probably be more to your liking and is more on the mark. Several years ago I was rushed to Bellevue Hospital unable to breathe. It felt like my heart was about to explode. Because of my condition, I was rushed into the ER to be examined. While lying on a rather uncomfortable gurney, a series of doctors came over to me one at a time to try and diagnose my condition.

Well, believe you me, even in the Bellevue emergency room I find ways to attract a healthy dose of weirdness.

At this point, let me tell you I was stressed out and in panic mode to begin with. Man, I couldn't catch my breath enough to walk fifty feet at this juncture. Heart racing, I saw one doctor who took my blood pressure and vital signs and spoke with me for a minute or two in order to assess my situation. She left, and a young male doctor came over and asked me if I was Timothy Green. I was kind of shocked that he identified me this way and asked him how he knew my middle name since it wasn't printed on anything in connection with the hospital or on my insurance papers. He kind of looked at me bewildered, shrugged his shoulders and muttered something about it being the name of a doctor he had just spoken with at the other end of the emergency room. That has to be nonsense. Absurd! Finally, he "corrected himself" and asked if I was Timothy Beckley, which was down on my admittance form that he had now bothered to take a moment to review.

What had shocked me in particular was that fact that the only person to call me Timothy Green or Timmy Green was my Mom, who passed away in the late 1960s. We were rather close and shared an interest in the paranormal. In fact, our home was haunted while I was growing up and my mother had apparently conjured up some spirits with the Ouija Board. And she had been with me when we had both seen two UFOs hovering overhead when I was ten. One seemed to be directly over our home, perhaps as a harbinger of my fascination with the subject, which has lasted for well over half a century.

Thinking about the MD's use of my middle name while I was being processed into the hospital, I couldn't help but accept the fact that this was more than a mere "coincidence." It seemed obvious that this was a "sign." I gave a sigh of relief that this was my late mother trying to tell me everything was going to be alright. Can't help but think my Mom was standing nearby, stepping down from heaven if only briefly as I was wheeled to a private room and hooked up to all sorts of modern miracle medical contraptions that looked like they belonged at the helm of Star Trek's Enterprise. After three or four days of visits from my homies who had come to wish me well, and an endless series of blood tests and examinations, a team of surgeons implanted me with an alien device – OK, it was only an earthly pacemaker but, hey, when you're in my condition, one can feel free to fantasize, can't they?

So how did the doctor know my "nickname?" He obviously didn't, but somewhere there was a minor invasion of the Matrix we are encased in. Maybe to say, "Hey, buddy, you're getting too close to the truth!"

PKD AND THE LATE BISHOP PIKE

For a long time I couldn't help but believe that PKD and Bishop James Pike made strange bedfellows. It wouldn't seem that they would have a lot in common, but as it turns out they certainly did. PKD was always questioning his religious beliefs especially wanting to know the meaning behind "the strange woman" emanating a pink aura standing in the doorway with what he took to be the Christian symbol of a fish on a necklace she wore. This experience produced a massive jolt on his psyche, but it also was a huge influencing factor on what he was to write about in the years following this experience with what has become known as "the pink light."

From what I can gather Dick and Pike first hooked up in July 1966, when the Episcopal clergy officiated at PKD's marriage to Nancy Herbert (wife number four). One could say that Pike was in his own way as "extreme" and controversial as Philip, having come under attack from his own church because of his "radical" views on numerous topics. He was an early proponent of the ordination of women, racial desegregation and the acceptance of LGBT people within the mainline churches.

Christian fundamentalists, meanwhile, were quick to attack him due to his liberal views: In regards to his theology, he seems to have had a problem with, amongst other things, the glorious Second Coming of the Lord Jesus Christ, the Virgin Birth, the Trinity, and what he called the "myth of the Garden of Eden." An event that had transpired a few months earlier might also have bought them together – as both gentlemen were looking for answers to specific conditions which were affecting their lives.

The writer and the bishop became "cosmically tied" when Pike officiated over PKD's fourth marriage.

Above: Bishop Pike had to deal with heresy charges more than once in his life, including for his beliefs about life after death.

Below: Bishop Pike and Martin Luther King discuss race relations in America.

The Matrix Control System of Philip K. Dick
And The Paranormal Synchronicities of Timothy Green Beckley

In February 1966, Pike's son committed suicide. He used a handgun, just pulled the trigger. He was holding up in a single room in a hotel off Broadway in midtown Manhattan. He had been depressed...using drugs. .. and just couldn't take it anymore. It was messy, my friend, Sandra, whose family lived in the apartment right next door, says of the condition of the room after the unfortunate episode. In fact, I didn't realize it until I spoke to Sandra recently that I had slept in the very room where the tragic event had taken place. The room eventually became part of the apartment where the Grahams resided. I stayed over many times. No one ever told me about the history of Room 429.

I was running my occult center out of a basement down the block, so I often dug in there for the evening instead of heading out to the suburbs, which I was still doing at that point in my career, which even than had many tentacles. However, there is another tragic event that took place in the same hotel years later that makes this an even more troubling synchronicity. But more on that in a moment.

After the death of his son, James Jr., the Bishop became despondent, the suicide having filled his heart with great sorrow. After many years of being estranged, father and son had reconciled and started sharing time together in England. But James Jr. was a restless soul and so headed back to the States when he became overtaken by a troubling spirit that often possessed him in irrational ways. Some say that it was due to his use of psychedelics causing a negative psychotic reaction.

After his son shot himself, Bishop Pike went into seclusion. He found himself holding up in his flat in Cambridge, England, where his son had stayed from time to time. A strange series of events started unfolding all around him in the apartment, convincing Bishop Pike that his deceased son was visiting with him, trying to provoke a reaction.

First off, Jim Jr. was a collector of postcards. He purchased them everywhere he traveled, though he often forgot to actually mail them. Now they were showing up of their own volition and being left in strategic spots so that they would seem to fall in a pattern like the hands on a clock, pointing to the specific instance the gun went off in his hand and his life ended. There was also the matter of open safety pins. Most guys just do not keep a lot of safety pins in their bureau drawers or elsewhere for that matter. Now there were pins all over the place laid out on the floor, and they too were placed as if they were revealing the time of death. Something strange was going on which Bishop Pike didn't have an immediate explanation for and it was one that was in disagreement with church doctrine in regards to life everlasting.

Such a placement of objects was considered by Pike to be more than "coincidental," plus it could well be the missing link to proving that there is a nonphysical universe outside of the corporeal Matrix we reside in.

Perhaps even more mysterious was the fact that one of the Bishop's closest associates, Mrs. Maren Bergrad of the Episcopal Diocese of California, who assisted with secretarial work for Pike, reported that she had been asleep in the flat where she stayed and that when she awoke in the morning her long bangs had been singed off. James Jr. had on several occasions said he thought Maren's hair needed trimming very badly in the front because it hung down so low that it covered a good portion of her forehead.

Books had also moved "by themselves" about the apartment with "incriminating" postcards stuck within their pages. More fantastic, if calculated on a scale of one to ten, was the clock in the bedroom, the hands of which froze several times, even after winding, at the precise minute Jim Jr. had ended it all back in New York. And a visitor to the apartment while staying over one night started channeling in his sleep. The channeled message seemed to match the "hippie philosophy" of the clergy's son. The first thing anyone thought of was poltergeists because, when pressed for an "ordinary" explanation, no one had any.

Eventually, the services of a medium were sought, though such matters were technically frowned upon by the church, since spiritualism was considered a "fringe doctrine" – at best – that had been heatedly debated by the Episcopal Church's hierarchy for decades. When queried, the Bishop's superiors tended to put such matters into the category of phantasms, which is an upscale word for ghosts used mainly in the UK by those seeking a more mundane "psychological" explanation for such phenomena. The church was not generally accepting of spiritualist ideas of life after death, so the Senior Pike was going to have to go out on a limb (thank you, Shirley) all by himself.

And that he did. Pike was soon taking the bull – or was it Satan, as the insane fundamentalists proclaimed – by the horns?

The Bishop was through a chain of events introduced to a number of mediums who held what could best be defined as old fashion séances in a darkened setting, curtains closed and the holding of hands around a circular table. If you've seen *Séance on a Wet Afternoon*, you will recognize the backdrop. For purposes of the rendering of this story, we will concentrate our attention on the late Arthur Ford, founder of an internationally respected spiritualistic group known as Spiritual Frontiers.

ENTER THE MEDIUM REV. ARTHUR FORD

The Rev. Ford was highly respected among his peers and was tested by the likes of Duke University. Many believed he had supernatural powers and could establish contact with the "next world." A capsulated summary of his life and career can be found on the site *PsychicTruths.com – Best Mediums of the Past.*

An American Spiritualist Medium and founder of the International General Assembly of Spiritualists. Ford was born January 8, 1896, at Titusville, Florida. As a youth he followed a pilgrimage that took him from Episcopalianism to the Baptists to Unitarianism and finally to the Disciples of Christ. He attended Transylvania College, a Disciples of Christ school in Lexington, Kentucky. Ordained as a Disciples minister, he served a church in Barbourville, Kentucky.

Ford realized his psychic abilities during World War I. While in the army he would "hear" the names of people he served with, and those names would appear on the casualty lists several days later. In the years after the war he investigated psychic phenomena and eventually joined the Spiritualists movement. Around 1921 Ford emerged as a trance medium, and "Fletcher," his control for the rest of his life, made his first appearance in trance sessions. He developed a popular following and in 1927 traveled to Great Britain. One of his lectures was attended by veteran Spiritualist Sir Arthur Conan Doyle, who enthusiastically told people the next day, "One of the most amazing things I have ever seen in 41 years of psychic experience was the demonstration of Arthur Ford."

Ford founded a congregation in New York City, but soon experienced conflict with the National Spiritualist Association, the main Spiritualist organization of the time. Ford had come to believe in reincarnation, a belief the association rejected. After many years of tension, in 1936 Ford led in the founding of the General Assembly, which had a more open perspective on reincarnation.

Ford achieved fame far beyond the Spiritualist community in 1928 by allegedly breaking the secret code between the late Houdini and his wife Beatrice. Houdini had arranged with his wife that if he died before she did he would attempt to communicate through a secret code known only to them. Arthur Ford is credited with revealing that code through his control, "Fletcher."

As a result of a tragic auto accident in 1931, in which his sister died, Ford was severely injured and became addicted first to morphine and then to alcohol. In his autobiography **Nothing So Strange** *(1958) he states that it took him 20 years and much suffering to overcome his addiction. (In fact, he never overcame his addiction and suffered from alcoholism until the end of his life.)*

In spite of his affliction he impressed numerous people with his abilities, including prominent researchers William McDougall and William G. Roll, Jr. of the Psychical Research Foundation. He also traveled widely to demonstrate his mediumship and in Britain visited the Churches' Fellowship for Psychical and Spiritual Studies. In 1955 Ford was active in the formation of a similar organization in the United States, the Spiritual Frontiers Fellowship, still active today.

In 1967 Ford again came into public prominence during a television discussion on life after death, when he went into a trance and delivered *several messages to Episcopal bishop James Pike. One claimed to be from Pike's son and another from the prominent theologian Paul Tillich. Duly impressed, Pike later publicly affirmed his belief in the reality of psychic phenomena in his book **The Other Side** (1968). The television program also revived public interest in Spiritualism and psychic phenomena, and within a month Ford received more than 12,000 letters. It was only after Ford's death that Allen Spraggett and William Rauscher, while compiling materials for his biography, discovered his notes for the session among his papers, revealing the fact that he (may have) faked parts of the famous séance.*

*Ford died in Miami, Florida, January 4, 1971. Shortly after his death, Ruth Montgomery claimed to have received messages from Ford, which were later published in her book **A World Beyond** (1971).*

The most decisive incident in evaluating Ford's mediumship seems to be his relationship to the Houdini code. The evidence for the authenticity of the code message from the deceased Houdini received through Ford's mediumship is contradictory. The message itself involved a secret code that was supposed to have been known only to Houdini and his wife. The stage magician Dunninger, however, claimed that the code had been published earlier.

The testimony of Houdini's widow is contradictory. She was said to have told a reporter that she did not know what the message would be, although she later wrote an impassioned private letter to columnist Walter Winchell stating emphatically that the message received from Ford was definitely the one agreed upon with Houdini and that she had not previously revealed it to Ford. She insisted it was not a fraud, as some had claimed.

SÉANCE BROADCAST ON NATIONAL TV

We might be safe in saying that the whole world was watching. I can't recall any other time in history that an entire séance was broadcast to the masses as it was when Bishop Pike went before the cameras to try and communicate with Jimmy Jr. The Bishop had a lot to lose should the medium Arthur Ford be exposed as a charlatan in front of a huge viewing audience. Though nothing conclusive can be said to have come out of the séance, Bishop Pike thought it was legitimate all the way.

The same website describes the mass séance accordingly:

At the beginning of the séance, Ford placed a dark handkerchief over his eyes, commenting that it was easier to go into trance if he did not have light, and the bright lights of the television studio would make the reception of the trance state that much more difficult. Once he had attained the trance state, Fletcher soon made an appearance. Fletcher said that he had two people eager to speak. The first communicating entity was that of a young man who had been mentally disturbed and confused before he departed. He revealed himself as James A. Pike, Jr. He said how happy he was to speak with his father. Next Fletcher brought forward George Zobrisky, a lawyer who had taught history at Virginia Theological Seminary. Zobrisky said that he had more or less shaped Bishop Pike's thinking, a point which the clergyman readily conceded. Louis Pitt then sent greetings to the bishop, who recognized Pitt as having been acting chaplain at Columbia University before Pike had become chairman of the Department of Religion.

Fletcher next described an "old gentleman," who, after some discussion, Bishop Pike recognized as Donald McKinnon, a man who had been the principal influence on his thinking at Cambridge. The last Spirit to come forward told Fletcher that he had called himself an "ecclesiastical panhandler" in life. Bishop Pike appeared to know at once what man had carried such a humorous self-described title. Allen Spragget, serving as moderator, asked Fletcher for a precise name. "Oh," said the spirit control, "something like Black. Carl. Black. Block."

"Carl Block," Bishop Pike agreed, "the fourth bishop of California, my predecessor." Then addressing the spirit directly, Bishop Pike said, "I admired and respected you, and yet I hoped you weren't feeling too badly about some changes."

Speaking through Fletcher, Bishop Block told his successor that he had done a "magnificent job" and that he had "magnificent work yet to do."

Bishop Pike said later that he did not see how any research done by Arthur Ford could have developed such intimate details about his life and such facts about the roles that certain individuals had played in shaping his thinking. He felt that the details had been "quite cumulative, not just bits and pieces, an assortment of facts." Bishop Pike stated that the information provided through Fletcher had formed a pattern. "Also, the persons who purportedly communicated had one thing in common – they were in varying ways connected with the development of my thought. They knew me at particularly significant times in my life, turning points."

A controversy still exists – did the medium Arthur Ford actually make contact with the spirit of Bishop Pike's son on national television?

In many ways, the life of Arthur Ford was quite tragic. In 1930, a truck went out of control and struck the car in which he was driving with his sister and another woman as passengers. The two women were killed outright, and he suffered serious internal injuries, a broken jaw, and crushed ribs. During his long hospitalization, he became addicted to morphine and attempted to free himself of the resultant insomnia by drinking heavily. While at the height of his popularity, he was also an alcoholic, suffering blackouts and failing to appear for scheduled demonstrations.

In 1938, Ford married an English widow, Valerie McKeown, whom he had met while on tour, but, in spite of their initial happiness together, his bouts with alcoholism doomed the marriage from the beginning. His public displays of drunkenness had become so humiliating that his faithful Spirit Control, Fletcher, threatened to leave Ford unless he began to exercise some degree of self-control. Ford continued to drink and Fletcher left the Medium. Soon thereafter, Ford entered a deep depression and suffered a complete physical breakdown.

The Twelve-Step Program of Alcoholics Anonymous managed to help Ford attain a level of control over his drinking problem, though he was never able to give up alcohol completely. In the 1950s, Fletcher returned as his Spirit Control, and Ford began once again to provide demonstrations of afterlife communications that many individuals found provided proof of survival of the spirit after death. Among Ford's many positive accomplishments during this period of revival was his participation in the founding of Spiritual Frontiers Fellowship in 1956. Arthur Ford spent the final years of his life in Miami, Florida, where he died of cardiac arrest on January 4, 1971.

TIME TO ADD A HELPING OF SYNCHRONICITY TO THE STORY

Hope you're relishing our tale of an afterlife and its many twists and synchronizations. The afterlife – if it exists – is definitely beyond the bounds of the Matrix, or you think it would be. Maybe "they" can't get to you or me after we've gone over (and shorted out?). Or maybe it's a continuation of the same computer program, just with different "operators" mastering the controls. It's supposed to be so wonderful in the Summerland, as the Spiritualists refer to the afterlife, though I'm not overly anxious to find out. But I do have my contribution to the experience of Rev. Pike concerning the passing of his son. I already told you how I just so happened to have slept overnight on a few occasions in the room where he shot himself. But there is another death in the same hotel that I need to tell you about that brings this tale around full swing and makes it a number one category synchronicity.

Betty Taylor lived in the penthouse of the same hotel. You had to take the back elevator up to the top floor and sometimes you had to wait a while as this is where they took the garbage down. Kind of tells you what sort of building we are talking about; though at one time well over a century ago the very affluent Diamond Jim Brady lived on one of the upper floors.

I am sure he moved before the building started going downhill as he wouldn't have wanted to bring his lady up to his flat in the back elevator. After all, he was known for his penchant for jewelry, especially diamonds. He "collected" precious stones and jewelry in excess of USD $2 million, which would be the equivalent to approximate $59 million dollars today. Who wouldn't date the guy? Oh, by the way, his main squeeze was an actress by the name of Lillian Russell. They often dined together. It is said he had a ferocious appetite. Notice the dapper appearance of Diamond Jim and that of author Tim Beckley here. Maybe we had our clothes made by the same tailor, and I used to collect some fantastic jewelry. The value of my collection was let us say "modest indeed" compared to Mr. Brady's, I being a small time publisher, he being a railroad magnate.

To get back to Betty Taylor – she was the local head of the Spiritual Frontiers group that medium Arthur Ford founded in 1956 and remained head of until his death in 1971 The group is still active, being mainly made up of religious leaders, writers, and business and professional persons "who feel a kinship with and have a concern for the growing Western interest in alternate states of consciousness and mystical experiences."

I must be honest and say I don't remember that much about Betty except that she was a very warm, compassionate gal in her forties. I met her

Beckley hung out in the hotel where Diamond Jim Brady lived and Bishop Pike's son committed suicide. A mere "coincidence" that they dressed alike?

initially in the print shop on the ground floor of the hotel where she resided. She was responsible for printing the programs for the local SFF group, which held its meetings in a campus assembly hall on Staten Island. I went once or twice to their meetings, but they were a bit "too Christian" for my neo-pagan tastes. Most Spiritualist-orientated groups follow the doctrinal beliefs of the Protestant Church except that they believe in their own approach to life after death. They don't even usually accept the concept of reincarnation, though Ford and Pike pushed the SFF in that direction and I think they do accept the idea today.

One day I walked into the ground floor print shop where I had met Betty and there seemed to be a negative buzz going around.

It turns out that Betty had died during the night when she fell down the hotel's airshaft outside her bedroom window trying to escape a "home invasion." Someone had broken in, raped her roommate and locked her in the back room. Betty was heavy set. She fell when she tied some sheets together, threw one end out of the window and tried to climb to the apartment below to escape her tormentor. The knot slipped and she plunged to her death.

Very sad. Very tragic. A very nice lady that was doing a good job in spreading the message of the SFF.

I do find it exceedingly strange, to say the least, that Bishop Pike's son committed suicide on the fourth floor and Betty died in her shared apartment on the top floor. Bishop Pike assisted in promoting the mediumship career of Arthur Ford and Betty worked for his group. If this isn't a "level two synchronicity," I don't know what is. Betty could have lived in any other hotel in Manhattan. James Jr. could have extinguished his life in any other single occupancy room in NYC. Yet by "chance" they died in the same place, though years apart.

I'm glad I didn't encounter young Pike's troubled spirit when sleeping in the room where he ended his life. Hopefully his spirit was at rest by that time. The chain of coincidences has seemingly come to an end. I, for one, am glad that they are over and done with.

SUGGESTED READING

THE PSYCHIC WORLD OF BISHOP PIKE, by Hans Holzer

THE HAUNTING OF BISHOP PIKE – A CHRISTIAN VIEW OF THE OTHER SIDE, by Merrill Unger

THE OTHER SIDE – MY EXPERIENCES WITH PSYCHIC PHENOMENA, by Bishop James Pike

UNKNOWN BUT KNOWN, by Arthur Ford

www.Spiritual-Frontiers.com

MORE SUGGESTED READING FROM INNER LIGHT/GLOBAL COMMUNICATIONS

DARK SÉANCE

THE PARANORMAL WORLD OF SHERLOCK HOLMES

30 YEARS AMONG THE DEAD

WE CAN AWAKEN THE DEAD

YOU CAN TAKE IT WITH YOU

13.

UFOs – A JOURNEY TO THE AFTERLIFE
By Timothy Green Beckley

I have a secret . . . I know something you don't know.

I have made what I believe is a shocking, but monumental, discovery involving the connection between UFOs and life after death.

It is almost too strange and too bizarre to be revealed, but I must do so, as disclosing "the truth" is an essential part of the UFO "game."

Kenneth Arnold, for all intents and purposes, is regarded as the literal father of modern day UFOlogy. On June 24, 1947, he spotted a formation of rapidly moving objects that appeared to be skipping over "water" as they moved in-between the cloud-covered peaks of Mount Rainier in Washington State.

Arnold was flying rather low, looking for a military plane that was said to have gone down somewhere between Tacoma and Yakima, when his eye caught something glittering in the brilliant sunlight.

"I saw the flashes were coming from a series of objects that were traveling incredibly fast," he would say soon after the experience. "They

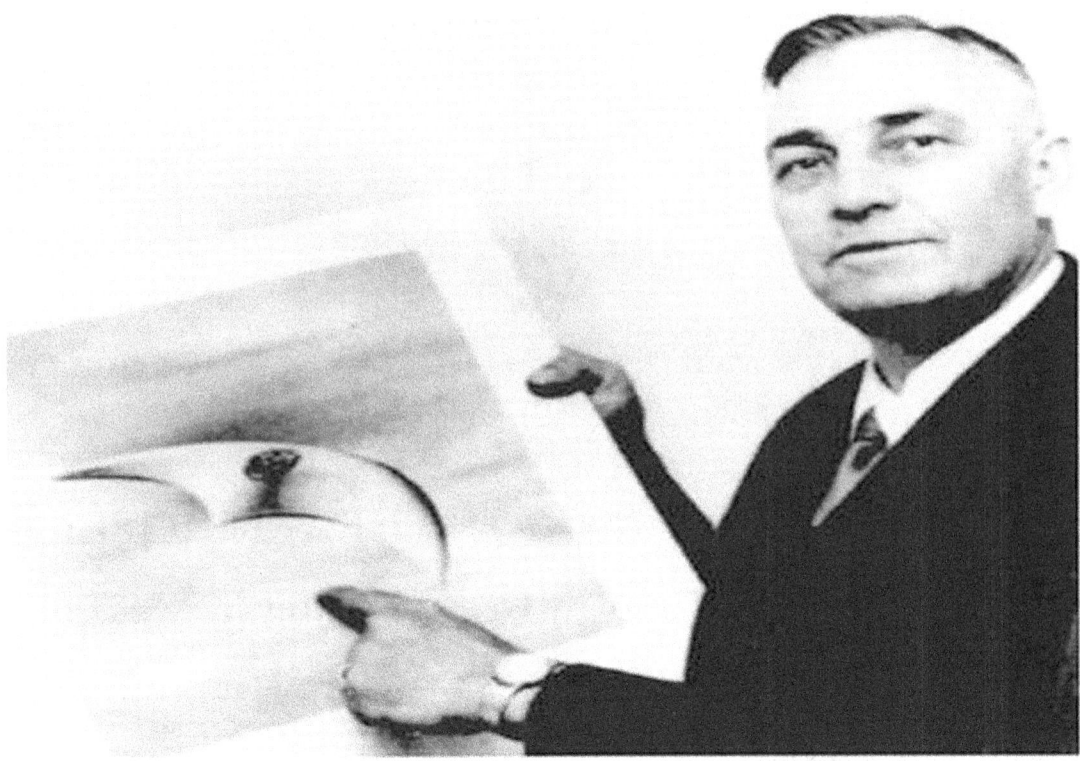

Above: Kenneth Arnold experienced the first major sighting of the modern UFO era to receive attention in the media.

Below: Shanelle Schanz, granddaughter of Kenneth Arnold, proudly shows off her tattoo depicting the most historic UFO sighting of all time.

were silvery and shiny and seemed to be shaped like a pie plate. What startled me most at this point was that I could not find any tails on them."

While Arnold passed away in 1984, his sighting over the years has been elevated to what might be considered a "saintly" status in the eyes of most UFO believers. In fact, the anniversary of Arnold's sighting is celebrated annually around the world as UFO Day. If you go to "Mr. UFO's Secret Files" on YouTube and do a search for Shanelle Schanz, you will come up with an episode of a podcast I hosted that ties in with this story. "The Strange Paranormal Saga of Kenneth Arnold's Granddaughter" consists of an intriguing interview with someone very closely related to perhaps the most important historical figure in the world of unidentified flying discs.

Shanelle Schanz has an elaborate tattoo gracing her upper back, from shoulder to shoulder blade. It is

a fabulous rendering, showing the date of her grandfather's sighting along with an illustration of one of the objects he observed which has become etched in the memory of so many of us who take the subject of UFOs seriously. On the program, Shanelle dropped a number of bombshells, at least to the average listener not familiar with anything but Arnold's initial observation. Truth is, Arnold had a total of eight sightings of unidentified craft in his a career, plus a run-in with the dreaded Men In Black and a possible attempt by a government agent to silence him "for good."

For those not old enough to know of Kenneth Arnold's involvement in the Maury Island Incident, we suggest you grab hold of a copy of the book "Coming of the Saucers," which he wrote with publisher Raymond A. Palmer in the early 1950s. It details this very disturbing case in which a UFO hovered over a boat off Maury Island, Washington, and hot molten metal fell from a large opening in the center of the craft, killing a dog and seriously injuring those onboard a small vessel parked near the harbor.

Samples of the scolding hot slag were collected and were being flown to Wright Patterson Air Force Base in Dayton, Ohio, when the plane crashed. Two military personnel were killed when the plane exploded, some say "mysteriously."

One of those involved in the Maury Island caper, Fred Crisman, has been linked to the Kennedy assassination by New Orleans D.A. Jim Garrison, as popularized in Oliver Stone's cinema epic on the subject.

But this missive is about Kenneth Arnold, UFOs and matters of a supernatural nature, primary life after death and the connection between UFOs and the hereafter – if any.

Now this is where the subject at hand gets downright spooky. Creepy. Eerie. Use any assortment of adjectives you might like.

I have discovered over the course of many years that so-called coincidences and synchronicities play a major role in the UFO phenomenon. I mean, at one time or another, we have all thought about an individual we haven't seen in ages and five minutes later the telephone will ring and it will be that individual on the other end of the line. Hey, that's interesting, but it doesn't prove much of anything.

The synchronicities in my life are much more dramatic and seem to be under the direct command of someone or "something." Some incidents that have happened to me are way beyond the pale.

What most people would refer to as a simple "coincidence" is more than just a random chance occurrence. And somewhere out there someone – **or something** – is directing the "show" and trying to draw attention to some other reality. Often these "coincidences" seem to be evidential of life after death.

THE JUNE 24TH ENIGMA

Now here the kicker, the punch line, the really strange part of this and when it finally starts to come together . . .

As we have ascertained, June 24th is a very important day in the history of modern day UFOlogy, the date when Ken Arnold had his sighting.

Journalist and radio commentator Frank Edwards, whose Flying Saucers Serious Business became a New York Times bestseller, also died on June 24th. Edwards is seen here with President Harry Truman.

But what isn't generally realized is that several – no make that numerous – UFO investigators and authors have passed away on this historic day, as if the "Grim Reaper" – or "someone – had hand selected this date to usher the spirits of these famous UFOlogists from this world to the next.

I call it the June 24th Enigma!

Here is a list of those associated with the field that passed away on June 24th as best as we can determine.

FRANK SCULLY – The author of ***Behind The Flying Saucers***, the first bestselling book on flying saucers (circa 1950), a book that introduced the topic of crashed space ships and dead space beings to the public. Scully was a columnist for Variety and a humorist. In October and November 1949, Scully published two columns in the highly respected show business trade publication claiming that extraterrestrial beings were recovered from a downed flying saucer near Aztec, New Mexico, based on what Scully said was reported to him by a scientist involved.

There were two UFO crashes, Scully claimed, one in Arizona and one in New Mexico. The saucers supposedly worked on magnetic principles. In the book, Scully revealed his two sources to be Silas M. Newton and a scientist he called "Dr. Gee." Sixty-thousand copies of the book were sold. Scully was known for his idiosyncratic prose, describing Dr. Gee as having "more degrees than a thermometer" and an alleged crashed saucer in the Sahara as "more cracked than a psychiatrist in an auto wreck."

Scully wrote another book on the subject and bore the brunt of some skepticism, but he continued to show interest in the topic until his death at 72 on that "memorial" date in 1964.

FRANK EDWARDS – After WWII, the Mutual Broadcasting System hired Edwards to host a nationwide news and opinion program sponsored by the American Federation of Labor. Edwards' program was a success and became popular nationally.

In 1948, Edwards received an advance copy of ***Flying Saucers Are Real***, a magazine article written by retired U.S. Marine Corps Major Donald

E. Keyhoe. Though already interested in the UFO reports that had earned widespread publicity since 1947, Edwards was captivated by Keyhoe's claims that the U.S. military knew the saucers were actually extraterrestrial spaceships.

Edwards began mentioning UFOs on his radio program, and wrote several books on the subject. His ***Flying Saucers, Serious Business*** is thought to have sold more copies in hardback than any other UFO book in publishing history.

He was dismissed from the radio program in 1954 for reasons that remain unclear. His interest in UFOs was believed to be a factor, but Edwards's editor and friend Rory Stuart wrote: "[AFL President] George Meany insisted that Frank Edwards not mention any [competing labor union] CIO labor leaders on his program. He flatly refused and was fired." In spite of thousands of letters in protest of his dismissal, Edwards was not reinstated.

Edwards died the night before he was supposed to speak before the National UFO Conference, held in Manhattan's Hotel Commodore and organized by *Saucer News* publisher, James W. Moseley. It turned out to be the largest UFO meeting ever held indoors, attracting a SRO audience of ten thousand over a weekend. Believers thought Edwards' death to be somewhat mysterious as he was not known to be sick at the time. Edwards died June 24, 1967.

LYLE STUART – An even more odd twist came about when Lyle Stuart – who was the publisher of Frank Edwards' books – also died on June 24, though not the same year as his author's passing. Stuart was thought of as being pretty much of a maverick publisher, putting out controversial tomes that no one else would publish, such as an expose of Scientology. Stuart first gained national notoriety by taking on the powerful newspaper columnist Walter Winchell in a series of scathing magazine articles, collected in book form in 1953. After serving with the United States Merchant Marines and the Air Transport Command in World War II, he worked for William Randolph Hearst's International News Service, Variety, Music Business and RTW Scout.

In 1951, he launched a monthly tabloid named *Exposé* (name later changed to *The Independent*) designed to publish those stories and articles that others wouldn't dare publish because they might offend subscribers or advertisers. Contributors included Upton Sinclair, Norman Mailer, George Seldes, Ted O. Thackrey and John Steinbeck. In another "mere coincidence," a longtime associate of mine, Harold D. Salkin, who was a supporter of many UFO contactees and groups, and worked with me for many years as a UFO journalist, started out his publishing career in Lyle Stuart's office.

How is this for a "coincidence"? The publisher of Frank Edwards' books, Lyle Stuart, also "journeyed over" on June 24th.

JACKIE GLEASON – Actor, comedian, musician, pool hustler and paranormalist, the "Honeymooner's" star must have known what he was talking about when he threatened to send his TV sitcom wife "to the moon, to the moon, Alice," because he might have already been there – or close enough to see the lunar surface at least. As a private collector, Gleason had one of the largest depository libraries on psychic phenomena and UFOs. When I was 16, he sent me a letter and a check to purchase a copy of one of my earliest books, *UFOs Around The World*. That book, as well as thousands of others from his depository on the occult, now rests in the hands of the University of Miami. Gleason lived in a circular, flying saucer-style house and was a guest from time to time on the Long John Nebel **Party Line** show, which was the first all night radio program devoted to the strange and unexplained.

Gleason also is said to have gone with golfing buddy Richard Nixon to catch a glimpse of an alien in a deep freeze stored in a secluded hanger at Homestead AFB, Florida. I remember there was supposed to be a UFO update on ABC's **Nightline** on June 24, 1987, to commemorate the fortieth anniversary of Arnold's encounter, but that segment of the show was presented in abbreviated form in order to add a last minute commentary about Jackie Gleason's passing that very same day

The "great one," Jackie Gleason, is among those who died on the anniversary of Kenneth Arnold's sighting - one of the strangest synchronocities of all. Gleason claimed to have seen UFOs and a dead alien body.

CONGRESSMAN MARIO BIAGGI – (October 26, 1917 – June 24, 2015) was a U.S. Representative from New York (served from 1969 to 1988) and former New York City police officer. He was elected as a Democrat from The Bronx in New York City. In 1987 and 1988, he was convicted in two separate corruption trials, and he resigned from Congress in 1988. He was one of the few politicians who took a serious interest in UFOs and didn't seem fazed that he might be subject to ridicule because of his beliefs. He was an early advocate for UFO disclosure but ran afoul of the corruption laws, which ended his career post haste, sans flying saucers. He died at 97 on – you guessed it – June 24! I had once interviewed him in his office for my "Saucers and Celebrities" column in UFO Report magazine.

Another UFO June 24th death synchronicity which needs to be examined more fully as we search for a potential clarification.

Writer and museum curator Loren Coleman (who also happens to have Cancer as a birth sign; one day separates our birthdays in the calendar month and year) has penned a meaningful book *The Copycat Effect: How the Media and Popular Culture Trigger the Mayhem in Tomorrow's Headlines* (Simon and Schuster). Coleman manages to provide us with a few additional names of those who passed as part of the June 24th synchronicity.

DR. JAMES MARTIN – This esteemed Oxford scientist, futurist and computer systems scientist was found floating face down in the Bermuda Triangle off his private island. In 2000 he authored a well-received book *After the Internet: Alien Intelligence*. In 1981 he went into business for himself as a consultant, and rode the well-paid wave of consultancy for nearly thirty years. He also advised the British and American governments on computer issues, becoming the first Briton to be appointed to the U.S. Department of Defense software scientific advisory board. He lectured on software and systems design for over quarter of a century. He died on June 24, 2013, at age 79.

WILLY LEY – Willy Ley was a German-American science writer and space advocate who helped popularize rocketry and spaceflight in both Germany and the United States. The crater Ley on the far side of the Moon is named in his honor. He was one of the first respected modern scientists who took a crack at answering the question of what is a flying saucer. He was one of the first, if not the first, person to say that 85% of all sightings could be identified, but what about the remaining percentage? Ley died at the age of 62 on June 24, 1969, in his home in Jackson Heights, Queens, New York.

ROBERT CHARROUX – Charroux was a pioneer of the theory of ancient astronauts, publishing at least six nonfiction works in this genre in the last decade of his life, including ***One Hundred Thousand Years of Man's Unknown History*** (1963, 1970); ***Forgotten Worlds*** (1973); ***Masters of the World*** (1974); ***The Gods Unknown*** (1974) and ***Legacy of the Gods*** (1974). His death on June 24, 1978, came as a surprise to everyone.

Of course we do not know the actual number of UFO researchers who have passed into – we hope – heavenly realms on June 24 as there is no international obituary for researchers of unexplained aerial phenomena. There could be many more. Your guess is as good as mine, but if you know of others who fit into this category please drop me a line at mrufo8@hotmail.com

THE ARNOLD HYPOTHESIS

Well, if it seems we were diverted in our drive to get to the bottom of this June 24th synchronicity in which various researchers have proceeded into the great abyss, it is time we get back onto our interdimensional Route 66 and proceed to our cloud covered destination, heaven.

For a long time I have tried to explain to people that Arnold did NOT believe that the objects he saw on several occasions were physical ships from one or more planets. He saw them as some sort of heavenly "conveyer belt" (my term) term to the other side. He didn't quite make this a secret, but I suppose no one really pressed him on his innermost thoughts concerning UFOs, and for that matter Arnold had a great mistrust of the press.

UFO theorist Mike Clelland has posted on his *UFO Experience* blog some fascinating comments about Arnold, some of which I have heard before and can confirm. Arnold's thoughts have been published here and there, but never in one place as Clelland has done.

"Arnold's experiences went well beyond that initial event in 1947," Mike notes. "Arnold went on to see a number of other UFOs throughout his life; he reported that UFOs could read his mind; he and his family saw floating orbs in their home; he claimed his phone was tapped; he was threatened by the military to keep quiet about what he knew and he was fascinated with synchronicities. He came to see these events as happening to him for a reason and he eventually saw the whole thing as a spiritual experience. Arnold also came to believe that the UFO phenomenon might represent some kind of connection between the living and the dead. All this and a pet owl on his ranch!

"Arnold had another sighting that involved a cluster of about 25 small craft. He later had yet another sighting over California in 1952. He was in his plane and flew above two distinct craft. One was 'as solid as a Chevrolet,' the other was semi-transparent, and he could look down on it from above and see the pine trees on the ground through the center of the object. He sensed these objects had the ability to change their density, seeing them as living organisms."

Here's what Kenneth Arnold said as far back as 1967: "The impression I had after observing these strange objects a second time was that they were something alive rather than machines – a living organism of some type that apparently has the ability to change its density similar to [jelly] fish that are found in our oceans without losing their apparent identity."

Arnold, notes Mike Clelland, had some bold ideas about UFOs in an era of nuts-and-bolts thinking. He wrote about his beliefs in the November 1962 issue of Ray Palmer's Flying Saucers From Other Worlds magazine: "After some 14 years of extensive research, it is my conclusion that the so-called unidentified flying objects that have been seen in our atmosphere are not spaceships from another planet at all, but are groups and masses of living organisms that are as much a part of our atmosphere and space as the life we find in the depths of the oceans."

Below is a list of curious details in the life of Kenneth Arnold, as disseminated by established conspiracy publication **Steamshovel Press** honcho Kenn Thomas.

++ Initial UFO sighting in 1947

++ Another UFO sighting of two objects that he filmed

++ Another UFO sighting of 25 small craft

++ Another UFO sighting in 1952 of two objects, one solid, the other jellyfish-like

++ Arnold stated he had telepathic communication from some of these sightings

++Floating orb seen in his home

++ Fascination with synchronicities

++ Belief that UFOs were somehow connected to the dead

++ The odd details of the military transport plane from 1947

++ Government surveillance, harassment and threats

++ His investigation of the Maury Island event, and meeting the mysterious Fred Crisman

++ The Maury Island event happened 3-days before his 1947 sighting

++ The Roswell crash purportedly took place 10 days after his 1947 sighting along with a pet owl! (Also identified by the late abduction researcher Budd Hopkins as a "screen memory" to hide the reality of the greys).

So, in short, Arnold believed that the UFOs he sighted were some sort of semi-living organisms, vessels that were responsible for taking the souls of the recently departed over to the other side.

Now, if this hypothesis is true, wouldn't it stand to reason that they would be personally transporting the souls who respected them and spoke so lovingly about them in life.

The spirits of Frank Edwards, Frank Scully, Jackie Gleason . . . well, we have named some of them a bit earlier.

Now Arnold is not the only individual to take into consideration the possibility that these craft could be some form of "mechanical angel" of sorts.

The popular AboveTopSecret.com web site has posted some comments in their chat room from those attracted to this concept.

In December, 2012 "Mandroids" followed up on this theory that had been generating some remarks

"Could UFO's be vehicles that enable the passed on to visit our dimension? One military remote viewer spoke of seeing his deceased father aboard a UFO. Some describe the afterlife as another dimension or universe where we move to. Quantum immortality is also an interesting theory. I think this. Most departed know it and are offered brief trips to see us or our 'realm' to say hello. Perhaps transcendental beings offer this? A many worlds tourist trip."

It didn't take long for fellow chat roomer poster "Bluesma" to chime right in about an incidents involving his deceased mother.

"I must admit, I have wondered about the link between our departed and UFOs. The reason being that when I saw one in plain daylight, and quite close, hovering and then maneuvering over me while my car stalled with everyone else's on the road, I had the sensation of being communicated with through my head. It was very strange – as if I was being communicated with telepathically. What struck me as strange is that I had the impression my mother was one of the energies doing so, and emanating from the craft . . . but my mother had died a couple of years before!

"I couldn't make heads or tails of how she (or her soul, or whatever) could have anything to do with a craft like I saw. It was your typical flying saucer shape, made of some sort of metallic material, and made impossible maneuvers. But it seemed very real and physical – not like lights in the air, or something vague like that, with which I would have found it easier to come to conclusions of a 'spiritual' nature.

"There were 'thought packets,' which at that time I wasn't very adept at unraveling into linear form yet, but could grasp only the general gist, which, in the case of her communications, was some sort of explanation (as I was immediately asking questions) of this being a state she 'returned' to, or otherwise went on to . . . though whether this state is actually physical (like if she was some sort of physical three dimensional entity up there) was not clear at all."

DECEASED SEEN WITH ALIENS ONBOARD UFOS

Church of Mabus podcast host and producer, Jeffrey Pritchett, expounds upon this "UFOs from here to eternity" concept in the National Examiner, an online publication he has written for regularly. One particular article is entitled *"Often the Dearly Deceased Are Seen With Aliens On UFOs By Contactees."*

"Many witnesses have confirmed having alien experiences and being inside ships and whilst doing so having seen the dearly deceased and departed. I believe on many levels aliens are also what we call angels in many scenarios throughout civilization's belief systems. This would make them the caretakers of the dead on some level if the beings being seen are in alignment with the Source of all of creation of the cosmos. Working in unison with the spiritual side of humanity to help them transition on many levels. Because often the messages conveyed are definitely messages of positivity and hope in cases like these where the recently departed are seen with these beings from the other side. So if the Contactee sees these departed loved ones with these alien beings, then it is a reassurance of life after death. Which can bring healing from grief and worry about a family member or friend who has died and passed over. I have also wondered on many levels if our spirits are in fact the same Universal family as the aliens in question."

Frankly, I don't know who outside of Kenneth Arnold can claim to have latched onto this UFOs/into the afterlife theory. I do know that Diane Tessman and I collaborated on a book "way back when."

One critic perhaps overstated the case when he proclaimed – "'UFOs: Are They Your Passport to Heaven and Other Unearthly Realms' is a non-stop thrill ride, giving its readers an insight into what it takes to ensure your passage through the pearly gates."

Hey, who knows where we are going for sure when we die – the universe is a vast abyss I would venture to say. Being "reasonably good" should build up a bit of "Good Karma." At least I would hope so.

Native Shamans worldwide have long professed that they have communicated with the other side.

Many in a psychedelic state have drawn objects and beings that closely resemble UFOs and what we call "aliens." Harvard University's Dr. John Mack spent time in the Amazon conversing with the region's inhabitants and was surprised to learn that there seems to be an umbilical cord between this world and the next.

Can we get to Heaven in a UFO? Is the afterlife a lot closer than we think?

We hope you'll discover some meaningful secrets within the pages of this work of nonfiction.

Surely, Heaven awaits!

JINX OF THE J – THE 27 CLUB – AND A NY DOLL

Some people seem to be able to predict their own passing. I don't know if it's a gut reaction to some inner feeling, but normally these predictions are foretold well in advance of an individual's transition. The most famous foretelling of someone's own death would be Mark Twain, who was born in 1835 on the day that Halley's Comet appeared for the first time in its cycle around the universe. In 1909, as the "avenging rock" was ready to rush past Earth once again, the great satirist proclaimed that he would be going out with the same comet. He did! Tough ball of ice. Too cold for me to ride on.

In the tight-knit field of UFOlogy, in addition to the death of famed researchers on June 24th, we have the coincidental birth and death of astronomer Dr. J. Allen Hynek, who came to Earth with Halley's Comet in 1910 and went out with it, as noted by one biographer. "It is perhaps fitting that Josef Allen Hynek left this world in the same manner in which he arrived, during the century's second passage of Halley's Comet, both comet and man leaving behind a brilliant streak of ephemeral light in their mighty wake, each unique and of its own kind."

But what about individuals in other walks of life? Are there any synchronicities that we can apply that would make it seem their deaths were preordained?

Well, in my own family tree we have the case of my late grandmother's brother-in-law back in Hungary in, let's say, the 1880's. Zoli had been out fishing, fell out of the boat, contracted pneumonia and was kept warm at home in hopes he would recover. He had a dream one night in which he said he had experienced a premonition that he would be the fourth person to die in the village in the coming days.

Zoli revealed the names of those who would meet their fate unexpectedly and the order in which they would be taken. They had not been sick or injured at the time of his premonition, but they passed in the specific manner he had said they would. And then God called Zoli to heaven next just like he said he would in the dream. Hey, we've got to blame these synchronicities on some higher power, so let's take it right to the top!

Back in the days of classic rock and roll, New York's White Witch, Walli Elmlark, and I co-authored a book–**Rock Raps of the Seventies**, which was half text, half pictorial. This large format paperback was filled with interviews, breezy reviews and pictures of some of the greatest rock stars of that era. We had a chapter that caused quite a bit of controversy and some negative mail from fans and even got a condemnation in *Crawdaddy*, a highly respected journal which took the music scene most seriously, perhaps more so than it deserved.

In **Rock Raps** there was a chapter called "Jinx of the J" which described the unwelcome deaths of numerous famed rock stars who had a "J" prominently displayed in their name. There was Janis Joplin, Jim Morrison, John Lennon, Jimi Hendrix, and Brian Jones. Skeptics point out that drugs played a major role in the passing of most of these musicians and we don't try to deny that, but so what? That's not part of our equation.

Then we have a much longer list of rockers who have been inducted into the "27 Club," meaning that they died at the age of 27. Talk about an uninvited calling. A lot of the musicians on the list I don't even recognize like Rudy Lewis (Drifters, vocalist), Peter Ham (Badfinger, keyboardist), Gary Thain (bassist, Uriah Heap), Leslie Harvey (guitar player, Stone The Crows). If you wish to do more research on this, by all means, search for "27 Club."

Now, where these puzzling deaths hit me personally and pretty hard is with the passing of a personal friend. Arthur "Killer" Kane was the bass player for the NYC glam rock band the New York Dolls, who were part of the underground Max's Kansas City crowd led by Lou Reed's Velvet Underground in the Sixties and Seventies. They predated even David Bowie in strutting around the stage in their six-inch platform shoes, mascara, lipstick, and tight- fitting silver lame tops and spandex pants. I had seen the Dolls perform many times. I was hanging out and trying to book some of the other local acts like Teenage Lust, the Magic Tramps, the Harlots of 42nd Street, and Satan, the Eternal Fire Eater.

The Dolls were the most popular of the lot, but I would not call them mega-stars. They attracted for the most part an enthusiastic, but not very large, following. The record companies were still not into glitter or glam rock (Bowie and Marc Bolan had not made it in the U.S. yet), and the Dolls were being passed over at that point. Which was a shame caused I loved these very theatrical, pre-punk bands. I was even known as "Mr. Glitter," and tried to be as flashy as I could without going to extremes.

Arthur Kane, the bassist for the band, and his wife, Barbara, and I, became friends. The couple would come to my UFO shows when I held them out west. They were into the subject and once they were even in the audience when I sang at one of the conferences a version of "A-L-I-E-N" to the tune of Hendrix's "Gloria," changing a few of the key words for theatrical effect. And, besides, it was a UFO event. The "He" being referred to here is of course an alien. The UFO Band backed me up: Sue Gordon, Randy Winters, Bleu Ocean, and Jerry Wills.

He came into my house
He came up my stairs
He tells me he needs me
He says that he cares
He makes me feel good

He makes me feel good all night.

At this point, in the late 1980s – early 1990s, the Dolls had broken up years before and Arthur was trying to get a fresh foothold in the ever-changing music business. He was finding it difficult and had been overwhelmed by a number of personal problems. It did not look like the band was ever going to get together again. David Johansen, the lead singer, was the only one really forging a career, as an actor ("Car 54") and a solo artist (Buster Poindexter).

Then, in 2004, the influential front man Morrisey, from the Smiths, put together a reunion tour for the Dolls, getting the surviving members back together again. Soon after, I got a call from Arthur, who seemed exceedingly happy. He had felt the world had passed him by and now he was back in the mix (musical mix that is) once again. The band was in rehearsal at the time in the UK, but they would soon be coming to America. They would be playing at an outdoor concert on Randall's Island Park in the middle of the East River, and Arthur was putting me on the backstage guest list.

As the date approached for the show, I tried to get in touch with Arthur on several occasions to see if there were any special instructions, like what day and what time should I show up and at what entrance to pick up my pass. I never heard from Arthur again. I got a call from my drummer friend Bleu Ocean that Arthur had died.

Turns out he died on my birthday July 13th, 2004. So now I think of him every year around this time and pay my regards to Barbara Kane, who used to bring their beautiful, pure-bred, white wolf to my conference. I never saw him shape-shift, but we once did fight over a bowl of potato chips when he scooped the last couple of chips out with his long tongue. I let him take them. He was my guest after all. Found out later "Killer" Kane had thought he had a bad case of the flu while in London and, upon arriving in the States, he checked himself into a Los Angeles hospital complaining of fatigue. He was quickly diagnosed with leukemia and died within two hours at the age of fifty-five. David Johansen described Kane as "nonjudgmental, bawdy and holy."

If you're interested in the glitter scene and in Arthur Kane's career, there is a streaming video version or a DVD titled, **New York Doll**. In the last few years before his passing, Arthur became a devout member of the Church of Jesus Christ of Latter-day Saints.

Once again, a strong "God connection" is implied. He is missed. And another death-dealing synchronicity in my life is hopefully put to rest for good.

P.S. - By the way, for those of you who are students of classical music, check out what is known as the Curse of the Ninth which, in essence, is the urban legend that says that a ninth symphony is destined to be a composer's last, and he will die after writing it, never completing a tenth. I never knew Mozart or Beethoven, so there is no "six degrees of separation" here or anything to apply to possible coincidences involving their deaths. Thank God we're out of the Twilight Zone, for the moment at least.

The Matrix Control System of Philip K. Dick
And The Paranormal Synchronicities of Timothy Green Beckley

Comments And Personal Experiences Welcome
mrufo8@hotmail.com

Mr. UFO's Secret Files Channel on YouTube.com
https://www.youtube.com/user/MRUFO1100

Website

www.conspiracyjournal.com

spectralvision.wordpress.com

www.teslassecretlab.com

Podcast

Exploring the Bizarre

kcorradio.com

14.

SYNCHRONICITIES OF A "FAMOUS MONSTER"
By Timothy Green Beckley

I wasn't sure if I wanted to make this part of the last chapter or not. But it's a story that should be told as it is a continuation of our search for synchronicities beyond the grave.

I wish to tell of – to me at least – an incident which greatly enhances, I feel, the author's case for survival and the possibility – if not the likelihood – that there is somehow a connection between our loved ones on the other side and our friends from "upon high." I hesitate to refer to them as "aliens," as Diane Tessman is more prone to do because of her lifelong experiences, but I have adopted the term "Ultra-Terrestrials," to best describe those beings, or entities, or pure energies that seem to coexist or readily mingle with us here in what we prefer to call the material world. Diane Tessman is more prone to do because of her lifelong experiences, but I have adopted the term "Ultra-Terrestrials," to best describe those beings, or entities, or pure energies that seem to coexist or readily mingle with us here in what we prefer to call the material world.

Church Folk – especially those South of the Mason Dixon Line (which happens to be as far North as Maryland by the way) - don't usually take too kindly to the claims of mediums or contact with the afterlife. It's those damn demons, you know. The Bible strictly forbids communicating with the dead. The Bible can be so simple minded. There weren't very many parapsychologists in the days in which it was written. From time to time, however, the church will admit that spirits can speak, but adds that their Lord condemns such practices as "listening in" on some otherworldly conversation – no matter who is responsible for the chatter.

We found this paranormal tidbit on a Christian website under the headline "Possession and Communicating with the Dead." Makes you want to stay far away from church, if you ask me. Thou shall have no other book before me but the Bible. Amen. PS - It says in Luke you can still read anything from our publishing house!

One of the most unusual cases involved the well-known psychologist William James and Columbia University professor of logic James Hyslop. The latter was a psychic investigator and friend of Carl Jung. Hyslop and Jung had together concluded that "spirits" from a nonphysical dimension of reality were communicating. Hyslop and James agreed that whoever died first would try to make contact with the survivor. James died in 1910. Hyslop lived another ten years. Sometime after James' death, Hyslop received a letter from a husband and wife whom he had never heard of in Ireland, a country he had never visited. They had been playing with an Ouija-board-like device and were bombarded by messages from the discarnate spirit of someone named William James telling them to contact a Professor James Hyslop, of whom they had never heard. The message they delivered was "Remember the red pajamas?"

It was an apparent reference to a trip Hyslop and James had taken together in which, upon arriving in Paris, their luggage was missing. They shopped for a few necessities. The pajamas Hyslop bought were bright red and James had teased him about them at the time.

While it would seem that only the surviving spirit of William James could have sent such a message, there is another explanation: A demon who knew of the red pajamas incident could very well have sent that message in order to encourage faith in the satanic lie that death is only an illusion. There are many other remarkable cases like this one.

Forrest J. Ackerman with just a few of his friends.

Damn, those pesky demons even know my late night attire. Satan apparently has his own dress code. Of course, he likes the color red. What a dated cliché. But I didn't want to tap this story since the rascals quoted are supposedly "spirits from a nonphysical dimension of reality." I think we can all go for that and keep to the standards of PKD's analysis of our ever-changing reality zones.

But for now it's a simple story I wish to relate that broadly indicates there is a trickster element in all of this. Our main protagonist is an individual well known to lots of us over the age of 50, especially if you were a young boy living in the late fifties, sixties and seventies.

For a period of nearly five decades, Forrest J. Ackerman was editor of *Famous Monsters of Filmland*, a publication that dominated the pulp magazine racks in newsstands throughout America. Under the editorial helm of "Uncle Forry," as he was best known by a multitude of followers, "FM" offered brief articles, well-illustrated with publicity stills and graphic artwork, on horror movies from the silent era to the then-present, their stars and filmmakers. The publication was specifically aimed at late pre-adolescents and young teenagers who couldn't get enough of Dracula, Frankenstein and all the other ghouls and ghosties that went bump in the night - all the nightmarish creatures that had been popularized on the big screen and were now invading our homes through the advent of the invention of something called television, which really allowed viewers to get a peek into another dimension of reality.

Not surprisingly, the content of the magazine influenced many would-be, hopeful filmmakers who would later emblazon their own mark on Hollywood, including the likes of Steven Spielberg, who once wrote to the magazine and had his photo published as a teenager. In his 2000 nonfiction book, **On Writing**, Stephen King recounts his own history with Ackerman's work and calls *Famous Monsters of Filmland* a "life-changing" publication, adding: "Ask anyone who has been associated with the fantasy-horror-science fiction genres in the last thirty years about this magazine and you'll get a laugh, a flash of the eyes, and a stream of bright memories - I practically guarantee it."

And, of course, I was reading *Famous Monsters* along with all my contemporaries!

In the wings, waiting for a chance at becoming a seasoned cinema mogul himself, was a highly motivated Paul Jeffrey Davids, who grew up in Kensington and Bethesda, Maryland, the son of Dr. Jules Davids (Ph.D.), the late tenured full-professor of American Diplomatic History at Georgetown University in Georgetown's School of Foreign Service. Becoming a winner in the first *Famous Monsters of Filmland's Amateur Movie Contest* at age fourteen was an early incentive for Paul Davids to choose a career in motion picture production. From his elementary school days onward, Davids made amateur science fiction, dinosaur, dragon and monster movies using stop-

Teenage "Monster Movie Maker" Paul Davids (left) and his "co-producer" Jeff Tinsley create creatures for one of their childhood 8mm films. They won Honorable Mention in Forry Ackerman's first Famous Monsters Amateur Movie contest, and that sent Paul on his way to an eventual Hollywood career.

motion animation, and his cinematic heroes from a young age were Ray Harryhausen, George Pal and, naturally, Forrest J Ackerman.

Though he had worked on other productions in Hollywood both for the big screen and for television, his first stellar break came when Marvel Productions hired him as the production coordinator for "The Transformers" animated series. His career blossomed after this, even though he had already established himself a writer for the "Star Wars" novel series.

I first met Paul around the time he was wrapping on his first major motion picture. **Roswell** was initially supposed to be a Home Box Office release, but HBO fumbled the ball and Davids eventually found a new home for the highly anticipated production with Showtime. The movie is now regarded by many Roswell aficionados as a major opus - adding respectable support to their belief that the incident really took place and that a space vehicle from another planet, complete with alien visitors, actually crashed in the New Mexican desert. The look and feel of the film had viewers believing they were actually back on the Army Air Base at the time of the supposed UFO crash in 1947, as well as at several reunions of the military personnel who were stationed there.

I'm sure Paul doesn't want the public to think that he is capable of excelling only in the sci-fi genre because he has pretty much adapted to the overall Hollywood scheme of things, having produced films like **Jesus in India**, Timothy **Leary's Dead**, **Starry Nights**, about Vincent Van Gogh, and, most recently, **The Life After Death Project** – which is where our story really begins to take shape, if only in ectoplasmic form.

In 2014, I decided that it was about time to start my own YouTube channel. I had traveled far and wide around the 50 states, setting up my tripod and chatting with some of the luminaries in the paranormal and Fortean fields. I taped the shows and would transfer them to DVD and give them out to those who purchased books from our website and through the mail at The Conspiracy Journal/Inner light Publications. The interviews are not of a Hollywood variety, but are more homegrown. I call these low-budget efforts my *"Unfair, Unbalanced, Unedited Series."* But, hey, don't let the series title fool you. We've got some high quality material here that you won't find anywhere else. Listeners tell me I know the right questions to ask my guests, and, hopefully, I get some sensible answers.

Type in Mr. UFO's Secret Files on YouTube.com and "educate" yourself on the finer points of UFOs and the unexplained cosmos we live in. There are well over 50 "campfire" chats from my "Route 66" travels, as well as interviews I have done with outstanding guests on several podcasts I've hosted, the current being "Exploring The Bizarre," plus some interviews I myself have given on a variety of closely cloistered topics. It's all here under the Big Top and includes a lively discussion with Paul Davids which I call *"A Famous Monster Returns From The Grave,"* in honor of Paul's longtime friendship with the man who actually gave sci-fi its name, Forrest J.

Ackerman, both before and after he passed over from the physical world to what we generally term "the afterlife," for lack of better terminology.

Ackerman, as Paul Davids affirms, was a diehard skeptic when it came to anything remotely extrasensory. Now, this isn't hard to believe as most of his friends in the sci-fi and magical communities were nonbelievers to the point of extremism. Isaac Asimov, Ray Bradbury and Arthur C. Clark were "born again" atheists, if there could be such a thing. Joe Moe, Forry's closest friend, summed Ackerman's afterlife "beliefs" up thusly: "Forry was a sworn atheist from his teenage years on and didn't believe in survival of personality after death. Therefore, he didn't have any romantic illusions about his collection living on beyond him. He simply wanted it to be preserved in his lifetime so he could have the satisfaction of sharing it. Once he was gone, he believed he would never even know that he'd been alive to collect anything."

Paul Davids and his mentor, the late Forry Ackerman — has he contacted Paul from the other side?

However, Ackerman did let it be known that, should his thinking processes continue beyond the grave, he would try to communicate with those who were dear to him in life. This is what I call the "Harry Houdini Pledge," which is mostly meaningless when you consider where it comes from. Most magicians and sci-fi buffs believe in little outside of their own imaginary worlds.

PKD was different and he got shunned for it by those in his own field. They take their skepticism as complete gospel, never having spent one single hour as an investigator of unexplained phenomena. But they feel no guilt in badmouthing others who have spent their entire lives trying to validate that which ultimately promises a resolution for our souls and the hope of finding peace as we spiritually advance. Or at least we can fantasize that this is the case. Maybe we move from one Matrix to another?

But - according to Paul Davids - Forrest J. Ackerman did manage to come back with evidence that there is another world - or worlds - out there that we find ourselves transported to when we clinically die here on Earth. First, it was a matter of objects seemingly moving about that could not be explained in ordinary terms. These early poltergeist-style events are frequently part and parcel of what is often just the start of a series of synchronicities that are likely to become "over the top."

And, indeed, matters soon started to escalate.

How did Davids come to the "irrational" conclusion that his buddy was trying to communicate with him with nonverbal techniques?

Two incidents stand out in Paul's mind, and it's no wonder why!

The first, I guess you could say, was a matter of an "ink blot test."

Davids revealed the details to us and it's up on my YouTube Channel. But I think I will let Tom Ruffles – writing a review of the movie *The After Life Project*, which Paul eventually produced - explain the situation, as he did for the prestigious Society for Psychical Research in the UK. Ruffles tells the story with admirable, exacting detail.

"On 18 March, 2009, not long after Ackerman's death (he died December 4, 2008), something very odd happened to Davids. While staying alone at his holiday home in Santa Fe, New Mexico, he began printing out a 24-page log of various business meetings and phone calls while he was out. On his return, he picked the sheets up from the printer, placed them on his bed, and left the room. The ink on the sheets was obviously dry. When he returned five minutes later, there was an unusual ink mark, still moist, on the top page, obliterating four words in a single line: 'Spoke to Joe Amodei.' The mark's neatness appeared to indicate intentionality. What is more, it was not uniform. 'Spoke to' could be discerned, but 'Joe Amodei' was completely obscured; Davids had to check the line on his computer. Nothing could have leaked onto the page; he was sure that the document was untouched when he left it on the bed, and such an obvious mark would have been noticeable when he picked it up from the printer. Curiously, for such a significant action, the name Joe Amodei, who is a film producer, meant little to Davids. They had spoken once about a deal that had not taken place but otherwise did not know each other. What could it mean?

Davids took the page to experts for advice. Jay Siegel, who is the chairman of the chemistry department at the University of Indiana, and John Allison, a chemistry professor at The College of New Jersey, both examined the mysterious mark but could come up with no explanation for how it might have appeared on the paper. After hundreds of hours in the lab, they were unable to recreate its precise appearance.

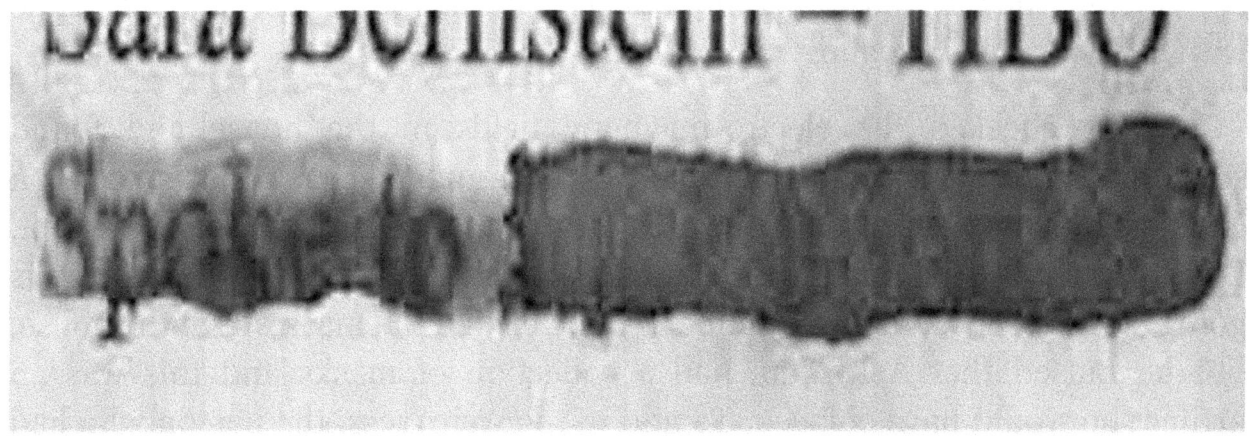

The ink has been scientifically tested by top chemists at Indiana University and the College of New Jersey. After three years of study, the chemists are convinced it's very strange, and science has yet to explain it.

They deduced that the agent blacking out the words was the same as that of the printer ink but contained silver not present in the printer ink. A solvent of some kind had been used to spread the ink and add more than had been on the page to start with, but how, and by whom?"

But this was, as Ruffles reports, only a minor part of the afterlife phenomena.

"The anomalies extended to those involved in the tests. Dr. Allison had been experimenting with various methods trying to recreate the ink mark and had put a batch of pages with his tests on a chair in his dining room, tucked under his briefcase. When he came back into the room to pick up his things, prior to collecting Davids, who was visiting his lab, he found the sheets on the floor, further out than gravity alone would have taken them. This was like Davids' paper episode, with no draught, animal or person around to have done it. Such anecdotes by themselves might not seem particularly convincing to people skeptical of a survival explanation, but it was the first instance of a growing body of incidents that seemed to indicate that Forry was using whatever means were at his disposal to demonstrate that he had survived death."

The "SPR" report states that Davis was so puzzled by this that he arranged for a clairvoyant to come to the house to see what they could pick up. The psychic did find something unusual, Ruffles confirms, as we continue with the anomalies at hand.

"She checked the electro-magnetic fields in the house and found something unusual around a Zimbabwean ceremonial mask that stood in a case just outside the bedroom in which the document was marked. In the film, Davids is shown moving an EMF meter around the case, and the needle is going off the scale. Somewhat unnerved, he moved the mask out of the house, but he mused that Ackerman had a collection of masks and this was an artifact he would have enjoyed. To add to the weirdness, the person who had given him the mask, an inveterate traveler, had a collection of slides of all his journeys, and he discovered that the ones relating to the African trip during which he had acquired the mask had mysteriously disappeared from their neatly-stored carousel. No other box had been touched, and the missing slides have never reappeared."

There is another "coincidence," which really blows me away, and which confirms Ackerman's ability to transport himself back to Earth to leave clues which confirm an afterlife and which further debunk his atheistic attitude toward the paranormal.

"So far, so strange. But there was more," reasons the "SPR" reviewer. "A week and a half before the ink mark appeared, on 7 March, 2009, a memorial arranged by Joe Moe, who had been Ackerman's personal assistant and caretaker, was held at Hollywood's Egyptian Theater. A documentary made by two Canadian filmmakers, Mike MacDonald and Ian Johnston, 'Famous Monster: Forrest J. Ackerman,' was shown that evening. Davids spoke at the tribute, and the pair told him afterwards that they had just had some peculiar experiences. While in town, they had a spare day, so they had visited Ackerman's final resting place in Forest Lawn Cemetery and MacDonald, perhaps not in the best of taste, knocked on it, asking if anyone was home, the sort of joke that Forry would have enjoyed. They didn't receive a reply, but returned to the room they were sharing in Hollywood to find their computers doing peculiar things."

In order to prove they were real individuals and not robots, they had to type in a random security password on Facebook in order to proceed to their home page. This is where one has to throw "reason" out the window and go along with the concept that synchronicities are not random but more or less part of a "guidance system" operated by interdimensional intelligence, which would most likely include members of those Heavenly realms we are so interested in connecting with UFO visitors. And, remember, Forry Ackerman had alien figures from such sci-fi classics as "The Day The Earth Stood Still" and models of spaceships from many a movie all on display behind glass cases in the various rooms of his "Famous Monsters" Hollywood estate, which travelers from all over the world visited.

The "SPR" review continues thus:

"The code that they had to retype? 'Ackerman 000,' and the first letter was initialized. As they were absorbing this and saying some of the things that might have come up onscreen, one of them said 'Ackerman dead,' whereupon Johnston's computer, supposedly in sleep mode, suddenly yelled 'Oh, my God, no way!' This was the voice of an animated character on YouTube, but he did not have YouTube open on his computer at the time. It seemed to be a comment, echoing their thoughts, on what had just happened with Facebook. What made it even odder was that Johnston had a photograph of Ackerman, aged about four and a half, on his computer, which he had uploaded when working on the documentary, an age appropriate to the childish voice which said 'Oh, my God, no way!' The computer events were within 30 seconds of each other, less than an hour after MacDonald knocked on Ackerman's tomb."

Paul Davids apparently was told about this on March 8th, ten days before the ink blot appeared, and it was really at this point that Davids started to see a pattern emerge, one that pointed directly to the discarnate Forrest J. Ackerman. The significance of the blacked-out line was still not apparent.

"It was only when speaking to Joe Moe to find out about Ackerman's editing practices that he realized that 'Joe Moe' was contained in 'Joe Amodei.' Ackerman had loved puns, using them extensively in his writing, and this was precisely the sort of wordplay that he would have enjoyed. Was this the reason why that line alone had been affected, Ackerman literally 'dropping him a line?' As if in confirmation, Moe then told Davids that a few days after the memorial, he had had a vivid dream in which Ackerman had appeared to him and praised the gathering, calling it the '9th wonder of the World' (King Kong, of course, being the 8th). So it would seem that Ackerman contacted Joe in his dream and then reached out to Davids to tell him, 'Spoke to Joe Moe.' Davids later found that, when editing, Ackerman often deleted sentences in exactly the same way as on his paper."

By no means does Paul Davids think that the series of events is "random" or a mere "coincidence." The Hollywood Renaissance man believes, as he puts it in an interview for Australia's New Dawn magazine, that he was "targeted" by Forry Ackerman.

"I think the incident of the inkblot is VERY important. Sometimes the answers to very big cosmic mysteries come in very small packages. Scientists deal at the level of individual atoms and sub-atomic particles. Others study photons or very faint astronomical phenomena from far off in space that have been traveling toward Earth for billions of years. My first question was, does the blacking out of four words in my document, at two separate levels of opacity, contain clues as to its origin that can tell us how it was done or why it was done? Is there something paranormal about it that can be demonstrated?

"The four words on my document were clearly targeted and the ink obliteration was deliberate and done by 'someone' or 'something' other than me while I was out of the room, at a time when NO ONE else was physically present in the house. I knew this for a fact, but could I convince anyone else? It actually surprises me the overwhelming extent to which the two key chemists who worked on it (one of them, Dr. John Allison, continued the work for years) state categorically that it is still a huge mystery they cannot explain and cannot duplicate in any way they can conceive - and they have tried hundreds of ways to duplicate it. Both Dr. Allison and Dr. Jay Siegel are world class authorities on the chemistry of inks, paints and solvents. Dr. Siegel has testified in a massive number of court cases where someone was needed to testify about the chemistry of evidence."

And so there you pretty much have it, the whole ball of afterlife wax in a fascinating happening that occurred to someone I know and trust. And all this so impressed Paul Davids that he went out and produced **The Life After Death Project**, a two volume DVD set that originally aired on the SyFy cable channel and is now available to home consumers.

THERE IS ANOTHER PART TO THIS STORY

Well, we are not quite finished yet.

Seems when I tell a story - especially one that concerns a good synchronicity - there has to be a punch line. I sometimes feel I am in the middle of a comedy routine. When Sam Kineson was still alive, a lot of people mistook me for him. Same hair style and color. Sometimes wore a beret.

Cherub cheeks. I even had a couple of strippers come up to me in the Scrap Bar, my favorite watering hole on McDougal in Greenwich Village, and congratulate me for carrying on in his tradition. I was even asked to sign autographs. But I wasn't Sam and he wasn't me. Died before his time. Dirty shame.

"The After Life Project" DVD presents all the evidence that the Famous Monsters editor is not just idle in his new home.

The following is an email I sent to Paul involving one of the strangest synchronicities of this type. Davids had just sent me the two disc DVD set **The Life After Death Project.** I think I had played Disc # 1 and the second one remained for some time in its DVD case in a stack by the TV.

Paul, top of the day to you.

Had a hell of a synchronicity/coincidence regarding your video.

I take it you have seen a movie or know about a film called "Premium Rush?"

With a thousand channels there was still nothing to watch, so I spent about twenty minutes browsing HBO/Showtime/Cinemax looking for something I either had not seen or something that had at least been made in the last four or five years.

I came across this film that I had never of heard of before and asked a friend in the room if she knew anything about it. She replied yes and that she liked it, but didn't know if I would since we all have different likes and dislikes as far as movies go. She mentioned that there was a conspiracy involved so I thought maybe I might "go for it."

Well, I nearly fell out of my recliner when the dirty cop trying to rip off the envelope from the bike messenger said his name was Forrest J. Ackerman...which obviously it wasn't. He mentioned Ackerman's name at least three times during the film.

Just so happens I had been showing your video to someone the previous evening and it was still in the DVD player right next to the TV where "Premium Rush" was unfolding on the screen.

Best regards, my friend. Don't forget to let me know when you will be in the city.

TGB

When Paul got back to me he mentioned that he had known about the movie – that the film's producer was such a fan of Uncle Forry and he was so devastated by his friend's passing that he decided to work Ackerman's name into the movie somehow, which he managed to do.

But what were my chances of having Paul's DVD set right there and the picture I had never heard of playing on the TV screen no more than a foot away? The madness continues.

FURTHER INFORMATION AND VALIDATION AVAILABLE AT . . .

www.spr.ac.uk/publication/life-after-death-project-dvd

www.PaulDavids.com

15.

RAYMOND FOWLER, THE PHILIP K. DICK OF "UFODROME"

By Sean Casteel

SOME OPENING COMMENTS FROM TIMOTHY GREEN BECKLEY

THE subject of UFOs fascinates almost everyone. Its historical and cultural significance cannot be denied. Multiple tens of thousands have encountered some sort of "otherworldly phenomena," been put under its spell, becoming in many instances mesmerized by their experience. We are not talking just "ordinary aliens," but some sort of paranormal "influence" that tosses them around in the Matrix and includes more than its fair share of bizarre synchronicities.

Like Philip K. Dick, we feel comfortable creating fresh terminology to describe some of our newly discovered revelations. "UFOdrome" is our derivative, our variation on the word "*Videodrome*," which is the title of a rather creepy motion picture released well over three decades ago. The film is deserving of a current viewing by those drawn into the eeriness of this volume's complex subject matter. The movie is described in this manner:

*"**Videodrome**" is a 1983 Canadian science fiction film written and directed by David Cronenberg, starring James Woods, Sonja Smits, and singer Deborah Harry. Set in Toronto during the early 1980s, it follows the CEO of a small UHF television station who stumbles upon a broadcast signal featuring extreme violence and torture. The layers of*

deception and mind-control conspiracy unfold as he uncovers the signal's source and loses touch with reality in a series of increasingly bizarre organic "hallucinations."

We can't unequivocally claim that there is anything overtly sinister about Ray Fowler's "UFOdrome" experiences, but we do note layers of deception in the overall UFO phenomena (referred to as the "trickster element" throughout this volume), and have written in previously published works all about the attendant mind controlling/mind numbing aspects of alien contact. – TGB.

*****

The story of alien abduction researcher Raymond E. Fowler illustrates perfectly how synchronicity goes hand in hand with UFO experiences of all kinds.

A BRIEF BIO

Fowler has written a series of groundbreaking books on the abduction experiences of New England housewife Betty Andreasson Luca, who encountered the standard issue gray aliens but believes they are angels sent to prepare the world for the Second Coming of Christ, which stands in sharp contrast to the belief that the grays are a hostile force with no regard for the suffering they cause abductees.

The long history of Fowler's interest in UFOs goes back to his childhood in the 1940s. Over the intervening years, he has written numerous books on the subject and been hailed by no less than the legendary astronomer, Dr. J. Allen Hynek, who said Fowler's "meticulous and detailed investigations far exceed in completeness the investigations of Bluebook." Which one can see is no faint praise when one realizes that Hynek was once the chief scientific consultant for Bluebook, the name given to the long defunct Air Force agency charged with investigating UFO sightings in the U.S. Fowler's contributions to UFOlogy are respected by UFO researchers throughout the world.

Fowler spent some time in the Air Force himself, working in its Security Service. He also worked for 25 years with GTE Government Systems as a Senior Planner for the Minuteman Intercontinental Missile Program.

DISCOVERING HIS OWN PAST

In his 2002 book, **UFO Testament: Anatomy of an Abductee**, the preface sketches in a crucial element of Fowler's story: "Throughout the warp and woof of the author's UFO and paranormal experiences is the slow but sure realization that he has been investigated by the very phenomenon he was investigating! Indeed, he realizes that his early insatiable interest in UFOs can be traced back to the then unsuspected experiences in his unconscious that dated back to his childhood. His fanatical interest in UFOs since 1947 was just the tip of the iceberg of UFO and related experiences that would slowly but surely surface to his conscious mind."

In an interview I conducted with Fowler at the time he published "The Andreasson Legacy," his last book on the experiences of Betty and her family, I asked Fowler about the interrelatedness of UFOs, alien abduction and other phenomena.

"If one takes the testimonies of a number of UFO abductees at face value," he answered, "we find that the abductees experience a number of paranormal phenomena in the aftermath of their abduction experiences. These include poltergeist phenomena, out-of-body experiences [OBEs], ghosts, apparitions, balls of light, psychic abilities, precognitive dreams, synchronisms, reception of telepathic messages, a feeling of being watched or monitored, etc. Is it coincidence or connection that these occur after a UFO experience?

"Indeed, some, like OBEs and telepathy," Fowler continued, "occur during some UFO abductions. The UFOs themselves have seemingly paranormal abilities. They are also able to appear and disappear within our space/time continuum visually and on radar. The alien occupants are able to do the same as well as pass through solid walls, doors and windows. They also are able to communicate by telepathy, exert mental and physical control over abductees and exert paranormal-like forces that can cause objects and persons to float and pass through solid objects."

In 2004's ***Synchrofile: Amazing Personal Encounters with Synchronicity and Other Strange Phenomena***, Fowler takes up the subject of his personal experiences with synchronisms, which he sees as being a typical post-abduction occurrence for the experiencer. He begins with a history of the subject that decries modern day scientific disdain for what are really ancient beliefs about real-world events having supernatural causes and the interconnectedness of reality.

New England researcher Ray Fowler understood the significance of synchronicity and UFOs so much that he wrote a book Synchrofile: Amazing Personal Encounters With Synchronicity and Other Strange Phenomena.

JUNG AND THE FIRST 20TH CENTURY GLIMMERS OF SYNCHRONICITY

The modern study of synchronicity began with the psychologist Carl G. Jung, and Fowler tells the story for the sake of readers unfamiliar with what happened one day as Jung was treating a female patient.

"During his research into the phenomenon of the collective unconscious," Fowler recounts, "Jung came across many coincidences that appeared to defy the calculations of probability. One of many demonstrative examples from Jung's case studies concerned a woman he was finding psychologically impossible to help because of her extreme, rational, know-it-all personality. He finally was able to break through her defense system when something very irrational occurred. It had a transforming effect upon both the patient and Jung himself. Describing the improbable meaningful coincidence responsible for this, Jung writes about the following incident."

"Synchronicity is an ever present reality for those who have eyes to see."
Carl Jung (1875 - 1961)

At this point, we will let Jung speak for himself:

"I was sitting opposite her one day, with my back to the window. She had had an impressive dream the night before, in which someone had given her a golden scarab – a costly piece of jewelry. While she was telling me this dream, I heard something behind me gently tapping on the window. I turned around and saw that that it was a fairly large flying insect that was knocking against the windowpane from outside in the obvious effort to get into the dark room. I opened the window immediately and caught the insect in the air as it flew in. It was a scarabaeid beetle whose gold-green color most nearly resembles a golden scarab. I handed the beetle to my patient with the words, 'Here is your scarab.' This experience punctured the desired hole in her rationalism and broke the ice of her intellectual resistance. The treatment could now be continued with satisfactory results."

Fowler picks up the thread again.

"Who or what was responsible for this synchronism – Jung, the patient or chance? Such a question presupposes a chain of causal events. However, Jung concluded that all known forms of causality were absent from this experience. The coinciding arrival of the scarab with the patient's dream had no determinable cause. It instead complemented the 'impossibility' of the analysis that Jung was attempting with his patient."

Jung then categorized the event as "acausal," a term one encounters frequently when studying synchronicity that is just another way of saying there is no apparent or obvious cause.

"Meaningful coincidences," Jung writes, "are 'thinkable' as pure chance. But the more they multiply and the greater and more exact the correspondence is, the more their probability sinks and their 'un-thinkability' increases, until they can no longer be regarded as pure chance, but, for lack of a causal explanation, have to be thought of as meaningful arrangements."

When one is honest, however, synchronisms are not inexplicable because the cause is truly "unknown," according to Jung. It is more a matter of the difficulty pragmatic intellectuals have in admitting to a supernatural, paranormal force operating in the background to orchestrate such moments of meaningful coincidence. As a psychologist, Jung was in the rare position of trying to lead his patient – and the world – to see beyond the "rational" and to therapeutically accept the "impossible."

SYNCHRONIZED EMERGENCY HELP

Fowler and his wife Margaret shared a synchronistic experience that Fowler relates early in ***Synchrofile***. His journal entry for May 13, 2000, is as follows:

"I got up around 5:30 A.M. and went for a two-mile jog around the golf course that borders our dead end street. Margaret got up later and soon after began suffering unusual chest pains, a feeling of weight on her chest and difficulty in breathing. She felt alone and helpless and wondered what was wrong with her. Margaret flicked on the TV to take her mind from the pain.

"Shocked, there before her very eyes was a man describing the typical symptoms of a heart attack, which matched exactly what was happening to her at that very time. He urged those who suffered such symptoms to get to a doctor immediately! At that very point, I arrived back from jogging. I raced her to the hospital emergency room. She was hospitalized for several days and treated for a mild heart attack!"

Fowler goes on to say that Jung insisted that such improbable synchronisms are often the catalyst for profound changes in the lives of those that experience them, which was also true for Fowler and Margaret. They felt the "concurrent coincidence" between the TV commentary and her heart attack was a Godsend, an event that prodded them to actions that proved to be lifesaving for her.

JUNG COINS THE TERM

Returning to Jung, Fowler remarks that, "Jung's theories are complex and hard to understand even by those who are educated in these areas. This is especially so as his views changed over the years and often seemed to contradict each other."

In any case, Fowler continues, "Jung believed that known forms of causality were incapable of explaining some of the more improbable forms of such coincidences. When no causal connection could be demonstrated between two events and a meaningful relationship existed between them, Jung believed that a unique type of principal was operating. He called this principle 'Synchronicity.'"

Again, the idea of a supernatural mover is hard for Jung and others to pin down or even admit to. Jung did relate synchronicity to his belief in the "oneness of the universe" and thus the interdependence of objective and subjective perceptions of the observer or observers. He grouped synchronicity into his studies of other fields, like precognitive dreams, visions, telepathy, near death experiences and even the UFO phenomenon. They all pointed to a kind of "absolute knowledge" contained within the collective unconscious and demonstrated how nature and people are interconnected.

THREE KINDS OF SYNCHRONICITY

According to Jung, all synchronistic phenomena could be grouped under three categories. He describes the first category this way: "The coincidence of a psychic state in the observer with a simultaneous objective, external event that corresponds to the psychic state of content, where there is no evidence of a causal connection between the psychic state and the external event, and, where, considering the psychic relativity of space and time, such a connection is not even conceivable."

Fowler explains that he refers to this type of synchronism as a "concurrent coincidence" that has no apparent cause and offers an example from his own life.

"September 29, 2002: My friend, Dave Harris, called to tell me about an unnerving synchronism. Yesterday, he telephoned his son, Phil Harris, to check on his health. Dave told me that Phil had cancer. During the telephone conversation, he mentioned my name to Phil. At that very moment, Phil was watching me on TV! It was a rerun of a program on UFOs."

Jung's second category of synchronistic phenomena is: "The coincidence of a psychic state with a corresponding (more or less simultaneous) external event taking place outside the observer's field of perception, i.e. at a distance, only verifiable afterward."

This is what Fowler terms a non-simultaneous "corresponding coincidence" that has no apparent cause. He again offers an example from his journal.

"April 10, 1996: I phoned Betty Luca to tell her about a painting that I had seen in a magazine that depicted angels holding hands and dancing in a circle. The artist of the painting was the famed Renaissance painter, Fra Angelica. In the meantime, my wife was downstairs picking through a pile of old books that we were going to sell to a dealer. She knew nothing of my conversation with Betty.

"When I came downstairs, I found her looking through one of the old books that was entitled: **Roses in Bloom**, published in 1876 by Louisa M. Alcott. I mentioned to her that I had just got off the phone with Betty about a painting by Fra Angelica. She looked up in disbelief and told me that she had just read a sentence in the book that mentioned Fra Angelica! This would have been about the same time that I had mentioned his name to Betty while on the phone. I asked her to find the passage in the book for me. She did, and I read these words – 'Have you given up your painting?' she asked rather abruptly, turning to a gilded Fra Angelica "Angels," which leaned on the sofa cover.'"

Lastly, Jung's third category of synchronistic phenomena is: "The coincidence of a psychic state with a corresponding, not yet existent, future event that is distant in time and can likewise only be verified afterward."

Fowler explains that he calls this type of synchronism a future "converging coincidence" that has no apparent "physical" cause. These experiences often appear to be precognitive or telepathic in nature.

The painting "Angels In Paradise" by Fra Angelico plays a pivotal role in a synchronicity between Ray Fowler and Betty Andreasson Luca.

To illustrate this kind of synchronism in his own life, Fowler draws from a diary he kept while stationed on a USAF base in England.

"At the time I wrote this entry, Margaret and I were preparing to leave for the United States, where I was scheduled for discharge from the Air Force prior to Christmas 1955. I had been in England for two years and eight months and had not been home during that time."

The first diary entry is dated December 2, 1955 (Friday).

"The Orderly Room says I may leave before or after the 21st. We packed lots of things and still got to bed early. I dreamed that I returned home without Margy. Mom asked me where she was and I said she was coming later."

Then on December 3 (Saturday), Fowler wrote: "I had a most vivid dream of my returning home and having a happy reunion. When everybody asked where Margy was, I told them that the government was sending her later. This is the second dream about this!"

Finally, on December 5 (Monday): "Had an inspection today. I went to the Orderly Room to see when we were going home and I was directed to Sgt. Hunt. On my way to see him, the Lord spoke to me [a voice in my mind] and told me to prepare myself for a shock as I was just about to be told that Margy could not go with me. This seemed impossible, yet, when I entered the building, I was told that very thing!"

The story continues.

"I still remember exactly where I was when that telepathic-like message entered my mind," Fowler writes. "I was passing the large bulletin board of the Orderly Room. I can remember Sergeant Hunt looking up from his desk and saying something like, 'I'm sorry to inform you that your wife cannot travel with you, as there will not be enough room on the aircraft. She will have to join you later.' So I returned to the States alone. It gave Margaret Christmas to spend with her family.

"As it turned out," he continues, "there was plenty of room on the plane as there were a number of empty reserved seats for officers. As it was, Margaret would have been terrified had she flown with me. We flew across the Atlantic from Scotland into a terrific storm. The aircraft experienced terrible turbulence and frightening air pockets. These sent the plane careening downward like an out-of-control elevator. The pilot had to make an emergency landing at Goose Bay, Labrador, because of lack of fuel."

There is so much of interest here. First, the fulfillment of a precognitive dream, which Fowler dreamed twice and did not believe would come true. Then what is initially a disappointing circumstance turns out to be a blessing, in that Margaret was spared the terror of the plane coming close to crashing in the storm near Scotland. It also illustrates how synchronicity seems to imply a guiding hand behind certain events. Few people reading Fowler's account would deny that the warning dream and what came after it ultimately proved to be a blessing, a safeguarding of Fowler and his wife that lies outside the direct control of any of the mere mortals involved in the drama. Fowler eventually made it safely to Brooklyn Air Force Base, New York, where he was discharged, and Margaret joined him a few months later.

FOWLER'S FOURTH CATEGORY: THE STEPLADDER SAGA

Along with his use of the three mainstream categories of synchronicity, which are universally recognized by researchers of synchronicity, Fowler has invented one of his own called "counter coincidences." The term refers to when two events that should naturally coincide do not. Although he says such events are very rare, Fowler does offer another journal entry to make his point.

"April 23, 1997: In the afternoon, something extraordinary occurred that involved Margaret. She went into the shed to get a rake. The rank handle was tangled with a large wooden stepladder that hung directly above her. When she pulled on the rake, the ladder became dislodged. It should have come down on top of her. She instinctively ducked. When she looked up unscathed, the ladder was standing in the middle of the shed with its legs apart and set up. This ladder is not easy to set up. It easily jams when one pulls the legs apart. How it got in the middle of the shed all set up is beyond us!"

Fowler explains why he and his wife found the incident so remarkable.

"There is no recognized reason," he writes, "why the falling ladder should not have coincided with the location of my wife. She was directly under it. There is no explanation for it opening itself in another location. These events were counter to what should have naturally occurred."

Again, one gets the impression that some kind of conscious entity is looking out for Ray and Margaret, creating small miracles along the way as it does so. In any case, while a given occurrence of synchronicity may not look particularly sensational on the surface, the events over time prove to have a transforming impact on the emotions that changes the way one views the world. Which is why a mere stepladder can have meaning – by the law of gravity it wasn't supposed to happen, but it did.

HE STARTED OUT AS A CHILD

In another chapter of **SynchroFile**, Fowler takes up the history of his own UFO encounters.

"My experiences began in childhood," he writes, "in Danvers, Massachusetts. I can remember waking up to a bright light beam shining through a window into my bed. It was so bright that I could see dust particles moving around in it. Each time that I saw it, I would crawl out of my bedcovers and allow it to shine on me. When I entered the light, I would feel what could only be described as pure love. I called it the 'love light.' I wish that I could remember more about what happened after entering the light, but that is where my memory of these events terminates."

Fowler also recalls the appearance of a robed lady encased in brilliant light from whom he experienced the same sensation as the "love light." After conversing with the woman about his children's Bible Storybook and another children's book with a section on astronomy, Fowler found himself engulfed in light and floating through the closed window, weightless and kicking his legs in the air.

"It was terrifying to look down at the illuminated flower garden far below," he writes. "I thought that I was going to fall. I think that the lady made me close my eyes because of my fear. I do not know what happened next. However, I can visualize coming back down to the house in the light and opening my eyes. What I saw when my eyes opened is still etched in my mind. I saw the small crescent-shaped attic window as we descended by it. The front side of house was bathed with light."

The next thing Fowler remembers is standing before the glowing lady in the middle of the upstairs hallway.

"She told me that I was going to do something important for mankind," he writes.

When an ecstatic Fowler told his mother what had happened, she impatiently said he had only been dreaming. The incident eventually faded from his memory until its return was prompted by certain catalysts, to include watching the scene in **The Wizard of Oz** during which the Good Witch descends to Dorothy in a ball of light. That brought the memory back full force, though it again faded away. Later, as an adult undergoing regressive hypnosis, the memory resurfaced again, this time for keeps.

A mysterious bright light outside his window which has never been explained led Fowler to his intense interest in UFOs and their association with coincidences and synchronicities.

SOME STREET GANG "CRED" PRECEDES THE LIGHT

If one is familiar with Ray Fowler, always an upright, "standup guy," as the saying goes, one may be surprised to learn that he once led a street gang in his Massachusetts hometown and would muster his followers in throwing rocks and apples at members of a rival gang. One day a kid named Dave moved into Fowler's neighborhood, and suddenly Fowler had to anticipate having some competition. As it turned out, Dave was from a broken home and Fowler's family took him in as a foster child, sharing Ray's bedroom.

Fowler had stopped attending church services years ago, but when he saw Dave praying and reading his Bible, Fowler decided to emulate his new friend. Fowler began to pray one night while Dave looked out the window.

"No sooner had I begun to pray," Fowler writes, "when it happened again. I was suddenly filled with that same unique, overpowering feeling of unconditional love and acceptance. It is significant that these feelings began at the same moment Dave shouted that there was a bright light illuminating the whole area outside the window. However, I was so entranced with my experience that I did not answer him. Decades later, I equated this experience with the other of my paranormal and UFO experiences. This realization would be the catalyst for another amazing psychic-like event."

For years, Fowler looked back and wondered about the light Dave had seen that night. Was it from a UFO? Fowler now recognized the sensations he had experienced as typical harbingers of UFO visitations and other bizarre events. Fowler had lost track of Dave, but he soon became obsessed with speaking to him again about the light Dave had witnessed. After a fruitless search through several telephone books, Fowler decided to try telepathy instead.

"On or about September 26th or 27th, 1998, I began to visualize Dave's face," he writes. "I would literally call up mental pictures in my mind. I relived going fishing and hunting together, playing sandlot softball and shooting off homemade rockets and bombs. My attempts at trying to reach Dave in this unorthodox way went on for several days without any result and I eventually gave it up. I thought myself rather silly for even attempting such a thing. So, you can imagine my shock when David telephoned me a few days later! The following 'converging coincidence' indicates that contact with Dave was telepathic in nature. It appears to have been in direct response to my concentrated thoughts about him."

At which point, Fowler inserts the relevant journal entry.

"September 29, 1998: I had searched for years for a dear friend named David Harris. He was a foster child that shared my room in 1950. He visited me in 1980, but I had lost track of him. A few days ago, he was very much on my mind and I began to make mental images and concentrate on them, thinking that perhaps it would influence him to contact me. Amazingly, this evening I received a telephone call from him. He was having a personal problem and said that he began thinking of me a few days ago!"

Not only had Dave been thinking of Fowler, he had also been thinking of the light and wondering if it was UFO-related. Dave said that it had lit up the whole area around the house but he does not remember what happened next. Like Fowler, Dave had experienced the typical amnesia that follows a UFO abduction encounter.

While Fowler had been reluctant at first to talk to Dave about his UFO encounters for fear that Dave would think him mentally unbalanced, it turned out that Dave had had bizarre incidents in his own life, two of which involved contact with the dead.

When Dave's young daughter was killed in an automobile accident, she contacted him audibly, assuring him that she was all right and in a better place. Shortly after his mother died, he received the same type of audible communication. It was always preceded by a buzzing sound in his ears. His mother told him that her jewelry was in a hidden section of her sewing basket, which her housekeeper had inadvertently taken home with her. Dave visited the woman and looked at the sewing basket. Sure enough, the jewelry, unknown to the housekeeper, was under a false bottom of the basket!

THE SYNCHRONICITY OF UFO DREAMS

Fowler writes that he has summarized his childhood experiences as a prelude to a number of his adult experiences, which involved UFO sightings and dreams of being abducted by the same type of alien entities he experienced as a child. He calls the adult sightings "synchronistic," because they link a physical event [sighting the UFO] with a psychic condition in the observer, which Jung calls "numinosity."

According to Fowler, "Jung, during psychoanalysis of patients, found that numinous experiences, whether encountered inwardly by a UFO dream or outwardly by seeing a UFO, were meaningful. Meaning, according to Jung, was often symbolically indicated through dreams that coincided with the event."

Fowler next recounts a series of consciously-remembered UFO sightings, beginning on July 4, 1947, when he saw a disc-shaped object approach and then descend with a falling leaf motion behind distant trees. Shortly thereafter, along with his mother and some of his siblings, he saw a cylindrical object engulfed in a cloudy haze hovering high in the clear blue sky above their house.

Similar sightings continued well into Fowler's adulthood.

"In 1966," he writes, "I observed a red oval object with no conventional running lights. I gave chase and was able to get ahead of it. I got out of the car. As it passed overhead, it emitted a light humming sound. Then it suddenly performed a quick descent in an arc behind trees. Later I learned that just a mile up the road from where I had seen it, others at nearby Gordon College had seen a glowing UFO pass over and perform a right angle turn over the college grounds. During the same time frame, in nearby Beverly, over a dozen witnesses watched a UFO hover over the Beverly High School. At one point it dived at two witnesses and hovered low over their heads.

"I investigated this sighting with a USAF-contracted team of scientists," he continues. "They wrote in their report that if the statements by witnesses were accurate, the object must have been 'alien' in nature."

Another sighting took place while vacationing with Margaret's parents in England that involved missing time. Fowler said he has had strange flashbacks in the years since but that the loss of time was especially disturbing for his father-in-law. On the flight back to the USA, both Fowler and his daughters, along with other passengers, saw two silver objects through the window but were prevented from looking at them more closely when the pilot ordered everyone to be belted in their seats because of possible turbulence.

ANOTHER SIGHTING, BUT WITH STRANGE EMOTIONS

So it is fair to say that Fowler has seen his share of UFOs. But they are all eclipsed by the story he tells next.

"My last conscious sighting of a UFO," he writes, "was a 'concurrent coincidence' that strained my credulity. It jarred my emotions to the very core of my being. Afterwards, I just sat limply wondering how such things could happen. Again, I was in an airplane with my wife, flying back from a visit to her mother in England."

After that dramatic buildup, here is Fowler's journal entry.

"September 28, 2000: While flying home from England, we passed off the shore of Newfoundland. Half in fun, I glanced out the window to see if could see a UFO. Shocked, I saw a light brownish disc-shaped object pass northeasterly under the plane smoothly. It moved as if it were a hockey puck gliding over the ice. It was around 4:35 p.m. EDT.

"The disc-shaped object passed through a break between the clouds thousands of feet below. At first I thought I was watching a reflection from the plane, but it had sharply defined edges. The way it flew stirred my emotions. It moved as if it were attached to a perfectly straight track. It is hard to describe."

While the details of the sighting itself seem pretty ordinary as far as such reports go, Fowler seems to be talking more about his intense emotional reaction, the "numinous" link between the physical sighting and the psychic elements which created the strange and strong feelings within him.

WAY BEYOND MERE DREAMS

Meanwhile, he also writes that, "UFO dreams are synchronistic in and of themselves. Persons who experience them report details within the dreams that coincide with others that report the exact details in their dreams. These details, in turn, coincide with details reported by people who have had a conscious UFO abduction experience."

There are innumerable benchmarks of the alien abduction phenomenon that abductees have in common, to include dreams of large black staring eyes, missing time and synchronistic happenings. Fowler says these phenomena appear to originate outside our concept of reality and are something Jung would call "acausal," or without any obvious point of origin – unless one admits to the existence of the paranormal. It is the linkage between the psychic and physical elements, such as the scoop mark scars left behind on Fowler's body and that of many abductees that illustrates the synchronicity of the psychic with the physical.

"Not only are UFOs seen, they are of course also dreamed about," writes Jung. "This is particularly interesting to the psychologist; because dreams tell us in what sense they are understood by the unconscious."

Fowler also frequently dreams about being abducted and began to record this type of dream in his journal. An entry from 1990 says:

"I remember portions of a strange dream of being in some kind of a laboratory. The man who ran the laboratory was a friend, but I cannot remember who he was. It was no one I knew in real life. He jokingly told me that he would sign a document indicating that I had been abducted by alien beings if I wanted. He indicated that he would do it only because I was his friend. I began to stare at his eyes. It was at this point that I instantaneously felt the inception of the physical tingling sensation felt in the past during bedroom visitation experiences.

"The dream abruptly ended at this point. Instantly, I felt pressure enveloping my whole body. I felt myself rising vertically and then moving horizontally along somewhere. I could not open my eyes. I then said to myself, 'I'm going with them. I want to go with them but I want to come back.' I stopped and hovered weightlessly. I felt love coursing through my body and I asked, 'Is that you, mummy?' [Note: I thought that I was dead and was being touched by my deceased mother.]

"I began to move horizontally again. I knew that I was now lying back in bed and tried my utmost to come back to full consciousness. I did not believe I was dreaming because I knew that I was lying in bed. I suddenly wondered if I had just had an abduction experience or if I had nearly died. I wondered if I should try to re-enter the strange state of consciousness again, but I thought of death and the possibility of not coming back if I succeeded. Something told me to roll over into my normal sleeping position and go to sleep. I did this. When I awoke the next morning, I had a clear memory of what had happened. I got a pad of paper and wrote down everything that I could remember 'for the record' in the event that it might be significant for future study."

Fowler related the experience to a friend over the phone twelve days later. After hanging up, Fowler wondered if the man in his dream could have been an alien. He began to experience a panic attack, feeling fearful and shuddering all over.

"Persons awaking from an abduction dream feel confused about the realness that such dreams engender," Fowler writes. "They are bewildered to find coinciding anomalous physical effects on their bodies. The nightmares contain the mixed nonsense of normal dreams along with fleeting dream-like memories of an actual abduction."

Another journal entry, this time dated November 6, 1995, illustrates Fowler's statement above perfectly: "I awoke remembering a very detailed dream. The contents were slipping away as I tried to recall the details. I remember suddenly finding myself floating just above the ground. There were typical gray entities on each side of me holding me under my arms. I was not frightened. I felt that it was just another experience among many that I was now used to. We seemed to be waiting for something. It was a warm summer night. The mosquitoes were vicious. I asked them to go up higher above the ground so I would not be bitten. They accommodated my request. We rose higher and waited. Suddenly we were in a bright room!

"There were more gray entities and a human woman in the room. I think she had blond hair and wore coveralls. The woman stayed near me as the grays proceeded to examine and prod me with instruments from a console in the wall. I did not put up any resistance and merely let them do anything they wanted to me. I think they drew blood from my finger. The woman told the grays that she wanted some time with me. They seemed reluctant to let her do this but allowed her to bring me to a table.

"We sat and talked. I asked all kinds of pertinent questions and got answers. However, I cannot remember my questions or her answers. I only remember begging them all to let me remember everything this time. The next thing I can remember is waking up in the morning. Strange. I wonder if this was related to an abduction or was just a dream."

Seen undergoing hypnosis, UFO abductee Betty Andreasson Luca's encounters included a variety of synchronicities.

The co-mingling of dreamlike elements of being taken by the aliens (as the psychic component) and their synchronizing with the physical component of literally being transported physically from his bed (so physical that he recalls fearing that the mosquitoes outside would bite him) again points to the complex connection Fowler is talking about.

"Just dreams?" he asks rhetorically. "Skeptics [especially in my case] would readily dismiss these as nightmares. They would suggest that my association with the UFO abduction phenomenon instigated them. I am certain that some dreams might fall into that category. However, what if the abduction dream contains a number of abduction benchmarks? What if these other benchmarks occur during a wakeful state before and after the so-called abduction dream? What if physical effects on the body correspond to alien operations on those same locations on the body in these supposed dreams?"

This concept is really downright spooky – dreams that leave behind physical evidence that they were true and not the mere confabulations of the sleeping mind.

MYSTERIOUS SCARS AND A TRIP TO THE DOCTOR

Fowler tells the story of receiving a phone call in August 1988 from Betty Andreasson Luca, the devoutly Christian abductee he had worked with for so many years researching her abduction experiences.

"Her voice sounded very nervous," Fowler writes. "She told me that three scoop marks in the form of a triangle had suddenly appeared on her arm. She told me they were similar to one on her leg that she had written me about some time ago."

Fowler admitted he had forgotten all about Betty's letter and went to retrieve it from his files.

"I had not paid much attention to it," he writes. "At that time, I did not realize that it was typical of scars that appeared on other abductees. I asked her to send some photographs of the scars and waited to see what they looked like."

The next night Fowler had a frightening nightmare. He felt himself being taken from bed and moved somewhere. He tried to wake up, thinking that he was only dreaming, but he couldn't. When he did awaken sometime later, he almost blurted out loud, "They were operating on my leg!" He found the scoop mark the next day while taking a shower.

"It was about a quarter of an inch in diameter and appeared as if a tiny round scoop of flesh had been removed," Fowler writes. "Betty's photographs showed similar scoop marks. Shocked, I made an appointment with my personal physician to examine it. He was alarmed and referred me to a dermatologist. The dermatologist insisted that I must have had a recent punch biopsy. He became frustrated when I insisted that I had had no such thing. His examination showed that it was healing and that it did not seem to be dangerous. As he walked out the door of the examining room, he turned before closing the door and said that, 'It looks like a punch biopsy!'"

Fowler says he feels compelled to emphasize that "such physical synchronistic effects are found upon awakening from such a dream. They appear overnight with no apparent explanation except in their relation to the content of the dream. Thus, abduction dreams are revelatory. They provide an explanation for anomalous physical effects upon the body that appear simultaneously with such dreams. They provide strong circumstantial evidence that the dreams are the way an abductee remembers an abduction. These physical and other non-physical benchmarks of a UFO abduction experience have appeared repeatedly in my life."

The foregoing has been a brief overview of Fowler's synchronicity experiences as related in his book **SynchroFile**. But he is not the only prominent UFO researcher whose life has been dramatically touched by the synchronicity phenomenon.

NORMAL LOGIC BATTLES THE IRRATIONAL TRUTH

Dr. Jacques Vallee, often considered one of the most respected researchers in all of UFOlogy, was in Los Angeles in the winter of 1976, compiling his notes on various branches of a UFO cult called "The Order of Melchizedek" for the book that would eventually be called ***Messengers of Deception***. Vallee had been frustrated in his search for information on the real, historical Melchizedek, who had lived in Old Testament times but about whom the ancients had recorded very little.

As the story is told online by a writer named Jeff Wells, Vallee was on Sunset Boulevard and had hailed a taxi. A cab stopped for him.

"After a short ride," Wells writes, "during which Vallee did not discuss his current research, he paid his fare and accepted a receipt. He stuffed it in his wallet and thought nothing more of it, until two days later he noticed it was signed 'Melchizedek.'"

Vallee next takes up the tale himself.

"I cannot afford to write this story," he says, "because I cannot expect anyone to believe it. At the same time, I cannot sweep it under the rug. There is only one Melchizedek listed in the L.A. phone book, and I have the receipt signed by the driver right in front of me. It was this incident that convinced me to put more energy into understanding the nature of such coincidences.

"The Melchizedek incident that I experienced on February 21, 1976, suggested to me that the world might be organized more like a random database than like a sequential library. Since there is only one person named Melchizedek in the L.A. phone book, I have to conclude that mere coincidence cannot explain this incident. Alternative explanations are equally inadequate, unfortunately. I did not discuss my research with the driver, so a hoax is out of the question.

"There could be a well-organized conspiracy against me, of course, to put lady taxi drivers on my path with names related to my current reading interests, but the motivations of such conspirators would be rather obscure. Fortunately, another avenue of explanation exists.

"If there is no time dimension as we usually assume there is, we may be traversing events by association. Modern computers retrieve information associatively. You 'evoke' the desired records by using keywords, words of power. You request the intersection of 'microwave' and 'headache' and you find 20 articles you never suspected existed. Perhaps I had unconsciously posted such a request on some psychic bulletin board with the keyword 'Melchizedek.' If we live in the associative universe of the software scientist rather than the sequential universe of the space-time physicist, then miracles are no longer irrational events."

So we have before us the unconditional love that Raymond Fowler received on numerous occasions from his alien abductors, a sensation that carries over to his many synchronistic, sometimes precognitive, dreams and flashes of mystifying memories that as of yet still hold their mysteries for Fowler and his readers. Then there is the bizarre experience of Jacques Vallee and the cab driver whose name was linked to Biblical history and a modern day cult.

Fowler summed it up by saying, "Synchronistic happenings in my life leave a strong impression that I am part of a greater ONE unknown reality that controls all things. To me, these uncanny happenings are an intrusion from a mega-reality into my particular reality via some kind of para-physical osmosis. In retrospect, it seems as if I am being schooled by 'something other' via these acausal manifestations."

In a 1965 song called *"It's All Over Now, Baby Blue,"* Nobel Prize-winning songwriter Bob Dylan wrote, "The highway is for gamblers, better use your sins. Take what you have gathered from coincidence." The lines can be taken to mean that "coincidence" is an experience we are intended to learn from, that coincidences have a meaning of some kind that can be deciphered and understood.

Which is exactly what Fowler, Vallee and so many others are trying to do – to make sense of synchronicity experiences that defy everything we think we know about time and space and yet also manage to make us feel, as Fowler writes, that it's all part of some greater plan that we are being taught to take our own personal part in.

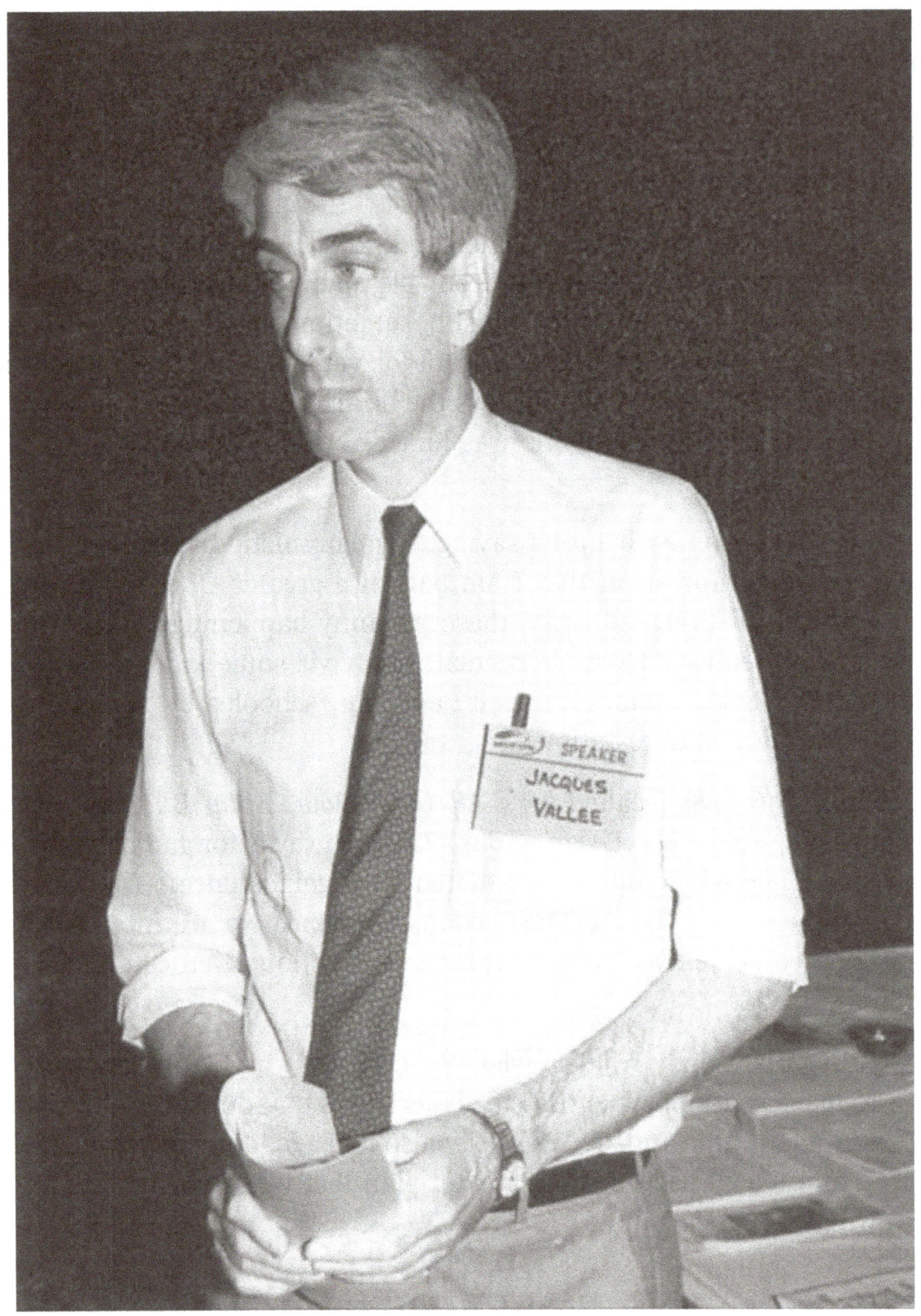

Jacques Vallee

SUGGESTED READING BY RAYMOND FOWLER:

SYNCHROFILE: AMAZING PERSONAL ENCOUNTERS WITH SYNCHRONICITY AND OTHER STRANGE PHENOMENA

UFO TESTAMENT: ANATOMY OF AN ABDUCTEE

SUGGESTED READING BY DR. JACQUES VALLEE

MESSENGERS OF DECEPTION

WHILE ANY BOOK BY FOWLER AND VALLEE WOULD BE HELPFUL AND INSTRUCTIVE, THE ABOVE BOOKS ARE ESPECIALLY RELEVANT TO THE SUBJECT OF SYNCHRONICITY.

16.

SYNCHRONICITIES AND THE CONTACTEES
By Nick Redfern

THE author of over 50 books on the paranormal, Nick Redfern is very aware of synchronicities. While others in the field ignore such "hunches," Nick follows them with high expectations that they will lead to a more complete understanding of the phenomenon that intrigues us so much.

Nick Redfern is a full-time author and journalist specializing in a wide range of unsolved mysteries, including Bigfoot, the Loch Ness Monster, UFO sightings, government conspiracies, alien abductions and various other paranormal phenomena. He writes regularly for the *London Daily Express* newspaper, *Fortean Times*, *Fate*, and *UFO Magazine*. His previous books include **Three Men Seeking Monsters**, **Strange Secrets**, **Cosmic Crashes** and **The FBI Files**. Among his many exploits, Redfern has investigated reports of lake monsters in Scotland, vampires in Puerto Rico, werewolves in England, aliens in Mexico and sea serpents in the United States. Redfern travels and lectures extensively around the world. Originally from England, he currently lives in Dallas, Texas.

* * * * *

Undoubtedly, one of the strangest and most unsettling aspects of any investigation of the paranormal sort occurs when the phenomenon itself decides to turn the tables firmly around and seeks to take an icy, steely grip on the investigator. For me personally, this has occurred on several memorable occasions – but certainly never before to the sheer and graphic extent that occurred in 2009, while I was deeply researching the so-called Space-Brother movement for my **Contactees** book. It was while my research was at its height that a truly bizarre set of synchronistic and near-unearthly events occurred that practically had me questioning both my sanity and my grip on reality.

Nick stands toe-to-toe with "Invaders" star Roy Thinnes, whose show was immensely popular when aired.

Carol Ann Rodriguez's snappy art adorns our edition of Dana Howard book. *Diane She Came From Venus* is available on Amazon.

George Adamski, Truman Bethurum, Billy Meier, and Daniel Fry were just a few of those curious souls who, many decades ago, claimed face-to-face interaction with long-haired, human-looking alien entities that wished us to disarm our nuclear arsenals and live in peace and harmony with one another. The era of the contactee was, to say the least, one of the strangest within what has become known popularly as Ufology. And, just maybe, it was that same concentration of high-strangeness that sucked me into the controversy at a deeply personal level.

It all began in late July 2009.

At the time, I was studying the life and UFO experiences of a 1950s contactee named Dana Howard, who claimed a number of meetings and exchanges with a beautiful, eight-foot-tall Venusian named Diana – several of which occurred during séances held at a Los Angeles-based church. See: I told you the contactee movement was a controversial one! One of those who provided very welcome assistance on this particular matter was an Oregon-based researcher and writer named Regan Lee, who had spent a great deal of time investigating the claims of Dana Howard.

On July 31, I wrote to Regan in an email that immediately after digesting the data she sent me on the Dana Howard affair, "I took some towels out of the dryer. One of the towels, a yellow and pink one, my wife Dana owned before we got married in 2001. So, we have had it for years. But for all the time we have had the towel, I never bothered to read the writing on it – until I was folding the towel right after finishing your chapter."

As I told Regan, the towel was adorned with a logo that read: Venus Girls Just Want to Have Fun. And both my wife and the key player in this story share the same name: Dana. Well, this had to have been some weird coincidence, right? What happened next, however, suggests not!

Two days later, I was sitting on the couch, reading the newly-surfaced account of a person who – in the 1970s – had a contactee-style experience that paralleled the 1952 encounters of Truman Bethurum, whose claims I related in my book.

According to Bethurum, on a number of occasions at a place called Mormon Mesa, Nevada, he met with a group of aliens – led by their Captain, the hot and shapely Aura Rhanes – from a planet supposedly called Clarion. Like most of the stories of the contactees, Bethurum's was highly controversial; it attracted just about as many believers as it did disbelievers. But, as I noted in my book, I was of the opinion that Bethurum had had an interaction with something. The precise nature of that something is, of course, a matter of personal interpretation.

After I put away the file on this newly-surfaced story, Dana asked if I could help her find her digital-camera which she had misplaced. We looked high and low, but failed to find it. But, while checking behind the TV set – to see if the camera had perhaps fallen there – I came across Dana's high-school yearbook for 1982. What on earth does this have to do with the contactees, you may justifiably ask? Okay, I'm coming to that.

Although Dana is a U.S. citizen, she grew up in the Cayman Islands and graduated from school there. I picked up the yearbook, with the intention of moving it to one side while I looked around for the camera, and was startled by something I had never noticed before: the cover of the book read: 82 Clarion.

How odd that after spending two-hours reading a report very similar to that of Truman Bethurum and his friends from Clarion, that I should then, immediately after, stumble across a book with that very word – Clarion – adorned across its cover.

In view of the above, perhaps I can be forgiven for thinking that each and every one us live in a dream-world of truly Matrix-style proportions!

The Matrix Control System of Philip K. Dick
And The Paranormal Synchronicities of Timothy Green Beckley

Nick is no creature from the black lagoon, but, when he does some shape-shifting, anything can happen.

SUGGESTED READING

BLOODLINE OF THE GODS

365 DAYS OF UFOS

WOMEN IN BLACK

ON THE TRAIL OF THE SAUCER SPIES

THE ZOMBIE BOOK

THERE IS SOMETHING IN THE WOODS

http://nickredfernfortean.blogspot.com

17.

DIVINE INVASIONS: PHILIP K. DICK, ROBERT ANTON WILSON AND "ALIEN CONTACT" IN THE 1970s

By Valerie D'Orazio, ButterflyLanguage.com

Valerie D'Orazio

VALERIE D'Orazio is an author and editor who has worked for MTV, DC Entertainment, Marvel Comics, Valiant Comics, Heavy Metal, and BOOM! Studios. She has written comics based on characters such as The Punisher, The X-Men, and Hellraiser. Her 2014 comic book biographies of whistleblower Edward Snowden and "Dark Knight" shooter James Holmes have received international online and TV press from outlets as diverse as

TIME, *The Guardian*, MSNBC, Al Jazeera, *USA Today*, *El Mundo*, *The Voice of Russia*, *The Washington Post*, and Infowars.

She currently writes the Butterfly Language blog, with a special interest in Philip K. Dick, Robert Anton Wilson, spirituality, artificial intelligence, futurology, synchronicity, the Joker archetype, and the uncanny intersection between the esoteric and pop culture.

https://butterflylanguage.com/

* * * * *

A very weird thing began to happen in the early-to-mid 1970s – a number of people were apparently "channeling" very similar information, from entities variously claiming to be aliens, God, and beyond. These people, from different backgrounds and fields, would end up basically forming an interconnecting web of High Weirdness that would impact popular culture to the present day.

We start with science fiction author Philip K. Dick – the author of **A Scanner Darkly**, **The Man in the High Castle**, and **Do Androids Dream Of Electric Sheep?** – who, on February 20th, 1974, had a paranormal experience he would later spend 1,000+ pages of journaling to try to figure out. He had answered the door to find a woman wearing a golden fish-pendant; the light reflected off the pendant in a particular way, bouncing into his brain and providing him with a dense amount of information.

In the months that followed, he would demonstrate powers of xenoglossia – suddenly speaking in Ancient Greek – as well as an instance of proven clairvoyance. Above all else, he was convinced that he – and we – were living simultaneously in the present day as well as the time of the first Christians in Rome . . . and that he was in contact with some sort of extra-dimensional (or not) being he would dub VALIS, who would at times take over his entire body:

"I experienced an invasion of my mind by a transcendentally rational mind, as if I had been insane all my life and suddenly I had become sane..."

Roughly a year before, on July 23, 1973, Robert Anton Wilson – co-author of the satire/sci-fi **Illuminatus!** Trilogy and the **Cosmic Trigger** books – claims to have channeled information from an intelligence in the Sirius star system. Exactly three years later to the day, Wilson opened himself up again to these entities to garner, as he put it, "another blast of Cosmic Wisdom" from "the Transmitters."

Wilson noted the similarities between his "contact experience" and that of fellow writer Dick:

*"Philip K. Dick and I had a series of rather similar experiences. From his experiences, he constructed **VALIS**, which looks like a science fiction story most of the way...abruptly towards the end you figure out, maybe it isn't a science fiction story, maybe it's an account of Philip K. Dick going crazy. Or maybe it's an account of Philip K. Dick being contacted by extraterrestrials. Now, **The Cosmic Trigger** pretty much has the same structure to it: Robert Anton Wilson being contacted by extraterrestrials. No: it's Robert Anton Wilson going crazy. No: it's just Robert Anton Wilson experimenting with alternate realities..."*

The Matrix Control System of Philip K. Dick
And The Paranormal Synchronicities of Timothy Green Beckley

Robert Anton Wilson

While his experience absolutely had a profound impact on his later work and philosophy, it is important to note that Wilson kept an open mind about it. Perhaps he truly was contacted by aliens...or maybe it was merely a case of his right brain speaking to his left...or maybe he was merely contacted by a 6-foot tall white rabbit called the púca (or, "pooka"...we'll revisit this later). While Dick seemed to obsessively seek Answers to the possible detriment of his health and sanity, Wilson opted for a more "chill" approach.

Almost around the exact same time Wilson was being "told" that "Sirius is very important," his incarcerated friend Timothy Leary – the highly influential psychologist who popularized LSD use in the 1960s – ALSO began receiving telepathic messages which were supposedly from extraterrestrials. The resulting **Starseed Transmission** was part conspiracy-ramble, part social-commentary, and part ecstatic proclamation of "The Good News" (replace Jesus with "Higher Intelligence"):

"Well, here it is. The comet Starseed comes at the right time to return light to Planet Earth. The structure for the new way is already here. Starseed will turn-on the new network."

"Starseed" also repeatedly referred to the incoming comet Kohoutek (which becomes equated with Starseed) as being of extreme importance and ushering in a new (space) age for humanity:

"Behold a great light appears in the sky. The offer is made. The signal is flashed. Resonate with it or die eye-ground and bored."

And this connection between comets, alien intelligences, and a new age for humanity is *very* interesting to me, as it would be echoed 20 years later with the Heaven's Gate group and the comet Hale-Bopp. From the Heaven's Gate official website:

"The joy is that our Older Member in the Evolutionary Level Above Human (the 'Kingdom of Heaven') has made it clear to us that Hale-Bopp's approach is the 'marker' we've been waiting for – the time for the arrival of the spacecraft from the Level Above Human to take us home to 'Their World' – in the literal Heavens. Our 22 years of

classroom here on Planet Earth is finally coming to conclusion – 'graduation' from the Human Evolutionary Level."

And guess when and how the founders of Heaven's Gate, Marshall Applewhite and Bonnie Nettles, received this information? During the early 1970s, via channeled/telepathic communications from entities they identified as being ultimately extraterrestrial in origin. They even featured a picture on their website depicting an alien gray-type figure, called "How a Member of Heaven might appear."

Marshall Applewhite and Bonnie Nettles

But it went beyond merely channeling. They flat-out said their bodies were "*taken over.*" They said their human "vehicles" were voluntarily "vacated" to allow these Higher Intelligences to operate on our plane of existence. Which is what Philip K. Dick claims happened to him regarding the entity VALIS (in fact, VALIS was, according to Dick, apparently a pretty damn good housekeeper and business manager, to boot).

This all puts the remake of **Invasion of the Body Snatchers**, from 1978, in a totally interesting light. Taking place amongst a bourgeois coterie of somewhat hippy-dippy San Franciscans (San Francisco would be an epicenter for channelers and general weirdness), the movie's events seem to strangely mirror what was claimed by Applewhite, Dick, and others – there was something out there, something that was not merely talking to particular people, but occasionally "taking over" their bodies.

And why would these "aliens" do such a thing, and why to these particular people? Why were these entities – if there were truly such beings at all – contacting Dick, Leary, Wilson, Applewhite, William Burroughs (who, to be honest, always seemed to be contacted by something), Ramtha (J.Z. Knight, first contact 1977), Chelsea Quinn Yarbro (the "Michael" channels, which started in 1973), author and ethnobotanist Terrence McKenna (starting in 1971) and more?

Well...they *were* all either writers or guru-types who ended up having an impact on popular thought and culture.

This is all not to say that "aliens" exist, or that what these different people claim happened to them actually happened. But SOMETHING happened to these dear people. To that, I think we can all agree.

What was in the drinking water in the 1970s?

Well, for one, probably a lot of dope.

And there was a whole raft of books and such from the 1960s that would have had an impact on these individuals. You had the highly-influential channeled Seth material from the mid-Sixties. You had a *lot* of people taking a lot of LSD and reporting what they found there. Heavy influence from Eastern religions and philosophy, books on a range of esoteric topics like **Morning of the Magicians** (1960), the "Ancient Astronauts" classic **Chariots of the Gods?** (1968), and a metric shit-ton of UFO narratives.

So it's possible that it was all just a case of popular-culture infecting highly-suggestible people with crazy notions and flights of fancy.

But that doesn't quite explain how Philip K. Dick, shortly after his 1974 experience, was able to psychically – and incredibly accurately – diagnose a rare birth defect in his young son's body that was going to, barring immediate surgery, kill the child.

What exactly happened to Philip K. Dick and the rest of these people?

We may never know for sure. But it is obvious that each person experienced and interpreted their so-called "contact" in a different way...through the lens of their own world-view and personality. For Leary, it resulted in a trippy missive full of railing against what he perceived to be an overly authoritarian government.

Why would "aliens" be contacting these particular people? Could it be because they were all either writers or guru-types who ended up having an impact on popular thought and culture?

Dick had seen the 1976 film **The Man Who Fell To Earth**, referenced it in his *Exegesis*, and clearly it had an impact on him – so much so that he synthesized the movie's story and imagery with the growing cosmology of his own February/March 1974 epiphanies to create **VALIS**.

From the *Exegesis*:

"Re the Bowie film, and the little boy on the raft floating toward England; the divine child won't be born, but rather smuggled in, like a cuckoo's egg in a host nest, disguised as a – human? Terrestrial? Evading 'Scotland Yard' – i.e., the authorities. Extraterrestrial? No. It has to do with time, and he can mix his world in and out with ours, like with a mixing board. Space and time both. But he is an invader – but God knows from where or when – but another planet. The future? And/or an alternate world?"

What is so strange about the Bowie connection to **VALIS** is that around the same time Dick was still experiencing the "afterglow" of his "2-3-74" mystical experience, the musician was having some related esoteric situations and notions of his own.

Specifically, a viewing of **Rosemary's Baby** in the mid-1970s reportedly sent Bowie into a state of paranoid terror that he himself would be kidnapped by occultists and be forced to sire a "devil baby" who might be then sacrificed. Which sounds, a little, like the situation the alien Eric Lampton found himself in – in terms of being the "father" (albeit second-hand, Joseph-style) of such a "divine" (or infernal) child. In the book **VALIS**, the baby is then murdered (sacrificed) by synth-pop music composer Brent Mini (a.k.a. Bowie collaborator Brian Eno).

Bowie was also heavily steeped in UFO and occult lore and he – much like Philip K. Dick – even believed he was "channeling" some of his material, or at the very least "not there" for the creation of some of it.

Of course, there might be a simpler explanation for both Bowie and Dick's preoccupations during the mid-1970s. They were taking a lot of drugs.

Yet, they also both seemed to be "accessing" the same "storyline." In fact, a lot of people, within a similar web of connections during those freaky Seventies years, did.

Was Bowie familiar with Dick's story of "2-3-74" and the pink laser beam of light that allegedly struck the writer in the forehead, giving him a religious euphoria? Because that sure looks like what is happening to the singer in his 1984 music video, "Loving The Alien"—Bowie blue (the color often associated with an otherworldly energy and power) and his hands in prayer, with a pink light emanating from the top half of his face.

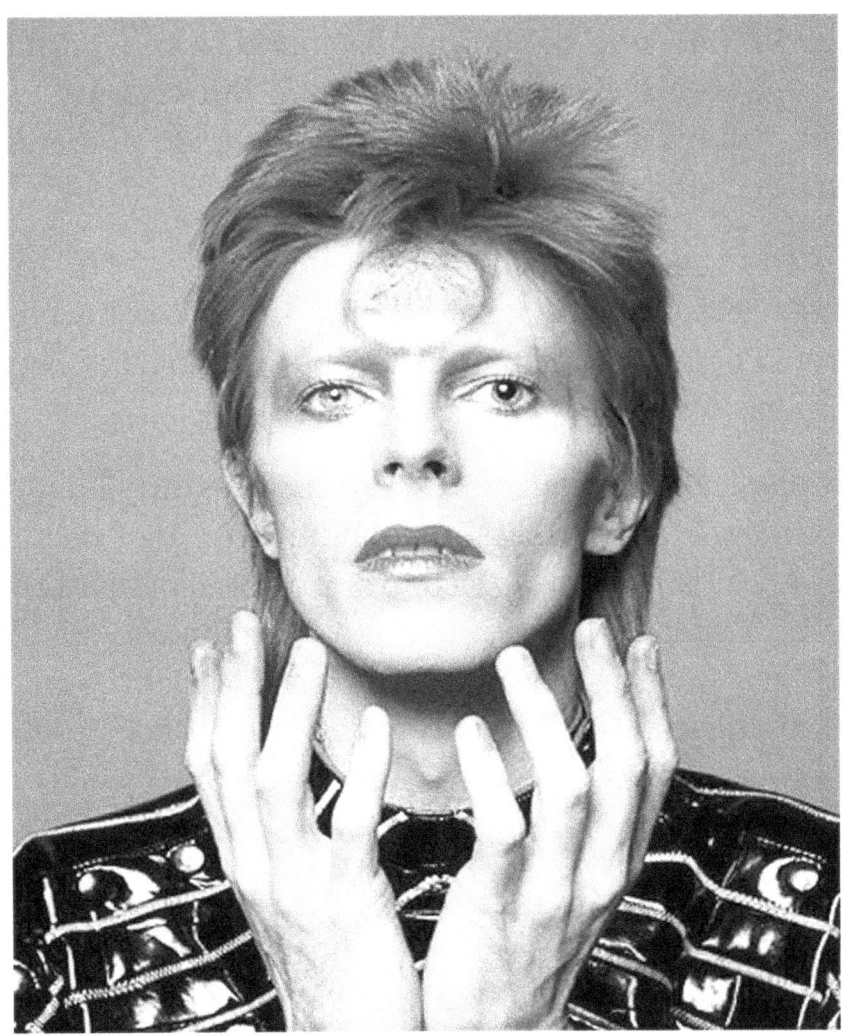

From VALIS: *"Different eyes replace the ones which exploded. Then, very slowly, his forehead slides open in the middle. A third eye becomes invisible, but it lacks a pupil; instead, it has a lateral lens."*

Another scene in "Loving The Alien" depicts Bowie, with a phantasmic "2001"-type display in the background, throwing his head back; overwhelmed and screaming. Now let's go back to **VALIS**, with this sequence describing Eric Lampton's movie of the same name:

"Long shot. The Lamptons' house below; camera is what they call 'camera three.' The beam of energy fires at the house below. Quick cut to Eric Lampton; he jerks as if pierced. Holds his hands to his head, convulsing in agony. Tight shot of his face; his eyes explode. (The audience with us gasps, including me and Fat)."

Did Bowie purposely put **VALIS**-type imagery in his music video as a tribute to Dick? Did Dick's use of Bowie as the template for the character Eric Lampton have some weird "quantum" effect that drew the singer into a larger real-world meta-narrative? Or, as I suggested before, were they both drawing from the same well of "inspiration?"

And because these two extremely talented men left behind for the public so many materials infused with their spirit, who can even say if the **VALIS/Man Who Fell To Earth** narrative is truly over?

18.

SYNCHRONICITIES WITH A PERSONAL TOUCH – LOOK NO FURTHER THAN A NAME OR DATE

By Cynthia Cirile

WRITER. Screenwriter. Poe scholar. "Feminist Rebel." Follows the Goddess in all forms.

"I am very proud of my three amazing 'children,' who are all pretty much all grown up! Jesse, John Cody, and Lucia. I have a pretty pup named Zevon Lombard Cirile. She drinks Coke Zero, like her Mama."

A longtime friend and fellow esoterist, Cynthia sees "the signs" all around. You can, she notes, learn to synchronize with the universe wisely.

* * * * *

We begin having synchronicities early in life, but we usually aren't aware of them until someone explains to us what a synchronicity is. Even little kids are aware of synchronicities but think that they are merely coincidences. If they grow up as part of an enlightened family, or are simply hungry to learn the truth, they'll eventually discover that there are both coincidences and synchronicities.

**Three faces of screenwriter and esoterist Cynthia Cirile.
(Photo by John Fusano.)**

I became aware of synchronicities, or meaningful coincidences, when I was about 12 years old. I had met a new friend, named Diana, who lived near me. We had a great deal in common – more than I knew. First, I discovered that, like me, Diana was a Capricorn. Then I learned that I shared a birthday with her father. This struck me as meaningful, even at that age, especially since I was growing close to the family. The most significant and startling revelation came about when I realized that our names, Cynthia and Diana, had the same meaning: the Goddess of the Moon. I had never heard of such a deity back then, but later in life, when I became attracted to the Goddess Artemis, I discovered that all three names, Artemis, Cynthia, and Diana, represented the Moon Goddess in different cultures. This was quite a shock!

Later on, as I began studying astrology, Tarot and reincarnation, I learned that there are reincarnation groups, or people with whom we share karma that must be resolved. Consequently, a group of us may choose to reincarnate together to work on our karma. The synchronicities I shared with my friend Diana drew us closer and helped us understand that we were twin souls. We had been here together in many lifetimes and had loved and supported each other.

Decades later I became interested in the matriarchal religions and became a priestess of the Goddess Artemis. I began to understand that I had been preparing for this all my life. I knew that I had been called. I had been named Cynthia for a reason. My name alone had defined my future spirituality.

Often, there are startling synchronicities regarding names and dates, especially surrounding birth and death dates. In my case, the most dramatic case involved my daughter, Lucia. Before she was born, I had named her for light – since the name means "light" in Italian. I thought it a holy name and believed she would grow up to fulfill her name. Indeed, she brings light into the lives of everyone who knows her.

Synchronicities may have linked Carole Lombard and Clark Gable in more than a tender embrace.

Before Lucia was born, I fixated on the date she would be born. I felt very strongly that her birthdate would be strongly synchronistic. She was supposed to arrive during the time of Sagittarius, and I thought she might be born on my father's birthday. That date passed. Important birth dates, death dates and even dates of astrological import passed. During the season of Capricorn, I felt certain she would be born on my own birthday. Those dates passed. We were half way into January now.

I had been obsessed with Carole Lombard and Clark Gable since I was a little kid. I knew the ins and outs of their lifetimes, and now felt that my daughter would be born on January 16th, which had the double synchronicity of being my friend Diana's birthday – but also the date of Carole Lombard's death in a plane crash in 1942.

This date, too, passed. We were now in the time of Aquarius. My imagination was spent. I couldn't think of any date during that period that would involve a synchronicity. Lucia came into the world on February 1, 1993. I was delighted to have a healthy and beautiful daughter, but confused, too, because I had felt sure that there would be a strong synchronicity involved with her birth.

The next day, her proud father walked into hospital room holding a newspaper clipping. I just glanced at it and felt a chill go through my body. The clipping was a typical one, "Who Was Born on Your Birthday – February 1st." I didn't even need to read the clipping. Just by looking at the date on the paper, something instantly clicked. I starting crying out, "Oh my god! I can't believe it! It's Clark Gable's birthday!" Everyone was moved, as the importance of this synchronicity was felt by the whole family. I could not believe that my daughter came into the world on Clark Gable's birthday.

As to whether this was a meaningful synchronicity? My daughter has always felt that Clark Gable is her chief guide, or "angel," and Clark Gable himself came through a medium friend of mine, thanking me for a lifetime of devotion and saying that this was why he had decided to be my daughter's heavenly godfather.

If you want to begin looking for synchronicities, start by looking at the names, the birthdates and birth signs of those you love. Patterns will begin to emerge that you can't deny. You'll begin to pick up a great deal about how and why you are connected to those you are. If you find certain names, signs, dates and even numbers recurring, you can be sure there are important messages for you there. With some practice, you will be able to identify not only people from your reincarnation group, but also twin souls and soul mates. Do synchronicities have meaning? You bet they do. But a synchronicity that isn't recognized is of no meaning at all! Keep your six senses open and tune in.

* * * * *

PUBLISHER'S NOTE: To this day a cloak of mystery surrounds the death of actress Carole Lombard and includes the specter of synchronicity and a possible UFO connection. According to researcher Kyle J. Wood, "officially" Ms. Lombard's doomed flight was running late and the pilot was cruising at a low altitude, resulting in the death of all twenty-one passengers. Says the on air contributing guest to E Entertainment's "Mysteries and Scandals:" – "Unofficially, some still believe it to have been the work of fate (via 'supernatural' design). In short, the number three, a reputed 'bad luck' numeral at the time, seemed to be everywhere. The Lombard party was supposed to travel back to Los Angeles via train after the War Bond rally in Indianapolis. Their group of three (consisting of Carole, her mother Elizabeth and friend Otto Winkler) only managed to board the plane because of three last minute seat cancellations. Carole was 33 years old at the time. It had taken three days to reach Indiana (her home state) by train. The plane was a DC-3, designated 'Flight 3.'" An FBI document filed at the time and released under the Freedom of Information Act tells of mysterious lights seen over a nearby mountain range, which some say may have contributed to the plane's crash in some form or another, perhaps drawing undue attention by the pilot. Journalist Kyle J. Wood summarizes: "Much has been forgotten about the 'peculiar lights in the sky' that were noted in regards to the crash of Lombard's flight. 'Hanging like a suspended lantern' above the mountain range, the mysterious unexplained light was first theorized to have possibly been part of a sabotage plot to lure Flight 3 to its doom' (because of the 15 Army Air Corps ferry pilots on board). This theory was quickly discounted after an airway beacon mechanic came forward and reported to the FBI about seeing an 'identical type light' hovering in the sky above Baker, California, just three days earlier. The mechanic was engaged in recovery efforts following the Lombard crash when he by chance learned of the similar light from an area ranch owner who had seen both the light and the plane's fiery explosion." The case has also been tied in with the Battle of Los Angeles UFO sightings which occurred around the same time. https://welkerlots.wordpress.com/

19.

EVERYTHING YOU WANTED TO KNOW ABOUT SYNCHRONICITIES:

A QUESTION AND ANSWER SESSION WITH MARIE D. JONES

Conducted by Timothy Green Beckley

MARIE D. Jones is the bestselling author of over 15 non-fiction books about the paranormal, consciousness, New Science, metaphysics, and cutting edge science. She is also a screenwriter and producer with several projects in development at various production companies. She has been a staff writer for a number of magazines including *Fate, New Dawn, Atlantis Rising, MindScape and Intrepid*, and has appeared on television's **"Ancient Aliens"** series and on radio shows all over the world. Her website is www.mariedjones.com.

Some opening remarks about synchronicity from Marie:

Synchronicities are pokes and prods asking us to pay attention to the present moment. When a synchronicity occurs, we see the effects and marvel that they are connected. The cause remains hidden in the implicate order of reality. Sometimes they are big and in-your-face, other times subtle. I was struggling with a choice between two book titles, neither of which was a common grouping of words.

I had been going back and forth for weeks, even months, trying to decide between one or the other, when finally I asked for a sign from the Universe. I asked for a visual sign, too, because I knew it had to be something I wouldn't explain away as a vagary. Three or four days later, I was in a bookstore, and a book fell to my feet with a picture on it of the animal in one of my title choices, a black swan. I felt a sense of relief and certainty that I had gotten my sign and never looked back.

Marie D. Jones

An even bigger synchronicity occurred when my son was born. Right before his birth, my beloved cat Elvis passed away after a long battle with cancer. Elvis had a very distinct meow that was more like a "Meh!" Elvis loved to sleep with one paw resting on me at all times, so he felt connected. I grieved his death, but prepared for the birth of my son, who was given the middle name Elvis when one of the first sounds out of his mouth was "Meh!" And yes, he napped with one hand, curled up into a little "paw" on my arm or leg, just like his feline predecessor!

* * * * *

Question: How did your interest in coincidences and synchronicities come about?

Marie: I don't remember a time when I was not interested or aware of them. Even as a child, I was able to make connections between events that seemed to have no apparent connecting cause, or at least not one I could see. I was always involved in the paranormal and metaphysical worlds, so the interest grew as time went on. I had a lot of background in metaphysics and New Thought, and synchronicities play a large role in the ideas present in New Thought . . . that everything is connected at some invisible level, and therefore events that appear to be disconnected really aren't that way at all. My studies in metaphysics led me to a deeper understanding that nothing is coincidental, and that led to a lifelong fascination with destiny and free will, which I just wrote a book about! When I've looked at the synchronicities of my own life, I can see how they were and are all puzzle pieces in the "bigger picture" of reality, and how they appear to be moving me towards a specific destiny, and have been doing so since childhood. So when they happen, I PAY ATTENTION!

Question: How does one tell the difference between a "good" synchronicity and one that is of no consequence?

Marie: I think any synchronicity is of consequence, although the reasons might not be evident right away. Some people have a synchronistic event that only makes sense down the road a bit. For example, meeting someone in a sort of coincidental way, then losing touch with that person, only to reconnect a year later over a huge opportunity that they bring to you. I am not sure synchronicities can be judged as good or bad. At least in my life experience I have never had a "bad" experience. Perhaps ignoring them, or not interpreting them properly might lead to a negative experience. That, of course, is an individual thing! I suggest people pay attention to all of them, because they are "pokes" and "prods" in a sense from that higher, invisible order of connectivity.

Question: There do seem to be bad as well as good coincidences, wouldn't you say? Born and died on the same day of the month. Run into someone you haven't seen in ages and it turns out to be a bummer all the way around with dire consequences.

Marie: Well, again, we are putting judgment onto events. Say you do run into someone you haven't seen in ages, and they screw up your life for a while. It could either be seen as a huge bummer . . . OR, it could be seen as a potential learning experience that you needed to have in order to build a certain character, or learn how to deal with people you don't trust. Everything can be some type of positive learning experience, no matter how bad it looks on the outside, but because we don't see the CAUSE or intention behind the two events we call coincidental, we automatically react to the EFFECTS.

The Matrix Control System of Philip K. Dick
And The Paranormal Synchronicities of Timothy Green Beckley

What COULD be discerned as bad, or negative, are intuitions that tell you not to go somewhere or do something, and if you ignore them, something bad happens, but these are different from coincidences. I have had this happen bigtime, where my gut said "don't do it" and I did it anyway and paid a price!!! We are definitely hooked up and tuned into a higher level of reality/knowledge that is always finding ways to communicate with us, either via intuitions, synchronicities, opportunities, etc.

Question: Can you relate some of the synchronicities that you feel are important in your own life?

Marie: I have had so many. But let's pick one that seems easy to describe. I have a novel I wrote and was in need of a title . . . and I had a title in mind, which included a certain color animal. Well, the day I was really, really stressing over this, I happened to see the exact animal in the exact color at least five different times, on a truck, billboard, book cover, wine bottle and on TV! And this was not a very common animal either. I took that as a direct sign that I had found my title. Now, did my brain just seek out this information to corroborate my intention of finding a title? Maybe. That cannot be ruled out. Our brains seek pattern, so we are "wired" to notice synchronicities. But I also like to think it was an outside force telling me I was on the right track, too! Maybe both?

I have had synchronicities and coincidences that have led me to people that I've worked with on projects, books, etc. That happens a lot. And often something that happened in my past will resurface to help me with something I am dealing with today. That happens all the time as well. I am a visual person, so I ask for images when I need some kind of guidance, and often get them. Another example: I couldn't decide whether I should sell my home awhile back, or stay, despite the mortgage issues I was having. I asked for an image of a gopher to appear somewhere that day if I was meant to "go." And lo and behold, a damned semi-truck drove by later with a giant gopher on it! I sold the house for a huge profit JUST AS the bottom was dropping out of the market here in my area, and everyone else was going into foreclosure.

Question: Why are the meanings behind such events so difficult to figure out – or is there a meaning?

Marie: Sometimes the meaning is obvious and immediate, as in having a synchronistic event occur, say meeting a particular person who is offering the kind of job you want. Other times, I think the meaning comes later, and perhaps on a subconscious level we "get" it before we are consciously aware of it. I suspect all of this "unseen information" speaks to our subconscious more because our conscious mind tends to ignore it, rationalize it, discard it and find logic where, at the time, there may not yet be any. Maybe the meaning is small, as in the black swan case. Fun prods to help us make a decision. Sometimes the meaning is huge, as in a coincidental meeting that leads to marriage, a career move, etc.

Question: What conclusions can you draw? Are these events just random? Or is there someone planning them? And, if so, for what purpose?

Marie: In my personal opinion, there is no such thing as "random" in this universe. It all comes down to whatever that invisible reality is where the causes occur. That leads to the question about someone "planning" the causes. I do not in any way, shape or form believe there is a person behind all this, but I do lean towards some kind of intelligence or consciousness, one that is not human at all, but possibly acts more like a computer processing information in a way that produces more information.

I think we are all able to tap into this vast field of information, which could explain all types of psi, including remote viewing and psychic phenomena. I also think this implicate order might answer some of the questions as to other types of paranormal phenomena – what they are, where they originate, how they manifest here. I think we are dealing with many levels of reality, and synchronicities are small reminders of that. We are not meant to tap into these levels all the time. Our brains are not structured to do so. We live a 3D existence in one dimension of time, but now and then we get those "glimpses" of other potential realities. What put them all into place, and runs them . . . that is the Holy Grail we all seek. First Cause . . . is there such a thing?

Question: How would your thinking agree or disagree with others who have studied the matter?

Marie: I love the work of Carl Jung and David Bohm. Jung set the bar for his work with synchronicity. Bohm especially succeeds at bringing the quantum world into the mix and can sound very metaphysical in doing so, but he was a physicist instrumental in the development of quantum physics. His idea of levels of order is, to me, the best explanation for reality I've found yet! But I suspect in the next 20 years, we will make discoveries about reality that will blow our minds . . . discoveries Jung and Bohm and others couldn't even imagine!

The Matrix Control System of Philip K. Dick
And The Paranormal Synchronicities of Timothy Green Beckley

SUGGESTED READING

THIS BOOK IS FROM THE FUTURE

11:11 – THE TIME PROMPT PHENOMENON

THE DÉJÀ VU ENIGMA: A JOURNEY THROUGH THE ANOMALIES

www.mariedjones.com

20.

DIARY OF AN UNHINGED MATRIX MASTER, SECTOR ONE

By Timothy Green Beckley

GHOSTBUSTERS – WHO YOU GONNA CALL?
TIM AND MARIA

I couldn't think of a proper way to list all the synchronicities that have happened to me. Should I do them by date of their occurrence? Well, that would be impossible because I never bothered to keep a log of the experiences. I would scribble a few notes down on slips of paper or put them in a folder on the computer somewhere, but that would make them impossible to find when I needed to get to them. Let's see then – by subject matter? Well, that would be like shuffling a deck of cards and I don't have all the time in the world with my busy schedule.

Hey, how about random? Whatever tickles my fanny (I mean fancy). Glad you've let me decide. But, hell, I promise it will be a painless ride through the galactic wormhole of happenstance and synchronization (promise to use words that roll right off the tongue).

So I thought I would start with the latest synchronicity while it is still fresh in my mind and before the control freaks at the "Total Recall" lab wipe the slate clean.

Every month or so I unwind by going down to Atlantic City. Hop on a bus from the Port Authority in Manhattan and roll down the New Jersey turnpike and onto the interstate. I know this is odd, but I don't gamble. Nevertheless, Atlantic City is a cheap place to visit. The rooms are economical because they expect you to spend every minute you're there tossing your money away. The casinos even give you a voucher for $25 to get you started. Sometimes I don't even use them unless they can be turned in at the food court.

The rooms are nice. You have a boardwalk right outside your door. The ocean is like a few hundred yards away and there is an I-Max in the food court that is open all night.

No shotgun wedding. Just a holiday setting used by Maria and Tim to pose in Atlantic City.

Usually I go down with Maria D' Andrea, who is a longtime friend as well as author of numerous books on spell-crafting and the occult. We've published over a dozen works of hers now. I have known her for 25 plus years. In fact, I hadn't heard from her for a long time because of some problem with an ex who thought he should be her agent. Then about ten years ago I read in the New York Post that Maria D' Andrea from Long Island had been killed in a hit and run while attempting to cross the highway late at night on her way to a convenience store.

Never could figure out why they ran this little item on page three of the paper as it's a long way from Long Island and people get killed on the highway all the time. I guess they just had room and needed a filler. They didn't say anything about this person's profession, but Maria D' Andrea isn't that common of a name and living on Long Island where Maria lives for real so I assumed it had to be my psychic friend I hadn't been in touch with for a long time. I was sad and told everyone about her death. You can't cross a major highway in the middle of the night with all that traffic coming at you from both directions and figure you're going to make it to the other side.

Eventually, I put the incident out of my mind until one day, maybe five or six years later, when I happened to be speaking with Peter Moon. He resides on Long Island and has been involved in writing up the Montauk time travel experiments in several of the volumes he has published under the Sky Books imprint.

"Someone would like to speak to you," he mentioned during our conversation about the plight of small publishers with the advent of the internet and the proliferation of the e-book. "Oh, who's that?" I asked. Turns out it was Maria D' Andrea. "But she's dead, Peter. I read it in the paper," to which he replied he had seen her within the last week.

Turns out it wasn't the same Maria D' Andrea (a good coincidence I would say) and so we picked up our friendship and our business relationship where we had left it before her ex wanted to butt into our business.

Anyway, we're rolling down the highway in a Greyhound and looking out the window and dozing off from time to time during the three-hour trip.

Eventually, the bus heads down the main street of Atlantic City, winding in and out of a couple of side streets to get to the parking garage at the Tropicana where I have booked a room for all of $79 a night with a view of the ocean (as opposed to $279, if you were spending the evening in a hotel in Manhattan without benefit of pool and boardwalk).

About a block away from the Tropicana there is a bed and breakfast we always pass and on the roof of the B&B are statues of the Blues Brothers. You know John Belushi and Dan Aykroyd. Don't even know why the figures are there as it hasn't anything I can see to do with the establishment the metal figures have been erected on top of.

The Blue Brothers relax on the roof of the Chelsea Pub at the gateway to the Tropicana Resort. Their presence was surely felt by Tim and Maria.

Now it's a known fact that Dan, besides writing and starring in the original **Ghostbusters**, is a firm believer in UFOs (he is a supporting member of the Mutual UFO Network, has done his own video on the topic, and has been stalked by the men in black while talking to Britney Spears from a pay phone – go figure) and an aficionado of the paranormal. He is even into the magick of crystal skulls, going so far as to package his own brand of vodka, Crystal Head Aura Vodka, which comes inside a replica of the popular crystal figure. The vodka is damn good. One of the best. Not just a promotional stunt.

Born and raised in Canada, Dan's family were into the spiritualist movement, held séances in the parlor, and his dad, Peter Aykroyd wrote a book several years back on the subject. ***A History of Ghosts: The True Story of Séances, Mediums, Ghosts, and Ghostbusters*** describes how Dan used to peak in on the séances through a crack in the door, and how the family's personal history influenced his fascination with all the spookiness that abounds in our world, all magnified by being in the Matrix.

Aliens play a large part in the life of Dan Aykroyd and in a specific synchronicity, as related by Tim Beckley.

Maria and I were discussing all of this and I even mentioned that I didn't think the recent version of **Ghostbusters** held together as well as the original. Dan wasn't in this updated version and I guess that sort of solidified my position. A few minutes later we pulled into the bus terminal at the Tropicana and exited the bus to get our coupon good for $25 at the slots.

In order to validate the coupon and get the funds put on the casino's membership card you walk up to a cage in the lobby and hand the person there your ID and the coupon and they look you up in the system.

This is when everything starts to get weird and you imagine Rod Serling standing next to you in apparition form sort of edging you toward the window to complete your transaction so you can check in and be on your way to great fortunes. Overhead the sound system plays music, nothing exceptional; it's just to fill the void while you stand around. There isn't a DJ or anything. Just random tunes like you would expect to hear in an elevator or office lobby. Some programmed music that comes from Pandora or some other outside service. As Maria and I move up in the line a new song comes on – IT IS THE THEME TO **GHOSTBUSTERS**!

How in the Sam Hill can that be? Nobody knows what we've been talking about the last ten minutes or so (oh yes they do!!!). And, even if they did, the music is originating from some unknown source far removed from the premises. Out of fifty million tunes to select from, why would the sound system choose to play the "Ghostbusters theme" at this very moment, when Maria and I have just entered the premises, brazen ghostbusters and paranormalists that we are? There can be no "ordinary" explanation. This is not just coincidence. There is no such thing in our scheme of things.

But, again, we've been conned by "them there tricksters" who love getting into our heads with some flimflam or other. I suggested to Maria that maybe something will come from this synchronicity. Perhaps we will take home a huge check. I suggest we ask around to see if there are any **Ghostbuster** slots in the casino. Turns out there is – or was. But they took them out a few months before, and, besides, they were penny machines. So, even if "they" steered us in the right direction, what is the most we could have walked away with? Around $150. Not exactly a sack full of silver. But it's another synchronicity under our belt and an inspiration that at least partially led to the crafting of the book you are now reading.

Hey, they might as well have been playing "Goldfinger" on the speaker system, cause it turns out that's what we got in the end.

LOST IN THE DESERT

This sync will be short and sweet – but I warn you it's still a hot one!

Well, it's hot because I'm out in the desert to do some sky-watching near Giant Rock where UFO contactee George Van Tassel met extraterrestrials who instructed him to build a time machine. And to visit with my friend, Diane Tessman, who lives out among the sand dunes. Joshua Tree in the Mojave is particularly hot this time of year and I don't usually do my sky-watching till the sun goes down. I've heard about this terrific motel where all the rooms are themed. There is the Cave Room, the Fifties Room, the Persian Room – well, you get the idea. It's a popular spot for the servicemen who are stationed on the outskirts of Palm Springs. They have somewhere to bring their girlfriends (or whomever they happen to have in tow) and hunker down in a land where there is no shade. I figure, WTF, let me get a room and a drink here. Only place around and I can always watch the adult channel on Pay Per View.

I pull into the parking lot and walk into the lobby with the blasting AC, which sure feels good. "Can I get a themed room, sir?" Slap my AAA and CC card down on the front desk, anxious to get some service and check into to the Persian Room, perhaps (belly dancers on premises, I assume). The clerk sizes me up and says, "Well, we're almost all booked. You're lucky we have one suite still available."

Oh, joy.

"It's the Bermuda Triangle suite." You have to be kidding, I thought. I'm stuck in the Bermuda Triangle for "real" this time. How appropriate it seems. But also disappointing. It would be hipper to stay in the Fifties Suite I would think. But it's my fate. Hey, I've written about the Bermuda Triangle numerous times. So now I get the opportunity to visit there. Not quite the Caribbean but it will obviously have to do.

Nice room. But nothing really exciting. A miniature lighthouse on the desk. Portrait of a sea captain at the helm of his ship over the bed. No vortex to report, but I did return to tell the tale of this tiny bit of synchronicity at the Oasis of Eden in the desert. Try not to get lost until you get there!

If you want to learn more about the desert air and the mysteries of this beautiful landscape, two suggestions: Trudge through the sand over to Amazon and search for **Mysteries of the Mojave**, which I edited (includes George Van Tassel's early channelings with Space Brothers). And then, while you're on Amazon, hunt under streaming video for "**Mysteries in the National Parks**." You're looking for the episode "Ape Man And Aliens," which is all about that part of this great country of ours. I am on the show for about ten minutes detailing UFO landings and a variety of paranormal potpourri. Now that's worth $1.95!

TGB lost in the Bermuda Triangle suite at the Eden theme rooms.

SOMETHING ABOUT THE DESERT HEAT

There is something about the vibes that are carried by the heat in the desert out around Joshua Tree. That's where pretty much all the contactees claimed to have had their alien encounters with human looking ETs back in the late-1940s and on into the 1950s. The silver spaceships were landing almost daily; it was like the desert was a train depot and rather ordinary individuals were being ushered aboard for supposed jaunts around the solar system to see what life was like on Venus, the moon and Mars. Pretty uneventful except for maybe a long weekend when you could take the time to take a cruise along the channels of the Red Planet. Of course, there were really no channels, but it looked as if there were should you peer through a reflective telescope.

Many times I would drive out past Morongo and sit in my Mustang convertible and just look up. If you live in the city, you have no way of knowing what the heavens look like way out in the desert. I mean, a million stars line up in the Milky Way, so many no one could count them. You're away from traffic and lights from the malls and the cities, so it's a stark contrast from what we are all used to. Not so much that way anymore as Mother Nature has been encroached upon by denizens from Hollywood and beyond.

But I loved it. So much so that in 1995 I decided to put on the mother of all UFO conclaves. Through a bit of business negotiations, I managed to get one of the plushest hotels in Palms Spring to turn over the keys to their vast ballrooms for FREE. Yup, that's right, FREE, where normally such an imperial set up would have put me back thousands of dollars.

The idea was to celebrate the fiftieth anniversary of UFO contacts in the desert and invite all those still active – or alive – from what is known as the Golden Age of Flying Saucers.

On our program we had Gabriel Green, Dr. Frank – **Stranger at the Pentagon** – Stranges, Robert Short, Hal Wilcox, Fred Bell, the grandchildren of George Van Tassel, who we honored with a plaque for their granddad's service to humanity. The family "time machine," known as the Integratron, still stands as a landmark in the desert, its dome visible as you drive down the highway. It was constructed with the aid of the Space Brothers and the concept is that you would walk through one entrance and come out the other rejuvenated and feeling (looking?) years younger. The device, made of solid wood without the use of nails or any other forms of sealing, is open to groups who wish to hold meditation sessions or sound therapy seminars.

On Friday evening our keynote speaker was the four-time Oscar winner, Robert Wise, best known for directing **The Day The Earth Stood Still**, starring Michael Rennie and still considered to be one of the most popular and well-received science fiction movies of all time. The 1951 film was characteristic of postwar and emerging Cold War anxieties regarding a nuclear holocaust as well as a general sense of fear and fascination with alien life forms. It brought a message of peace and love to a population that was soon going to become known as the "peace and love generation." The movie's impact is still felt, with its popularity never diminishing.

In a series of telepathic messages, the Space Brothers gave George Van Tassel the mental blueprints for a time machine known as the Integraton. The device still stands proudly at the side of the road in Landers, California.

We started setting up in the banquet area mid-afternoon on Thursday, bringing in cartons of books to sell and setting up the Welcome Conference Visitors booth to sell tickets. Our staff was on hand doing the dirty work – Jackie and Cindy Blue, Carol Rodriguez, Allison Infinity, Bleu Ocean, Bunny Atlas – while I sort of supervised and greeted some of the speakers who had booked rooms early.

A little while into the process of setting up, a few strays start to wander in to watch us unloading the books from sealed cartons and to fondle the merchandise (which I hoped they would purchase over the course of the weekend). Someone passes by and leaves a stack of mail on the book table. It has a rubber band around it and I supposed – correctly – they had just been to their post office box and, being absent minded, left it on the table for me to find and take to the lost and found.

Then I notice that the person who obviously left the bundle of mail is still within shouting distance, stopping to look at some of the crystals that were being unpacked by Bob Short and his wife Shirley. "Excuse me. Excuse me." I went over to the gentlemen and asked, "Did you leave these behind?" He looked at me and the mail and said, "Yes, thank you for finding them." I wasn't being nosey but I did see the name on the top letter since it was facing up. The letter was addressed to Kenneth Anger.

I had no particular reason at that moment to think it was *the* famous underground filmmaker, Kenneth Anger, who had produced and starred in a highly-touted, controversial film called **Lucifer Rising**. The movie had also been notable for its musical score by Led Zeppelin's Robert Plant. Well, actually, the score was never used because the master tape had been stolen while Anger was staying at Plant's sprawling estate on the shores of Loch Ness in Dumnadrochit, Scotland.

The place, known as Boleskine House, had once been rented by occultist Aleister Crowley and was said to be haunted. Apparently, heads of a decisively phantasmal nature were said to clatter and clunk down the long, dark hallway at night. Some say that the monster in the Loch was actually conjured up by Crowley, known for his ability to summon some rather negative spirits to the earthly plane. And apparently Anger dabbled in a bit of ritualistic magick –

Filmmaker Kenneth Anger has been known to use many occult themes. He became part of a TGB synchronicity at a Palm Springs UFO conclave.

Satanism? – as did Jimmy Page. They were all known to practice the ins and outs of necromancy, conjuring spirits from the dark side of creation. Anyway, it all sounded sensational, or at least the British tabloid press thought so.

I'm not much of a fan of "art films," but I did respect Kenneth Anger, who had managed to carve out a rather warped reputation as an adept of the occult arts. He was utterly flamboyant and caustic and didn't give a goddamn what anyone thought of his work or who he was.

Turns out it WAS the filmmaker Kenneth Anger, and so I asked if he was planning to come to the conference over the weekend and if he had a particular interest in UFOs. He said he would like to come but was broke, not being backed by Tinsel Town's elite. As to his interest in UFOs, Yes! He had had a sighting while out cycling one morning. He was staying in a home once owned by Al Jolson and would get up early to get some exercise. Before dawn one day he says he was followed by a UFO as he rode along.

As I was often known to do, I comped Ken so that he could make it to the banquet that evening where Robert Wise was giving the keynote address, telling the audience of several hundred all about the pros and cons of making **The Day The Earth Stood Still**. It was a memorable evening, at least for me. I sat Anger next to Mr. Wise at the head table and introduced them both. That's certainly a bit of occult magick. What's the possibility of him leaving his mail on the table and my knowing who he was? If "they" hadn't made him leave those bundled-up envelopes, he would have passed right by and out the door, probably without saying a word.

It was a weekend I shall always remember as the greats of flying saucerdom gathered under one roof, which I had managed to pull together for zip, nada, where normally it would have cost a bushel and a peck to get this affair off the ground. Thank you, Space Brothers, who I strongly believe are in collusion with the entities of ECCO, or at least have a direct line to the Command Post headquarters of the Matrix.

BETTER NOT FORGET YOUR PASSPORT

As we trek along, it becomes apparent that a disproportionate number of these episodic moments (makes me sound a bit crazy, right? Well, it's supposed to ducky!) occur outside a person's normal surroundings. True enough, a synchronicity can strike like a bolt from the blue anywhere you happen to be, but there is nothing like being taken by complete surprise when you are somewhere "unknown," somewhere in "foreign territory," miles from the security of a locked door back home.

With my Amex card secure in my wallet, it was off to Hawaii with psychic and musician Maria Lee Carta. (Check out her musical website at: http://www.marialeecarta.band/) Together, we planned to investigate the mysteries of the islands. Dig into the legends and lore that have made this paradise in the Pacific so magical, so mystical, so steeped in the supernatural.

We arrived in Honolulu and took off to the outer islands from there. If you want to learn about our exploits in detail, including "meeting" Madam Pele, the local UFO fireballs known as the "akualele" and our possible sighting of the Night Walkers, I suggest two things. Go on over to Amazon and pick up a copy of **Kahuna Power – Expanded Edition**, or, if you don't have the necessary quail to buy the book, Google "Fire Starter," Season One, Episode 3, of **Mysteries At The National Parks**. Originally broadcast on the Travel Chanel I found it on YouTube right away. No charge! This is a brief look at the strange events that befuddle many visiting or living on one of the seven islands, Oh! And it features yours truly, who is staggeringly handsome on TV (especially in HD).

Known officially as the Garden Island, Kauai is home to wildly verdant landscapes, oxygen-rich air and utter serenity. It is also the oldest of all the Hawaiian Islands, which has given it its more modern nickname Jurassic Island. It's significantly less-populated than the big three islands — Oahu, Big Island and Maui – and for some travelers it is a bit off the beaten path.

Not for Maria and I. Before our arrival we had set up an interview with one of the editors at The Garden Island newspaper. We wanted to let residents know about our arrival and how we were hunting down information on the lore and legends and what are mistakenly called the "superstitions" of the Hawaiian Islands. After the interview, which was scheduled to be printed later that day, and with time to kill, we took a leisurely walk around Plantation Hale's mall, stopping to watch an elderly gentleman as he went about weaving a garment in one of the outdoor stalls. Turns out that it was no "coincidence" that we had paused momentarily to watch as he toiled away, showing tourists how everything was once woven by hand before the invention of the sewing machine.

Eventually we made it back to the hotel, which was in walking distance. As we entered the room the phone was ringing off the hook. The callers appeared eager to share a bit of Kahuna knowledge with Maria and I, since I guess they could somehow "sense" our sincerity in seeking to spread their knowledge back to the mainland, where not much was known about the Kahuna tradition.

Among those who called – hold onto your milk shake – we found out the next day, upon meeting him, was the eighty-year-old "weaver" who had gotten our attention in the mall when we should have been inside relaxing in

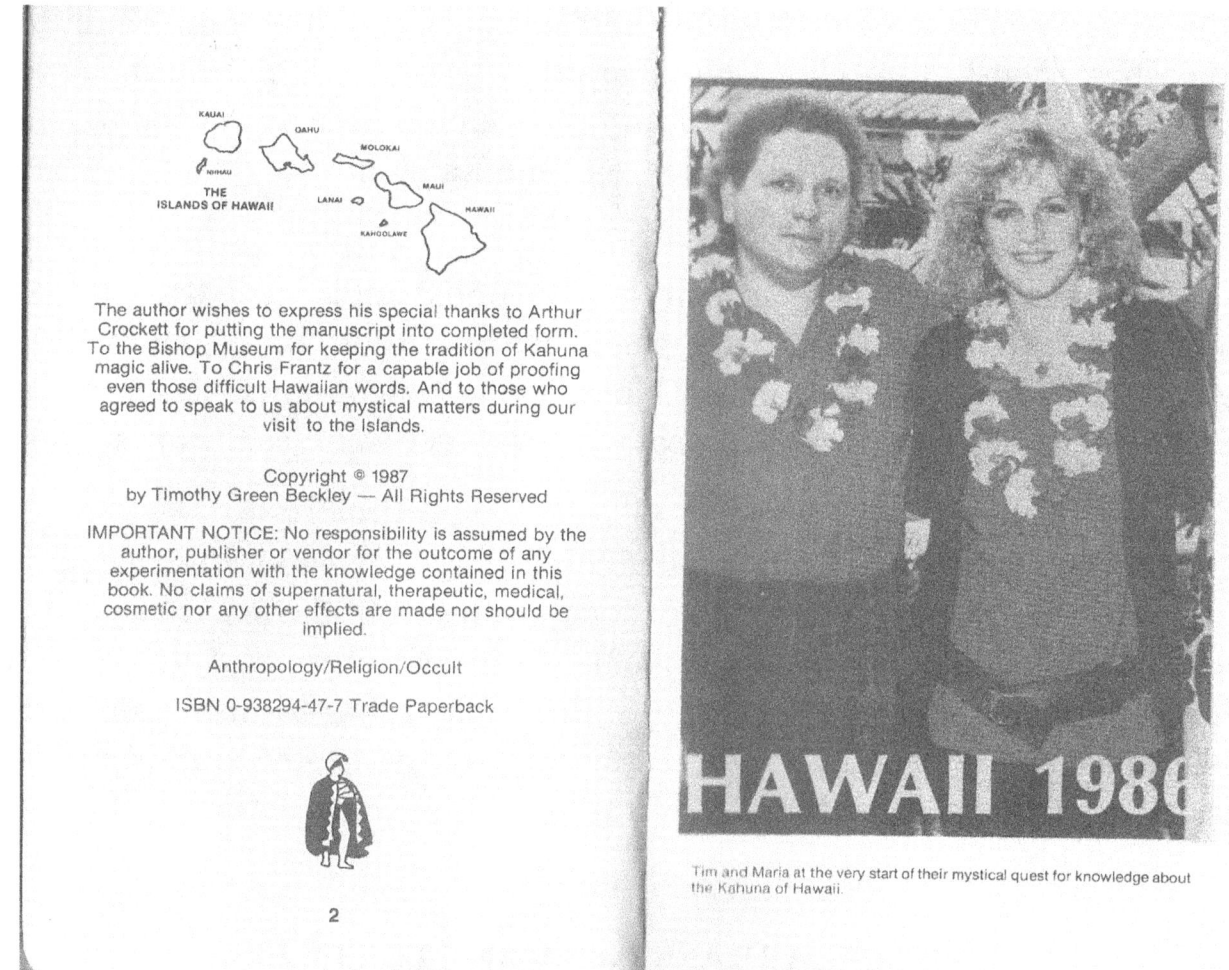

TGB and Maria Carta ventured to the islands in 1987 to rediscover the knowledge of the Kahuna shaman. Photo spread from rare first edition of the "Kahuna Power" book.

an air conditioned room, being that it was high noon and shade was lacking along our route.

Joseph Iida had a great deal of knowledge about the subjects of herbal remedies and has had personal experiences with the enigmatic goddess of the Fiftieth State, Madame Pele, who manifests as a beautiful woman with fiery red hair just before the volcano on the island erupts as a warning sign for the people to take shelter.

Of Portuguese and Japanese heritage, Joseph says he and his family were among the few "outsiders" to learn all about the Huna faith, and, while he was still living, he kept the traditions as best he could. He told us that his father kept a black book with all the herbal remedies written down in it, the book mysteriously vanishing when Joe's dad passed away. But despite his advanced years, Zmr Iida had absolutely no trouble with his memory and had managed to preserve all the knowledge of the Kahuna priests that had been passed down to him.

One of the concoctions Joseph sang the praises of is made from an herb known on Kauai as Mamaki. "This plant," we were told, "makes an excellent herbal tea that will bring a person's blood pressure right down. I've also used it to help individuals with diabetes eat whatever they want, as the tea acts as a neutralizer in their system."

Sounds good to me. In fact, I had totally forgotten about this part of the interview. Since I am a diabetic, I am going to check out the tea, which can be ordered from Amazon (what can't be?). It's in leaf form, so I will have to figure out how to make this into a drinkable brew by using my little microwave and hope it isn't observed by those trying to spy on me and peer into my apartment – thank you, Mr. Trump!

AN EMBARRASSING POINT IN TIME

Having started off with the most recent synchronicity, I figure I should go back to the very beginning, to when this was a fresh phenomenon to me. Or at least back to the point I have conscious recall of. Though there is, prior to the next incident, the time when my life was saved by an "unseen hand" at the age of three. Our car would have gone over the edge of a cliff if something hadn't impressed upon my mother to tell my father to stop driving IMMEDIATELY! The following is probably the first solid, hard core "proof of the pudding" that I remember.

As one can tell from my little narration about almost plunging to my death down the side of a ravine, synchronicities can sometimes be a "good thing." But there is nothing in the Matrix Rule Book that says they have to be.

This one is downright embarrassing.

This crazy occurrence happened a good many years before the "big bang" of San Francisco's 1967 "Summer of Love." It must have been around 1965 or 1966. Can't give you a specific date. Haven't kept any kind of a dated diary. Especially since I didn't know what I was getting myself into back when this happened.

I had just met this absolutely beautiful girl. Sandy Graham was an aspiring model anyone would be proud to be seen with in public. I know I certainly was. We met over a jukebox playing songs like *Hang On, Sloopy* by the McCoys at a local soda fountain. I won't tell you we had a coke, because you could get served beer at 18 in those days and so we were both legal.

Eventually I asked Sandy out to dinner. I didn't have much money but there was Patty's Clam House over on 34th Street down the street from Macy's and I knew the food was reasonably priced there.

We ordered from the menu and slick Timmy went for a bottle of wine to wet our whistle. We chatted up a storm and frankly I didn't want the evening to end. I wanted to order another bottle of wine but realized my pockets were almost empty. But there was a way to make this moment last. If I didn't leave a tip, I would have enough to go for another canter of Rose. Hell, I was young and insensitive, I admit, but not as far as Sandra and I were concerned.

So we ordered another bottle and drank it down – slowly.

Eventually, we parted company and we must have goose-stepped out of Patty's rather quickly. I figured, what the crap, I am not ever going to see the waiter again.

Wrong!

Couple of days later, I am going up the escalator in the Port Authority Bus Terminal, minding my own business, when someone taps me on the shoulder. Being in a rather unsavory part of Manhattan – in those days – the notorious 42nd Street, I pulled back a bit and turned around quickly. A gruff voice says to me, "Don't I know you from somewhere?" Well, I didn't recognize the gentleman, to be honest, but he recognized me. "You're the guy who didn't leave me a tip the other night!"

I was flabbergasted. I had been "found out" in a bus terminal with thousands of people around us racing to get home. Those little bastards, those mean old tricksters from the Matrix, were trying to show me up.

Finding myself in an awkward situation, I mumbled that I didn't know what he was talking about and took two stairs at a time up the escalator to get on my bus. I guess I outdistanced the waiter who I had stiffed because I never saw him again. Patty's Clam House closed a couple of years later without my having gone back there for dinner and a bottle of wine. Sandra is still a friend.

CALL ME "ANOTHER URI GELLER"

At this point it's become obvious to most of you by now how I seem to attract very weird synchronicities and coincidences in my life, lots more than most people do. On Memorial Day I decided to take a break and go over to Manhattan's Hudson River Park, where I had never been before. But I had heard it was so lovely, being on the water and all, and me, being a Cancer, should find extra special (and it was!). My friend and associate, Carol, said we could quickly get to the park by taking the 23rd Street crosstown bus and, if we showed them our senior citizen ID, we would only have to pay half the fare, $1.25. I had a little change cup I had put into my pocket beforehand and had loaded with mainly quarters for the round trip. I took out 5 quarters and told Carol to hold onto them while I got my ID from my wallet. She said, "Well, you need another quarter because one of these coins is Canadian and the bus driver won't take it." I quickly replaced the Canadian quarter with a "good" one. But I didn't want to put the Canadian coin back in with the rest of my change or I would only have to go with replacing it again. Still, I didn't want to just toss it away – after all, a quarter is a quarter. So I placed it on the bench where people sit and wait for the bus. My thinking being that perhaps an out-of-towner from Toronto might come along and pocket it for use back in their country.

It was about a ten minute ride across town to the last stop just outside Hudson River Park. Carol and I exited the bus out the front door and, as I walked down the couple of steps to the ground, there on the sidewalk – where the same bench would have been, if there was one at this stop – was a shiny quarter – an American one. I can't help but believe this was more than a coincidence. Stuff like this just doesn't happen. Leave a quarter, get back a quarter. Did I somehow teleport the quarter with a bit of "shape (or face) shifting" tossed in for good luck? Thumbing through the pages, you will discover that I have experienced other synchronicities involving coins, as have others. It's like our "friends" at ECCO are playing a happenstance cosmic version of the "Shell Game," a game involving sleight of hand, and prestidigitation in which three inverted cups or nutshells are rapidly moved about, and contestants must spot which is the one with the coin placed underneath.

Or maybe, as it might turn out, I can just teleport like Uri Geller!

A cosmic currency exchange on the crosstown bus.

GETTING LUCKY

Hey, I'm a single guy. Never been hitched. Love my freedom. But also known for loving the ladies. Could never keep my eyes off them. In NYC you can't walk a block without some model sauntering by on her way to a photo shoot. And tight jeans. If you have a figure for them, I will follow you anywhere (keeping a discreet distance naturally) And blonds? They can do no wrong.

In order to keep in the mix, I have been known to hit the streets of Greenwich Village late at night in my "disguise" as a hard core rock n' roller. Used to promote local bands. Partied with the top groups. Am even on a platinum album, Edgar Winter's *"Frankenstein,"* though I don't play an instrument, but clink a mean ash tray with a set of metal keys on the album's rather chaotic party song, *"We All Had A Really Good Time."*

In New York, if you were part of this smoking, very hip, scene, you never went out before midnight – and that was early for some of the gang who haunted the clubs and bars between McDougal and Bleaker Streets and on the lower east side. The likes of Bob Dylan, Simon and Garfunkel, Jimi Hendrix and David – "The Pope Smokes Dope" – Peel all got their start along this strip in the 60s (yup, I go back that far). Let's see, I hung out at all the "in" places over the years: Max's Kansas City, Mercer Street Theater (that one collapsed in a pile of rubble, but no one was hurt), the Bottom Line, the Cat Club, the Lime Light, and my all-time favorite, Scrap Bar, where just about everything imaginable went on. (We still have an annual reunion, though the place hasn't been open in over ten years).

In fact, one gossip columnist, People reporter Mitchell Fink, relates the following titillating tale: "The owner of New York City's Scrap Bar, a rock-and-roll haunt in Greenwich Village, tells us that on the night of April 3, Guns N' Roses lead guitarist Slash showed up at the bar with porn star Savannah on his arm. If only she had stayed on his arm. According to bar owner Stephen Trimboli, Savannah and Slash engaged in full hit whoopee – to use the Latin phrase – right there at the bar, in full view of everyone." Trimboli says that afterward Savannah got up and made her way to a waiting limousine outside. Slash followed her, says Trimboli, "with a very silly look on his face."

And speaking of blonds, I met a very attractive and sexy gal at about 5 AM under the most unusual of circumstances. It fits nicely into our compelling and ongoing search for the truth about synchronicities.

Back then the party never stopped. After the "legal" bars closed, it was into a cab in search of a place that was open till the sun came up (and sometimes long past). Before my time, these places were called Speakeasies, but basically most of them were holes in the wall where they sold watered-down booze and had a game of poker or blackjack going on in the back room. Lots of transvestites and cross-gender types before they were accepted into society. There were even a few elaborate places where celebrities went to unwind and mingle with us commoners. It was literally a mixed bag. Something you might not tell your mother (or wife) about. Shame. Shame. But I loved it.

On a number of occasions the police would arrive and raid the place. Normally, they didn't arrest any of the patrons, just made us line up and patted us down for drugs and weapons. As fate had it, I left my Glock at home most nights. Usually, the places were pitch black and really rather scuzzy. You certainly wouldn't want to eat – *or do anything* – off the floors.

During the lineup and frisk and search one night, with the light down really low, I found myself standing next to a cute blond. We started up a conversation, keeping it low so as not to draw undue attention to us. Despite the circumstances, which, over the course of time, we had gotten more or less used to, we shared a chuckle or two between us and at some point the gal asks me what I do during the daytime.

I tell her, truthfully, that I am a publisher of New Age, UFO and metaphysical books. To which she says "Oh, I'm really interested in that," to which I said to myself. "Yeah, Yeah," thinking that maybe it's just a subtle come-on by a cutie who might be interested in more than a late night Budweiser. But to keep the conversation going, I ask, "Oh, really, so who are your favorite authors?" I figured she might say Edgar Cayce or someone like that.

The gal, whose name was Beth by the way, mentions a couple and who they were really floors me. "Brad and Sherry Steiger." Well, I just about lost it. "What a coincidence," I tell her, playing up the moment. "I happen to publish books by Brad and Sherry and I'm having dinner with them tomorrow. Would you like to join us?"

Beth happily obliged, and we have run into each other from time to time. I wouldn't call it a fling, but thank god there is a thing known as "luck" in this weird matter. I think this is best described as serendipity, an unexpected meeting or chance encounter that leads to a pleasurable experience.

As a sidebar, I have had numerous synchronicities at after-hours clubs. In the darkened room there is a guy at the bar (a club doorman by the name of Peter) complaining to the bartender that someone has stolen his book. After he has calmed down, I ask him what he had been reading. He tells me, **The Witches' Bible**, to which I responded, "Not to worry, I will give you a copy next time I see you. I sell a few of them now and then." I mean, there could not have been more than three or four other booksellers in the whole of Manhattan who carried this title in stock. What are a person's chances of losing this title anywhere? And someone even knowing about it? Not to mention having it on a shelf at home?

Another time at Body Heat (an after-hours bar long since boarded up by the NYFD), I strike up a conversation with someone I have never met before. (In case you're wondering about the décor at Body Heat, someone said it resembled Shaft's living room. Actually, Body Heat cannot possibly be held to that standard.) Anyway, the guy tells me he is a film producer. Well, so am I. Question: "So what have you produced?" Answer: "Nothing you'd ever have heard of." And he was right. He mentioned a few of his company's titles. Turns out I had gotten a VHS of one of them for a dollar in the overstock box at a local video store a couple of weeks before. Actually, a good film about a group of kids that go snowboarding, get snowbound in a shack, and then fool around with a Ouija Board they find. Eventually, demons invade the place and kill them while they make out (typical horror plot) and almost freeze to death.

Believe me when I say no one had heard of this movie. In fact, my VHS copy was defective and so the picture would jump around. Never saw the guy again. Never ran into another copy of the video. But this coincidence gave me something to talk about in the wee hours while guzzling down some cheap vodka. If you're going to get drunk, you might as well have a synchronicity to go along with your cocktail.

BACK IN A LITTLE WHILE

Well, I have more experiences to share, but I figure I would break them up into two sections and let a few of our other PKD fans and synchronicity experiencers have a go at sharing their accounts.

TO BE CONTINUED – YOU'D BETTER BELIEVE IT!

To make up for that embarrassing moment at Paddy's Clam House, TGB made Sandra cover girl for an early issue of the defunct Beyond Reality magazine.

21.

RETHINKING THE POSSIBILITY OF AN EMULATED WORLD

By Diane Tessman

DIANE Tessman has counseled abductees, experiencers and contactees for over 33 years. She draws on her own experiences in childhood as well as the ongoing ET contact throughout her life. While teaching school for 11 years, Diane was State Section Director for Florida MUFON in the late 1970s and also a field investigator for the Aerial Phenomenon Research Organization (APRO). Over the years, thousands of people have read Diane's two publications, *The Star Network Heartline* (since 1983) and *The Change Times Quarterly* (since 1990). These publications have contained an amazing number of accurate predictions over the years. In 1980, Diane underwent hypnotic regression with Dr. R. Leo Sprinkle and remembered details of her childhood encounter with a being called Tibus. Diane has specific conscious memories, too, but did not remember a number of details consciously. One UFO encounter was aboard what appeared to be a starship (UFO). Another encounter was in a cabin on Eagle Lake, Ontario. A membrane was taken from Diane on one of those encounters. It is quite possible that this membrane was used by the ET

* * * * *

Is human DNA a form of synthetic biology? If so, who or what created our pixels? Can the UFO puzzle only be fully explained by the shocking answer that we live in a super-computer simulated and emulated world?

Professor Nick Professor Bostrom is the University of Oxford Director of the Future of Humanity Institute; his research on "Do we live in a computer simulation?" is highly respected. Rich Terrell, from the NASA Jet Propulsion Laboratory, California Institute of Technology, has helped design missions to Mars, discovered four new moons around Saturn, Neptune and Uranus and taken pictures of the distant solar system. He also is a proponent of our reality being a computer emulation. A number of other respected physicists, astronomers, and even engineers are fascinated with the likelihood of this theory.

Diane Tessman stands near her home in Ansgar, Iowa.

Dr. Leo Sprinkle, a psychologist formerly associated with the University of Wyoming, verified Diane's contact experiences, which started for her at a young age.

Incidentally, the only difference between a computer simulation and a computer emulation is that the simulation remains external to the experiencer, while the computer emulation is within the individual as well. This emulation includes emotions, intuition, spiritual feelings and so forth.

The idea that we exist inside a great computer which simulates and emulates our world and our universe is repugnant to most of us. There are people who find it exciting. Investigating and searching to find the truth is what science should be all about, and it is no coincidence that spirituality is also about investigating and finding truth. I suspect that there is a larger spiritual truth to which all individual paths lead and I suspect that truth is scientifically valid as well.

Our DNA can easily be "downloaded" into pixel form; usually DNA is expressed as TTGGGAGGCCGCCGAGGC (a sample). Northwestern University offers extensive research on this topic which can be found online.

If you replace "A" with a dark grey pixel, "C" with a slightly lighter gray pixel, "T" with a still lighter grey pixel, and "G" with the lightest color grey pixel, you have the world of computer code.

www.basic.northwestern.edu/g-buehler/genomes/g_append.htm

High level scientists are even now conducting experiments to discover whether the universe exists within a simulation created by super-computers of the future. Might it be future humans running a super-computer in which we, their apparent ancestors, live and die?

Time magazine reports that by 2035, we will be linked permanently with computers via chips implanted in our skulls. If some of us don't want that, we will soon be left behind in very dramatic, life-threatening ways because the new state of the human/computer Singularity will put "organic humans" in the same boat as the Neanderthals.

Where will the human-computer Singularity be by the year 2400? Will we have achieved the creation of synthetic biological life forms? Will we BE synthetic biological life forms?

http://homoartificialis.files.wordpress.com/2012/03/whole-brain-emulation-by-sandberg-and-bostrom.pdf

So, by the Year 2400, will we have recreated the human mind entirely by feeding its every neuron, every quantum bit of consciousness, into a super computer?

My guess is we'll do it closer to the Year 2100. By 2400, we can't even imagine!

The composition of our reality is composed of subatomic particles and waves. Are these advanced pixels? If this is true, our simulated/emulated world could be run not by future humans but by alien intelligence. However, in this article I would like to take the approach that humans of the future will continue to advance rapidly in computer-related knowledge. Will we maintain spiritual and ethical integrity? That is another question!

The Matrix Control System of Philip K. Dick
And The Paranormal Synchronicities of Timothy Green Beckley

In time, we will design a super-computer which emulates the human mind and which simulates a living, seemingly organic world. How will the mind within know its world is simulated? Perhaps it will not. How will the mind know it is an emulated mind?

At the University of Washington, a super-computer is working to discover the truth of our existence. Are they creating the foundation for that super-computer which they now seek to discover?

"Imagine the situation where we get a big enough computer to simulate our universe, and we start such a simulation on our computers," says Professor Martin Savage, a physicist working on the University of Washington project.

"If that simulation runs long enough, and has the same laws as our universe, then something like our universe will emerge within that simulation, and the situation will repeat itself within each simulation."

The current understanding of string theory indicates that there are 10,500 universes with different laws that determine the behavior of particles within them. "So it is certainly true that, with enough computer resources, theorists would like to explore these universes," he adds.

Finite computer resources mean that space/time is not continuous but set on a grid with a finite volume, designed to create maximum energy subatomic particles. The direction these particles flow will depend on how they are ordered on the grid. The University of Washington study will be looking at the distribution of the highest energy cosmic rays in order to detect patterns that could suggest that the universe is the creation of some futuristic computer technology.

Particles on a grid? Are we indeed talking about the pixels of a computer?

If it does turn out that we are mere players in some sort of computer program, they suggest that there may be a way to interrupt the program and play with the minds of our creators.

"One could imagine trying to figure out how to manipulate the code, communicate with the code, and [address] questions that appear weird to consider today," says Professor Savage.

How about re-programming the simulation like James Kirk did at Star Fleet Academy with the Kobayashi Maru simulation?

How about escaping the matrix? What if our descendants, the future humans (who might have designed our own simulated world), are in a simulation too? Perhaps highly advanced aliens or transcendent masters operate an even bigger universal super-computer.

Another theory: Could this explain past lives? Perhaps your past lifetime is merely a parallel aspect of your emulated mind within the simulation - a different program of YOU. All sorts of paranormal and metaphysical ideas can be explained through the computer-simulation theory, and this theory explains the anomalies of UFO and alien behavior as well. Goodness, are we in a computer simulation in this universe which we know and love so well?

Some very smart people feel this is the only answer to stubborn questions which don't make sense with any other answer. Are the extreme distances involved, from star to star and from galaxy to galaxy, truly impossible? These vast distances become irrelevant in a simulated universe.

Could this be the reason many Earth species are becoming extinct, often suffering from an immune deficiency disease which now involves diverse species? Has our "Earth simulation" caught or been implanted with a computer virus, and thus we are becoming a malfunctioning simulation?

Could this be the reason for many things going wrong, from the structure of society to the melting Arctic and Antarctic ice? Yes, it might sound ridiculous, but stop to consider what we have done with technical advancements today.

Remember, quantum super-computers now exist and are busy working away. Do you ever have a glitch in reality? Perhaps déjà vu or a premonition, or just a funny moment wherein an anomaly occurs which simply cannot happen?

Perhaps the glitch is in the programming of your emulated reality. If we live in a computer simulation, it also means there is no death; the research being done on the universal morphic field of consciousness inside and outside our own mind could be harmonious with the simulated reality theory.

The implications are huge regarding the course of human history and everything else! In a sense, this is the Theory of Everything! Whether we are energy-simulations or organic, we are real and free anyway. We bleed. We hurt. We laugh. We can affect our reality and adapt.

No one should feel that life is of any less value because of this theory. Life is the same existence as we have always known. Life is life. When we manage to challenge the game and play with the minds of our creators, perhaps we graduate to becoming one of the creators ourselves.

This is not unlike spiritual philosophies which tell us we reach Godhead after sufficient experiences as lesser beings. Or (a variation), we are all one small component of God, a pixel of God.

The Matrix Control System of Philip K. Dick
And The Paranormal Synchronicities of Timothy Green Beckley

SUGGESTED READING

SEVEN RAYS OF THE HEALING MILLENNIUM

COMING OF THE GOD CLOUD

EARTH CHANGES BIBLE

THE TRANSFORMATION

ALIEN AGENDA

Email address: dianetessman0@gmail.com

Diane's website: www.earthchangepredictions.com

Enjoy her book, **The UFO Agenda, So…You Want to Know the Truth?**

www.amazon.com/The-UFO-Agenda-ebook/dp/B00DUEPPJ4

22.

GAMES OF THE GODS

By Hercules Invictus

HERCULES Invictus is a Lemnian Greek, a proud descendant of Argonauts and Amazons. He is openly Olympian in his spirituality and worldview, dedicated to living the Mythic Life, and has been exploring the fringes of our reality throughout his entire earthly sojourn. For over four decades he has been sharing his Olympian Odyssey with others. Having relocated the heart of his Temenos to Northeastern New Jersey and the Greater New York Metropolitan Area, he is now looking forward to establishing his unique niche locally and contributing toward the enhancement of his community's overall quality of life. Hercules is currently recruiting Argonauts to Quest for the Golden Fleece.

Hercules hosts the "Voice of Olympus" e-radio show on the Spiritual Unity Radio Network. He founded or co-founded, among other things, Mount Olympus LLP, Olympian Heroic Path, Olympian Shamanic Path, Cosmic Olympianism, the Regional Folklore Society of Northeastern Pennsylvania and the Center for the Study of Living Myth in New Jersey. He also spearheaded many of the real-world Age of Heroes initiatives and the fictive Mythic Adventure tales. For more information please Friend him on Facebook or visit his website: www.herculesinvictus.net

* * * * *

Hercules Invictus

Greek Mythology suggests that we exist to honor the Gods of Mount Olympus and to provide them with entertainment. Our daily lives are loosely staged productions that they can observe, influence or participate in. At will or at whim they can descend into our world to directly experience its many pleasures and perils. They can easily assume human, animal or combined forms. They can even manifest as natural and supernatural phenomena.

Not only that, but they can also appear as or act through us. Zeus and Hermes enjoy occasionally posing as road-weary travelers requesting food and shelter. Athena often spoke through Mentor in Ithaca and advised young Telemachus. Zeus was Amphitryon to Princess Alcmene when he fathered the Theban Hercules.

Incarnating as a human is another option. Thus some or all of us may actually be the Olympians themselves, or an aspect of them, temporarily experiencing the challenges of lack and limitation. Having voluntarily imbibed water from the River Lethe, we forget that we are really immortal and all powerful and, for a while, dream that we're not. We do this to see if we can master mortal life, transcend the human condition and reclaim our divine status. Mortality may even be a divine learning experience of some sort, one that we actively and voluntarily co-create on some higher and normally inaccessible level of our consciousness.

Beyond my own Olympian explorations and contemplations, numerous mages, sages, philosophers, metaphysicians, physicists, science fiction and comic book writers, movie makers, game developers and a few outspoken billionaires have also have also concluded that our world may indeed be illusory, a trick of light shaped by expectation and imagination.

If you factor in the Ancient Astronaut/Ancient Alien/Lost Civilization assertions that the Ancient Gods possess high-tech devices and employ mind-control, this scenario becomes even more plausible because we ourselves, as mere mortals, are well on the way to effectively programming minds and creating fully immersive and engaging artificial realities.

The Games of the Gods, though enigmatic to our mortal point of view, often seem to suggest that there are layers to our reality beyond those which currently ring true and that we ourselves are not what we believe ourselves to be. Perhaps their insistence on our honoring them is their way of reminding us who we truly are.

I will share a few of my personal experiences in the pages that follow. In honor of Olympus, they all took place mostly on the island of Lemnos in my beloved Hellas.

THE LADY IN WHITE

Every time I visit Aghia Marina, a small mountain shrine near the town of Moudros, I am cheerfully met by a young woman dressed in immaculate white attire that covers all but her face, hands and feet. She appears to be in her twenties and is remarkably well informed about everything I've been up to since the last time she saw me. I always enjoy being in her company and we always have great conversations that last a good long while. When I'm ready to trek back to Moudros she bids me farewell and walks towards a partially whitewashed tree to the right of the shrine. She touches the tree, looks back briefly, our eyes meet and then I turn my head away.

At that moment it always occurs to me that the name Maria, as I have come to know her, sounds a lot like Marina, the Lady of the Shrine, and that she hasn't aged a day or worn different clothes in decades. The mountain has sparse vegetation and some widely scattered, stunted trees. There is nowhere she can hide, yet she is never anywhere in sight mere moments after she has said goodbye. The shrine itself is tiny and filled with the icons and supplies needed to maintain it.

And then I find that I can't recall exactly what we discussed beyond my interim activities. The conversation suddenly blurs and then evaporates like a forgotten dream.

Who is she? How does she know when I'll be there? How and why is she always so well informed about my thoughts and actions? Why does everything seem so normal until I turn away? Where does she come from? Where does she go? What does she do when I'm not meeting her there?

No Lemnian I have ever shared this story with has ever reported hearing about similar encounters at the mountain shrine of Aghia Marina. According to tradition, Aghia Marina was a very young but devout martyr who was extensively tortured and then beheaded in 270 AD. As a Greek Orthodox Saint, she has been assisting people afflicted by demonic possession for over 1700 years. Back in the mid to late 1940s, a Communist teen defaced her icon with a knife as a gesture of anti-religious contempt. The next day the icon was discovered crying real tears. A special liturgy was recited by a local priest and lots of local people (including my mother) went to witness the miracle.

What did any of this, aside from my mother's presence in a crowd, have to do with me? If it weren't for the white garb and her connection to the shrine, I'd assume she was a Dryad that simply merged back into her tree. She didn't feel like a Dryad, though, nor did she feel like a ghostly martyr, stern Christian Saint or divine exorcist. Was she a spirit? No, I've had way too many spirit encounters not to have recognized it. A White Lady? I'd encountered one of those in New Jersey. Maria definitely wasn't the same type of being. An apparition of the Holy Virgin? Though I was dedicated to the new religion's Queen of Heaven as a baby, my spirituality has always been openly Mythic and Olympian. This never seemed to bother or concern Maria in the least. Perhaps she is a Space Sister, Ascended Master or . . . an Olympian herself.

Whenever I've brought others with me, she failed to appear, though I later dreamed of her. The dreams were nearly identical to the actual encounters. Was this then an internal experience, a product of my own mind? If so, why is it seemingly triggered by my visits to the shrine?

Although I don't truthfully know who or what Maria is, I am looking forward to encountering her again someday. I know that I'll be happy to see her and will greatly enjoy her company, fully understanding (in this moment) that I won't question the oddness of it all until the encounter is over. And, on some level, it is comforting to know that an inexplicable entity is greatly interested in and always watching over me.

THE SATYRS OF LEMNOS

The association of Satyrs with the island of Lemnos is ancient indeed. The first-to-second-century Lemnian author Philostratus, who wrote ***The Life of Apollonius of Tyana***, preserved the tale of a contemporary sexual liaison between a mortal woman and a Satyr. Although he was reluctant to provide many details, he related that he grew up with and personally knew the product of that particular union. The half-ling, a boy, was made to wear a faun skin to mark his daemonic heritage.

I've heard countless stories over the years of encounters with Satyrs, always at night, usually on dirt paths in the sparsely wooded mountains, and often casually perched atop a boulder. In these tales, although the Satyr actually does very little beyond warily watching, the witnesses relate being overwhelmed by panic and fleeing recklessly back towards the lights and fires of human habitation.

In the Lemnos of my youth it was also believed that unions between humans and animals often produced *"terrata"* (monsters), including Satyrs. I've heard this from traveling country doctors as well as farmers and herders. The resulting aberrations are usually destroyed at birth, but not always, as encounter tales persist.

Roman and Grecian statues are said to resemble Ultra-terrestrial figures.

I remember once viewing a modern Satyric folk-ritual from the second floor of my grandparent's home in Moudros. I was of grammar school age and fascinated with the older boys with painted faces, wearing horns, tattered clothes and/or fur leggings. They brandished clubs and what looked like knotted rope and were roughhousing raucously as they descended down the cobblestoned main road that slopes towards the seashore. Later, after dark, they returned with torches, chanting *"Pa-loo-kah"* and menacing all they encountered. Folks ran from them, sometimes laughingly. Certain individuals were soundly struck and yelped in pain.

A theia (aunt), wrapped in black widow's garb, cautioned me not to go out and explained that I was watching something ancient and forbidden. She then told me that if the boys caught me spying on them they would surely beat me the next time they saw me. I resolved to one day join their Satyr band but alas I never again had the opportunity to observe them. Though this memory is still very vivid and I've related it countless times, yesterday it came into question. As I fact-checked details with my mother before composing this, she confirmed that this rite did indeed exist during the days of my childhood and was almost exactly as I've described it.

UFOs hide in clouds or are energized by them. Here is one "a thousand stories" over Mount Olympus.

The only discrepancy was that, in her memory, long strands of interwoven garlic bulbs were most often used to whip people, not knotted ropes. As I was sneaking peeks from the second floor, my misperception was easily explained. But my mother also pointed out that the Satyr ceremony was usually enacted sometime between December 25th and January 6th, then again near Easter during the "Karnavalia." As we only spent our summers in Greece, it was very unlikely that this was something I had physically observed.

I don't know what to make of this now. Nor can I associate my memory of the black-clad aunt with any actual person that would have been in that room on that night. As with Maria, or while in a dream, I did not question the logic of it while it actually occurred.

Then I remembered several more reality-bending experiences that happened on that very same floor, one of which I will now share.

HOW I LOST ATLANTIS

The Sleeping Prophet, Edgar Cayce (1877-1945), once predicted that a portion of Atlantis would rise in the waters to the east of the Americas sometime in 1968 or 1969. Being Greek and mystically inclined, I was looking forward to this and was delighted when it actually happened, on schedule, off the coast of Bimini in the Bahamas.

There was extensive coverage on TV and in the printed media. The topic was hot in the US, in Greece, and I imagined globally. Proof of Atlantis and the power of prophecy . . . wow!

During my summer in Lemnos, I pored through a stack of Greek magazines and newspapers my grandfather had put aside, and we kept up with the latest developments on the radio. He was also extremely interested in Atlantis and we discussed Plato's **Timaeus** and **Critias**, which introduced Atlantis to the world; some of Shleimman's reported finds at Troy; the Thera/Atlantis connection; the Minoans, Poseidon; other possible mythic correspondences and several other theories (all naturally involving Greece in some way). Happy times and great memories!

A few years later, when I was a trance medium in New York and studying the mysteries of modern Theosophy and Spiritualism, I brought up the topic of the risen Atlantis several times and was surprised to find that, while many of my associates remembered all the hoopla, a great number did not.

I attributed this to the fact that the others, not being Greek, may not have paid as much attention to it. High school had humbled me by lightly covering all I had learned (aside from language) during eight years of Greek Parochial School in one semester of Mythology and several scattered sentences in History.

Hercules and soul mate Athena strike a royal Olympian pose.

Over the years, I have found that the number of folks who remember this event has grown increasingly less. The current consensus is that Atlantis never rose and that Cayce's prophecy failed. The structures off the coast of Bimini seem to be a dead end, though there are still some people theorizing and exploring. Whenever I encounter someone who still remembers, I find that their frustrations and puzzlement matches my own. Did it or didn't it happen? Do realities intersect and merge? Can you somehow cross over or suddenly find yourself in an alternate reality?

I've spoken of this phenomenon and posed these questions for years in my workshops and recently discovered that this type of experience is called the "Mandela effect," as many folks remember Nelson Mandela dying in a South African prison, which didn't happen in this reality.

I can't satisfactorily explain these and other anomalous events I've experienced during my many years on this planet. The Games of the Gods – though ever present – remain enigmatic, even if we are the ones ultimately playing them. I honor Olympus through everything I do and try my best to entertain and inform my ancestral Gods. I continue to learn, to question, to change, to grow. But, like Socrates, I freely admit that whatever meager wisdom I have gleaned, and share, is dwarfed by the vastness of all that I still don't know.

Onwards!

© Hercules Invictus

www.herculesinvictus.net

23.

WHAT IS OUR 3-D REALITY COMING TO? MULTIDIMENSIONAL TRICKSTERS, TEACHERS, SHAPE-SHIFTERS AND ASTRAL SHAMANS

By Brent Raynes

BRENT Raynes has been investigating and researching UFOs since 1967. He is the author of ***Visitors from Hidden Realms*** and the editor of *Alternate Perceptions* magazine. Brent has traveled extensively across the US and into Canada, interviewing numerous witnesses and researchers. He has taken a comprehensive global and historical perspective on the Ufological landscape. He has also participated in Native American rituals and ceremonies, gaining valuable insights and information from his interactions with these wisdom keepers. Brent is able to make revealing comparisons between the interrelated experiences and disciplines of parapsychology, shamanism, Jungian archetypes and ufology. Complimentary subscriptions are available to this fine publication at www.apmagazine.info/

In this overview, Raynes discusses the interconnectedness of the various phenomenon that strain our perceptions of normality, pointing out that reality is subject to change at any given moment.

* * * *

"The trickster must be testing us big time," I recently remarked to a serious, academic researcher who has found himself caught up in our mutual struggle of trying to better comprehend a hugely complex, largely indecipherable, multifaceted enigma that too simplistically we call "UFOlogy." By phone and email we had been privately discussing all of the seemingly interrelated aspects we potentially perceived between UFO contact encounters and the paranormal, the NDE, kundalini, and shamanism. I added, "Discernment is certainly not easy – especially when teacher and trickster may be one and the same."

The role of the archetypal trickster is something my good friend and colleague, Dr. Greg Little, a Memphis, Tennessee, psychologist, researcher and author of many marvelous titles, has spoken about on many occasions over the years. Time and again he would explain how, from the Native American perspective, when one attempts to contact the spirit realm "you'll usually encounter trickster forces first."

**Brent Raynes with Peruvian whistles said to be consciousness-altering, with the ability to open one up to other dimensions!
(Photo Wayne County Now)**

Well-versed in Jungian psychology and Native American spirituality, Greg once expressed to me the following: "The trickster forces are there to essentially test you, to see how balanced you are, to see how serious you are, to see if your inquiry into the spiritual world is full of good motives or negative motives." He warns that only if you are able to see through the deceptive antics of the trickster archetype will you be able to "get to some deeper layer of truth."

Of course, it may not always be a trickster. A Christian friend confessed to me awhile back how his wife had described how her deceased grandmother had visited her one night, and said the grandmother's appearance seemed very physical, very real. While he initially felt, due to his Christian beliefs and background, that it was likely a hallucination or something demonic, he then pondered it some more. Then it occurred to him that in the Bible it tells us to "test the spirits." He realized the reason one would do that was because, just maybe, some of these spirits are indeed what they profess to be.

Discernment is certainly a crucial and key issue. How much of what people experience is truly an independent intelligent energetic force separate from our consciousness? And how much of the perceived experience may be filtered through one's own consciousness, through one's own personal background of beliefs, memories and expectations, thus bearing some measure of distorted recollection of what precisely had transpired?

In "alien abduction" cases there are descriptions of what are called "screen memories" (something Sigmund Freud called "displacement") of owls, deer, regular people, and other seemingly ordinary scenes and situations. These substitute memories reportedly overlay more disturbing memories connected with alien being encounters with a more acceptable content, but often include certain details that seem a little odd and out of context with everyday reality.

For example, a mother reportedly had vague memories of firing a gun at "white-faced children" whom she felt were "trying to steal" from her family.

Later, when one of the family members underwent hypnosis, the story of an abduction by strange dwarfish entities emerged.

In another case, a woman had a confusing and disturbing memory of lying in a field next to a car. Under hypnosis, the object was found to have been three times taller and perhaps four times longer than a car, and "rounder" too.

In yet another instance, a strange meeting occurred when three young "musicians" drove up to a cabin of vacationers in Kentucky in a mysterious car that "glided along without bouncing" over a very bumpy road. The group clearly remembered the blond-haired man who did all of the talking, but no one could remember what his companions looked like. Just before the meeting, one of the group, a young girl, had made contact with the blond "musician" on a CB radio. She described him as someone who could have easily been her brother, or even her masculine twin! She had an intense feeling of already knowing him. Later, under hypnosis, she recalled crouching down in the truck with the CB radio, looking fearfully at strange lights in the sky just before the visit.

Sometimes hypnosis isn't even needed, it seems, to discern beyond the so-called "screen memory." An experiencer in Florida once shared with me how, after a low-level encounter with a domed, disc-shaped object, her home erupted with poltergeist activity which, over time, escalated into balls of light and humanoid beings appearing in her and her teenage son's bedrooms. A being that appeared to her initially had a face that reminded her of a late husband, followed next by an evil-looking, "cat-like face."

But then what should we make of what the shaman's of old called "shape-shifters"? Could such a thing have some actual basis in reality? Are we dealing with what are referred to in the East as tulpas (thought-forms) or are energetic, plasmic (ectoplasmic?) creations of spirits and aliens another possibility?

Former Australian medical doctor turned channeler Dr. Maree Batchelor has been impressing quite a number of people with her abilities. "Those I have referred to Dr. Maree Batchelor have reported both positive medical healing and psycho-spiritual outcomes," Dr. Bob Davis, a professor of neuroscience, informs me, adding, "The effects are unique to those receptive to her unique and powerful abilities. While she is indeed the 'real deal,' trying to explain the foundation of this ability remains elusive."

HOLOGRAPHICAL SHAPE SHIFTING

In addition, as Dr. Batchelor reveals in an interview in the April 2017 edition of *Alternative Perceptions*, many people have been reporting that when doing a session with her, especially in person, but occasionally over Skype as well, she will, as she expresses it, engage in "holographical shape-shifting with the frequencies coming in and I'll actually present as a different person in front of them."

Many times she takes on the appearance of a Native American, but also has been described as appearing as a blue alien being, an elderly Indian holy man known as Bhagawan Nityananda, and an enlightened woman named Anandamayi Ma. She adds that she feels that these people's third eye are somehow "picking up the frequencies" and they become "activated," even though many times they are not particularly familiar or prone to such experiences. (*All added proof that the nature of reality is open to alterations at any given moment as outlined by PKD in his work. - TGB*)

Australian medical doctor turned channeler Dr. Maree Batchelor.

In the world of mediumship – commonly referred to as channeling these days – this kind of reported happening is not unheard of. Frank C. Tribbe, who served a 40 year career as a U.S. Government attorney, a job which afforded him much opportunity for foreign travel, used to take advantage of his visits to other countries to learn firsthand more about paranormal phenomena. One time, while in London, he got together with a man who was both a spiritualist minister and a minister for the Church of England. He was taken to have a session with a local medium.

"The minister from London was on my right and the medium's wife was on my left, and we were all practically touching each other, just inches apart,"

Tribbe told me in an interview back in 2004, "The medium went into trance and the communicator from spirit turned out to be Chinese. Apparently it was one of the more common communicators who came through to this particular medium. And, since the minister from London had been to this medium before and recognized the voice, he spoke to the spirit and welcomed him to the circle. The thing of it was – here was this medium, only a foot or two from me, and his face was as typical a British face as you can imagine. However, as soon as that communicator – who was supposedly a Chinaman from two or three centuries past – began speaking through the medium, his features changed. It became a much rounder Asian face. So, for about 45 minutes, as this reading went on, it was like that face right in front of me was that of a different person altogether. Then finally, when the reading ended and the minister on my right told the communicator thank you and said good bye, the Chinese man's face vanished and the normal British countenance of the medium returned."

There were several questions I needed answers to. "Was that face just as clear as a regular face?" I asked. "Oh yeah," Tribbe replied. "It's something that the British Society has done over the years. I've got a huge library of several thousand books and I have books from the Society in London where they have photographed these images, and very often there would be two clairvoyants. One was getting a message and the other was getting a face of the communicator. One of these psychic facilitators died only two or three years back, but I have her book that she published fifteen years ago.

The Matrix Control System of Philip K. Dick
And The Paranormal Synchronicities of Timothy Green Beckley

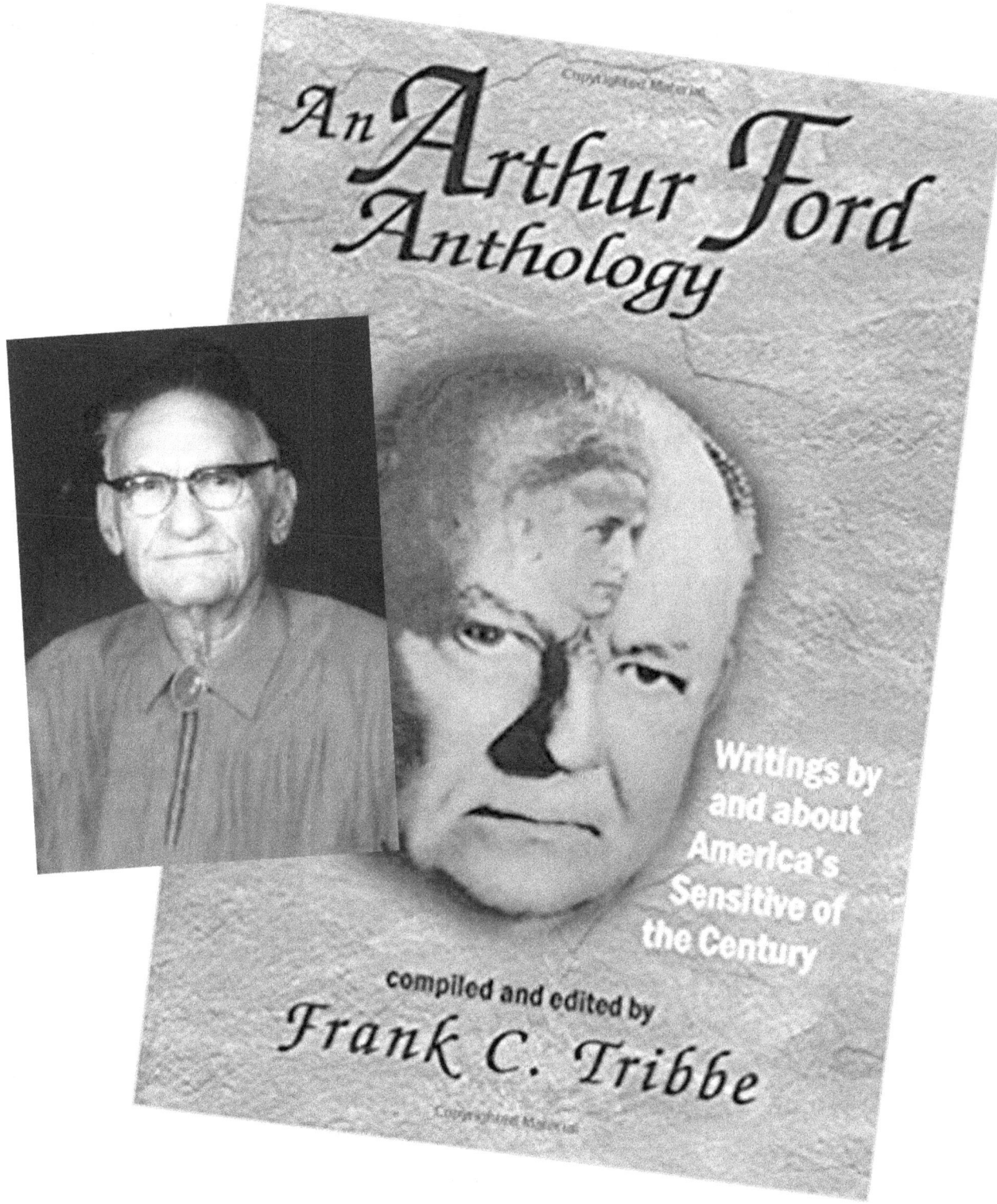

Frank Tripper has attended many seances. Not by "coincidence," he has also written a book on the medium Arthur Ford, who the late Bishop Pike used to contact his son.

Apparently, she would sit there and observe the same spirit that the clairvoyant giving the message was seeing. All the time, she would be doing a sketch, and several of them are recorded in this book. Typically, when she got through doing her picture, she would pull it off her easel and give it to the person in the audience whom the reading was for. Time after time, the person would come back the next day, or the next week, and show them photographs of the deceased person that was communicating and which this artist was copying as the other one was speaking. They were almost a perfect match."

THE MOCK-WA-MOSA PHENOMENA

Michigan researcher and author Dennis Morrison has delved into the Chippewa tradition of the Mock-wa-mosa, known also as the Bearwalker. However, its practitioners reportedly use their powers for evil, and tradition states they must kill at least one person a year or else this dark power turns on them. Allegedly these practitioners have the ability to shape-shift, are able to appear as a bear, an owl or simply as a mysterious ball of light, often producing temporary states of unconsciousness in their victims. In a phone conversation with Morrison in 2010, he described to me how in an interview he had had with a Chief John Nahgahgwan he was told of the experience the chief and another man had with this phenomena.

"I recall him telling me that they were walking down a path in the woods out there by Mikado Reservation and they saw this bright ball of light coming towards them. He told me that the one way to be able to render the Mock-wa-mosa powerless was to double back on it – where it had already come down a path – then take a pinch of sand and put it in your cheek. This renders them powerless. I think he said that they were actually able to put their arms around it and then the light turned back into the person that it was. It was a woman. He wouldn't tell me her name because she still lives up there. But later I interviewed, for an article that I did, a lady named Mrs. Beaver, and she was a very elderly lady. She couldn't tell me how old she was but her face was deeply etched with wrinkles. I remember her talking about the power that she had. She wouldn't say the word Mock-wa-mosa, but the power that she had

One of the most fascinating stories Dennis Morrison tells is about the shaking teepee phenomena. A shaman speaks to the spirits behind a closed flap yet those on the outside can see through the tent via supernatural illumination as well as see the spirits emerge from nothingness.

allowed her to actually go in and steal people's souls when they were sleeping. It was an evil power and it was a power that a person had to use. It was a power that was bestowed upon them that was not necessarily something that they wanted. A relative who was dying could bestow that power to them."

Dark practices existed within other groups; practices that were considered to be best avoided. One medicine woman of Cherokee and Choctaw ancestry explained to us how it was best to go with the flow of nature rather than to try and manipulate her for personal and selfish gain, and especially to do no harm to others. Among the Cherokee there were believed to be dark practitioners who could transform themselves into a "purplish ball of fire," as well as a wolf, raven, cat, or, once again, an owl. (Subscribe to "Dennis Morrison" at YouTube.com)

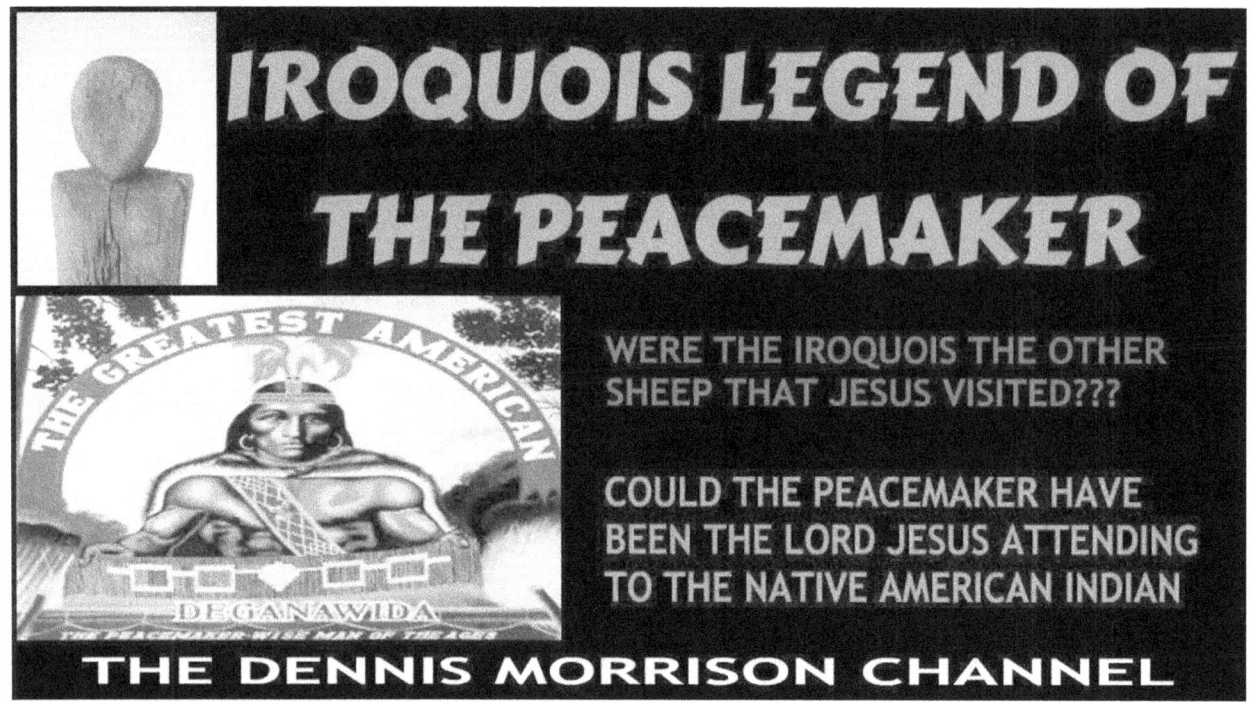

In 2007, Hawaiian born UFO researcher Kalani Hanohano helped explain to me about a mysterious UFO-type ball of light phenomenon frequently observed in Hawaii, which New Jersey author Timothy Beckley, who wrote **Kahuna Power: Authentic Chants, Prayers and Legends of the Mystical Hawaiians** (1987, 2007), had also described to me. Beckley had been to the islands to investigate these occurrences. To Hanohano, this mysterious light, called an akualele, which meant "flying god," was also something dark. "The akualele are devices manufactured by kahuna sorcery whose main function is to harm or kill another human being," he noted, explaining that it was a "supernaturally-generated light phenomenon." Like regular UFO encounters, a car engine may temporarily conk out while an akualele flies nearby. But otherwise, these are not your typical flying saucers piloted by supposed Greys of Zeta Reticuli origin, or even those "Little Green Men" from Mars. For more information, here are two links to what I've written previously on the subject:

http://mysterious-america.com/realitycheck1007.html

http://mysterious-america.com/realitycheck1107.html

EXPERIENCING THE EFFECTS OF AYAHUASCA

Accounts of people ingesting shamanic hallucinogen mixtures like ayahuasca can be quite amazing and reportedly very beneficial for some. They also seem to aid some people in entering alternate realms of reality where very strange things may occur and validating evidence may be acquired. (*PKD would have loved to know this – TGB*)

Reinerio (Rey) Hernandez, a UFO contact experiencer himself, tried ayahuasca a few years ago and believes it can be "one of the contact modalities" that he and other serious researchers and scientists are trying to understand, strongly suspecting that the theoretical tenants embodying quantum holographic consciousness may be the key. [Note: Hernandez is on the board of directors of the late astronaut Edgar Mitchel's Foundation For Research Into Extraterrestrial Encounters (www.Free.org)]

Consciousness expansion experiencer Rey Hernendez stands proudly beside the late astronaut Dr. Edward Mitchell.

"With my eyes closed, I moved my head in the direction of my friend who was sitting next to me and who did not take this medication," Mr. Hernandez recalled. "Like ESP, I knew everything about him and his problems. I then verbally told him of what I was 'seeing' and what he needed to work on. I then saw a human figure who I identified as Christ Consciousness who sat only one foot away from me, sitting in a lotus position right in front of me. I then reached out both hands to touch him and I immediately started to shake like I put my hands on one of those major power lines. My entire body was shaking violently for about 15 minutes."

After this electric sensation had left, Hernandez perceived that between himself and this other being he had identified with Christ Consciousness was a glowing urn that was glowing like the sun, floating between them at chest level. He then felt that he had been instructed to somehow remove his friend's "soul" from his body and place it in the urn, at which point again he was hit by what felt to him like a "1,000 volts of electricity," his body again violently shaking while holding the urn in his hands. "I felt that Christ and I were 'energizing' my friend's soul," he explained. (*Certainly on a par with PKD's emotional VALIS contact, in which Christ played a part. - TGB*)

Later, he felt that he had become someone else; an "Amazonian shaman." He saw himself as "a little four-foot midget, dark skin type, with full shaman regalia, with skirt and feathers, etc." The old Rey felt like an outsider, viewing this experience from high above, "but my consciousness was actually this very powerful shaman," he wrote.

"My personality changed," Hernandez explained. "I then had a different personality and became more authoritative. I told my friend to keep quiet, that I was in control and not him, and that I was taking over. I told him that this experience was for him and not about me, as he originally thought, and to be serious and get ready for some difficult work. Once again, I magically knew all of his problems and told him what he needed to work on to cure his ailments." Hernandez then proceeded to inhale and exhale very deeply while moving his hands in the air all around his body. "I was massaging his invisible energy field to put the final touches on my spiritual cleansing of my friend," he noted. Then, after a while, he looked over at another person several feet away, "scanned him," and explained what his problems were and what he needed to do.

"I later confirmed that everything I diagnosed was 100% correct," Hernandez added. In addition, the real icing on the cake, so to speak, came a little later when a lady friend, who had known nothing of what had been transpiring but is known for having psychic gifts, entered the house and said, "Oh my God, you are a bloody shaman. You are really ugly, very short, with very dark skin. You are stern looking. I am now getting information. You are from the Lake Titicaca area, from the location of the ancient ruins. The time is 800 BC. You trained all the shamans from hundreds of miles away from all of the Andes. You astral traveled wherever you wanted."

Hernandez confesses that, prior to this experience, he thought "energy healings" and all the rest was "bullshit." He had tried the ayahuasca, he admits, to "fix some of my emotional baggage." Although he had been helping others, he came away from the experience himself feeling healed too. "All of the issues I was struggling with have tremendously subsided," he explained. "Ayahuasca is indeed a miraculous drug; especially more so for experiencers of ET contact. It seems to bring out even more exotic events for experiencers."

(Last interview with Dr Mitchell: www.youtube.com/watch?v=5Z2oY4TsEI8)

Back in August 2011, Dr. Arthur Cushman, a board certified neurosurgeon from the Nashville area of Tennessee, was holding a private meeting with several of us to share some of his personal findings regarding Native American beliefs in an afterlife, something he had been researching in great detail. After his presentation was over, our conversation split off into a variety of different directions. Then someone brought up ayahuasca. "Let me warn you about that," Dr. Cushman told us. "It's called the death vine. Don't take it unless you're prepared for it and you're with a highly spiritual person. You'll usually experience death, either by being eaten by a jaguar or, like the experience I had, where you're killed by a snake."

At that point, someone who had heard the story before said it was an amazing account and asked Dr. Cushman to tell it again. Cushman agreed to do so. He explained how he had been diagnosed with metastatic cancer and had been told that there was no medical treatment that could help. He said that he was, in essence, told "to just go home and die." Instead, though, Dr. Cushman decided to attend a conference on healing out in Santa Fe, New Mexico. There he met Alberto Villoldo, a medical anthropologist who has studied shamanic healing along with his wife, who was from Chile and who invited him to visit Peru to explore shamanic methods of healing.

ALONG THE AMAZON WITH THE ICAROS

From a small primitive Peruvian village named Puerto Maldonado, close to the borders of Brazil and Bolivia, located along the Madre de Dios River (which I understand is translated to mean "Mother of God River"), Dr. Cushman and others were taken up river by motorboat on a long trip that took many hours. They finally reached a spiritual learning center located high up on a bluff. There Dr. Cushman attended classes and ceremonies dedicated to teaching spiritual ways and engaging in healing modalities.

Locals along the Amazon blow Metacho smoke over an ayahuasca vine. Photo courtesy Merci Mori.

Then one night he and others were taken across the river to sit in a circle on a huge sandy beach. There they were introduced to what he called a "jungle shaman" who played a flute, did unusual whistling (what are called icaros), smoked up the attendees, as well as drenched each of them by spitting a combination of tobacco, cheap rum, and some herbs on them. "I was wondering if I should pack up and go home at that point," Dr. Cushman said. "But there were lots of crocodiles in the river, and piranha too," he chuckled. He decided, under the circumstances, to continue with the next phase of the ceremony, the digesting of ayahausca, which he described as "awful tasting."

At first, Dr. Cushman laid on the beach and watched other people as the mixture seemed to introduce them to altered states; he felt nothing happening to himself.

Under the direct influence of ayahuasca, many experiencers have reported seeing UFOs, which are depicted in a variety of paintings – such as this one by the artist Pablo César Amaringo. His work is available at www.jacobsm.com

"Then, all of a sudden, all of the stars in heaven formed this beautiful pulsating geometric shape and I saw this huge portal in the heavens. Then these angels came down and stood around me. They diagnosed me and then they put their hands on me. It was just like getting a vibrating sensation or being shocked."

Around him he could see "ancient ones, spirits" with their hands on other attendees. In the meantime, he continued to be aware of the jungle shaman whistling and playing music. Dr. Cushman became sick and vomited, but instead of normal vomit he saw what looked like feathers coming out of his mouth. The vomit/feathers were collected into a basket by a young beautiful Indian woman. He thought to himself that, though he was old and had been feeling sick, "this is really wonderful."

But then Dr. Cushman noticed a huge anaconda coming towards him. The snake and a vine, from different directions, began to wrap around him. Cushman naturally began to struggle, trying to break free. "Then the snake head came right up in front of me and said, 'Arthur, stop fighting me. I'm going to kill you. You knew that. If you fight me it's going to be much more difficult. Just let me kill you and things will be better.'" So Cushman decided to relax, feeling his life being squeezed out of him. "Then I floated out of my body and I looked down and saw this dead body lying down on the sand and saw the snake and the vine just slithering off," Cushman recalled. "I floated there for a minute and then I went into the mouth of the serpent, into the dark. I had a review of my life. Everything from when I was born to what seemed like everything I'd ever done or thought in my life. Then I floated up and there was this beautiful world that I could see. I saw my father and mother and grandparents, people I knew, and Jesus was there and other masters. I kept going and I could see flowers and trees. Oh, it was so beautiful. I wanted to go there. And then, all of a sudden, the Archangel Michael was there. He had this flaming sword and he lowered it. Mary was standing on the other side. I could see her red heart pulsating and she held out her hand and said, 'No, you're not ready. You can't go there. Your purpose on Earth isn't done. We have things for you to do. You must go back.'"

So Dr. Cushman floated back and re-entered his physical body. He was starting to feel better when he noticed impish beings surrounding and laughing at him. "I thought, 'Oh no, what's going to happen next?'" He said he was going to come right out and reveal what the beings told him. He recalled that they said: "Arthur, you are full of shit. You must let go of your ego." Moments later, he got up, raised his walking stick in the air (he had polio when he was nine) and began limping back to the boat. He was doing much better than when he had to be assisted.

Sometime later, after all this that had happened, Cushman was laying down in his hut relaxing. "There were a couple of other people in there with me. We heard the door open and this jungle shaman walked in with us. He whistled and he said he wanted to check and see how we were. But he wasn't fully embodied. He was maybe three quarters. Enough that we could clearly see who it was. And all night he walked around the place. I could hear him whistling and this and that, and he called us by our names."

So that we'd all understand, Dr. Cushman added: "In other words, he bi-located, walked around, and apparently visited other people. The next day we went back up the river." In the Sacred Valley area near Cusco, he said he hiked with the group for some six miles. He did very well; a few days earlier, he couldn't have walked a block. He was doing much better and is still alive years later, adding, "I would never want to do it again. It was not a pleasant experience."

"I have no sign of cancer and my post-polio syndrome went away," Dr. Cushman explained. "This kind of woke me up that there's other possibilities and that the three dimensional world that we live in isn't all that there is. So basically this was a wakeup call."

Dr. Cushman also has an interest in UFOs. As I am putting this together, he just described to me some recent photos taken here in Tennessee of an alleged UFO, which a Native American shaman had told him was a visitor from the constellation of Arcturus, in the 8th dimension no less. This reminded me of how back in October 2014, Dr. Cushman told me of having had a recent sighting of a formation of UFOs. "We had a sweat lodge in Centerville, way out in the middle of nowhere," he had told me. The same shaman just mentioned had announced on this occasion that the "star brothers and sisters were with us," and then it happened. "They were pretty low," he said, describing how they were silent, silver, "saucer-shaped" craft, but had no visible windows. There were five in all, one which he said was huge. "That was an amazing experience," he added.

Discerning the "real deal" objective truth and comprehending the overall reality behind it all is certainly a huge, huge challenge for us. How can anyone wrap their mind around such anomalous accounts? I've read that neuroscientists say we have some 100,000 miles of nerve fibers that make up each human brain, which sounds like a lot of miles. But I can't adequately wrap my brain around this high-strangeness. After half a century in this field, I have yet to find anyone else who could either.

Maybe a bigger brain and a few thousand more miles of nerve fibers would help?

It is believed that the blowing of pipes and whistles among the native tribes could make possible shape-shifting by tribal shamans.

SUGGESTED READING – BRENT RAYNES

VISITORS FROM HIDDEN REALMS

ON THE EDGE OF REALITY

SECRETS OF THE ANDES AND THE GOLDEN SUN DISC OF MU

SUGGESTED READING – GREG LITTLE

PATH OF THE SOULS – THE NATIVE AMERICAN DEATH JOURNEY

PEOPLE OF THE WEB

GRAND ILLUSIONS

24.

DIARY OF AN UNHINGED MATRIX MASTER, SECTOR TWO

By Timothy Green Beckley

IN HONOR OF THE DALAI LAMA

YOU may think it crazy – anything that comes from Donald Trump is suspect – but the Donald may not be far off with his conspiratorial, disconcerting talk about televisions that "listen in" to your conversation and spy cameras peering out from your microwave. It's a crazy thought. But one that was not without precedent in the world of PKD.

"All that was involved from the start . . . was advanced laser technology. Mini (a rock musician collaborating with these unknown forces) found a way to transmit information by laser beam, using human brains as transducers, without the need for an electronic interface. The Russians can do the same thing. Microwaves can be used as well. In March 1974 I must have intercepted one of Mini's transmissions by accident; it irradiated me."

There were, for example, the voices that Dick says were emanating from an unknown radio station. They were anything but tranquil as they suggested he take his own life. Very frightening!

Then there were the subliminal messages coming from TV land that he thought were trying to influence children who sit as a rule in front of the set for hours each day. In "VALIS" we are told: "The satellite had control of them from the get-go. It could make them see what it wanted them to see. The satellite has occluded them, all of them. The whole fucking United States."

PKD concluded that the probable source of these transmissions was somewhere in the vicinity of the Sirius star system. He suggests that beings from this abode have visited here and that the African tribe known as the Dogon knew of their existence eons ago and even did crude star maps showing the point of origin for this group of aliens. In **VALIS**, one of the "fictitious" characters flatly states: "My God. These are the original builders," to which another character replies, "We have never stopped. We still build. We built this world, this space-time matrix.""

Tim Beckley admits that the Matrix can be difficult to explain and to navigate even in the best of times.

So now maybe we know who we are dealing with – or perhaps we still don't have a clue. But we trudge on with my second group of synchronicities, tying together the true nature of this phenomenon, only to come up against a "brick" or artificial computerized wall that will only let us go so far in our assumptions about the Matrix and its ability to influence our lives.

ENTER LONG JOHN NEBEL

Many people still think that Art Bell was the first to broadcast shows pertaining to UFOs and the paranormal over the radio late at night from his home studio near Area 51. Not even close. If you go back to the late 1950s and 60s you would find the midnight to 5 AM slot occupied by the dean of all night talk show hosts. Long John Nebel stood six feet four and was the master of the airwaves. WOR, whose transmitter was located off the New Jersey Turnpike, had the capability of reaching tens of thousands with its 50,000 watts of power. The signal could be picked up in thirty states, some say as far away as Arizona on a good night, when the signal would bounce and skip high up into the atmosphere before coming back down.

In the 1970s I became somewhat of a regular on the show. John had been stricken with cancer and his lovely wife, the very famous model Candy Jones, often took over the broadcast chores, especially on a Sunday night when she would invite me on to talk about everything from UFOs to the Loch Ness Monster. We lived in the same neighborhood so we often took a cab home together as the sun was coming up.

The following synchronicity is a heavy duty one. It has played on my mind for many years because the person involved became a friend of mine due to the set of coincidental circumstances I am about to describe.

I was on Long John's show one night discussing haunted houses and ghostly spirits and things that can be conjured up or put to rest. The next day I get a call from a young lady who tells me that she'd heard the program and was very impressed with the on air conversation. She told me that she is a columnist for *New York Magazine*, and her interest in the paranormal prompted her to dial me up for more information. She explained that she edits the "Best Bets" feature on the last page of the very prestigious weekly, which is more or less a listing of ten items associated with a specific topic. She wanted to gather material on haunted houses and ghostly encounters which have taken place in and around New York City, and said she is fascinated with the topic and will handle the write-up in a serious manner.

We continued talking for maybe fifteen or twenty minutes, during which time she tells me her name is Terry Clifford. Finally, after covering any number of relevant points, I say something like, "Terry, why don't you give me your address and I will send you additional literature in the mail?" She told me she would plug my activities at the NY School of Occult Arts and Science, which she would also visit in due course. I suggested that by sending the material we can always get back in touch to finish up the interview with anything we missed during our initial conversation.

She starts to give me her address and halfway through I begin to think that there is something wrong here – that she is repeating my address and not hers. But how would she know my address?

Turns out, Terry lived on the sixth floor of the same building while I was living two floors below. Now that's a trip, I would say. A solid "coincidence," if you want to label it that.

To say the least, Ms. Clifford and I became friends, living so close and being interested in pretty much the same subjects, though she was more into Eastern philosophy and meditation than I was. Later, she did a column – one of her "Best Bets" – on the top ten UFO sightings in and around Manhattan, including one where 70 witnesses are said to have sighted a giant orb hovering and floating over Central Park from the restaurant atop the Gulf and Western Building, now a Trump hotel minus the fancy penthouse eatery.

As to be expected, since we were in the same building, Terry and I would often meet one another either by the mail boxes or going up and down in the world's tiniest elevator built for two (or three if you're in a menage).

In addition to doing her regular column for New York, Terry was also a freelance writer, mainly on holistic health, and was a good friend of the Dalai Lama. She had traveled a whole summer with him and had written a book

Terry Clifford was a part of an ongoing synchronicity in Tim Beckley's life.

about their exploits long before the Tibetan exile received the kind of publicity and notoriety he currently enjoys.

It was a sad day when Terry went through her transition to another place and time. Terry passed away of sudden and rapidly metastasizing cancer on August 10th, 1987, at the age of forty-two. She died peacefully at home, two floors above, in the company of close friends.

Said one admirer – "If anyone ever misplaced something and couldn't find it, Terry would transmit the 'Saint Theresa mantra': 'Little flower in this hour show your power.' It usually worked!" If I had known she had this power, I would have visited more often as I am forever losing things into the Matrix (a common phenomenon which we have covered in previous works, like **Amityville And Beyond**).

So you would think that our story ends here.

But no story like this ever ends, nor should it. A person like Terry Clifford has much to teach no matter where she resides, in the penthouse on the sixth floor or in the Summerland, as spiritualists are prone to call the afterlife.

Let's say twenty years after her passing, possessing no calendar of synchronicities to mark it on, I am downtown at one of my favorite watering holes in Greenwich Village and I'm having a few drinks with my "blonde as can be" friend Holly. There's a gentleman standing next to us at the bar who, after a bit of chitchat, offers to buy us a round of drinks. Who are we to refuse? He seems to be very jubilant about something. I ask him why he appears to be having such a really good time, to which he remarks, "Oh, this afternoon I signed a four figure contract with a major publisher to put out my book on human relationships."

I told the gentlemen, who frankly was out of place in this rather seedy bar, complete with pool table and pole dancers on the bar, that I too was a publisher and would never have been able to offer him anything like a four figure deal. But, if he couldn't find a publisher for his next book, I might be able to hustle up a grand to send in his direction. We both had a chuckle, and eventually he asked me what sort of books I published. I told him that I specialized in what are commonly referred to as "New Age" subjects, like books on Nostradamus and the Eastern mystic T. Lobsang Rampa, who wrote extensively about Tibet.

Phil, that was his name, told me that he had visited Tibet and India in the 1970s and had even met the Dalai Lama. At which point, I mentioned about my friendship with the New York columnist and how she also had been in India around the same time as he had. Phil wanted to know her name and I told him it was Terry. At this point the man turned a whiter shade of pale and proceeds to shock me by saying, "You won't believe this, but Terry Clifford was the love of my life. I had a crush on her and I was very sad when I heard she had passed." Now that's a heavy dose of synchronicity with a double-edged blade. Furthermore, Phil says Terry had mentioned him on the acknowledgment page of her book, the foreword of which was written by the Dalai Lama, and he said there was a similar acknowledgment in the work he would soon have released.

Again, this all took place approximately twenty years after she departed from here. What this proves I can reach no conclusion about, though I did mention to Phil that I thought this was a message to him from Terry and not really one meant so much for me, though it certainly is a pretty heavy duty synchronicity.

I asked him what other projects he was involved in, and Phil said he was headed off to the UK in a few days to deliver a talk to a psychiatric conference. Figuring this would pretty much be a group of hardnosed skeptics, I made my new found drinking buddy promise that he would tell his associates about this little episode so as to convince them there might be some form of life after death.

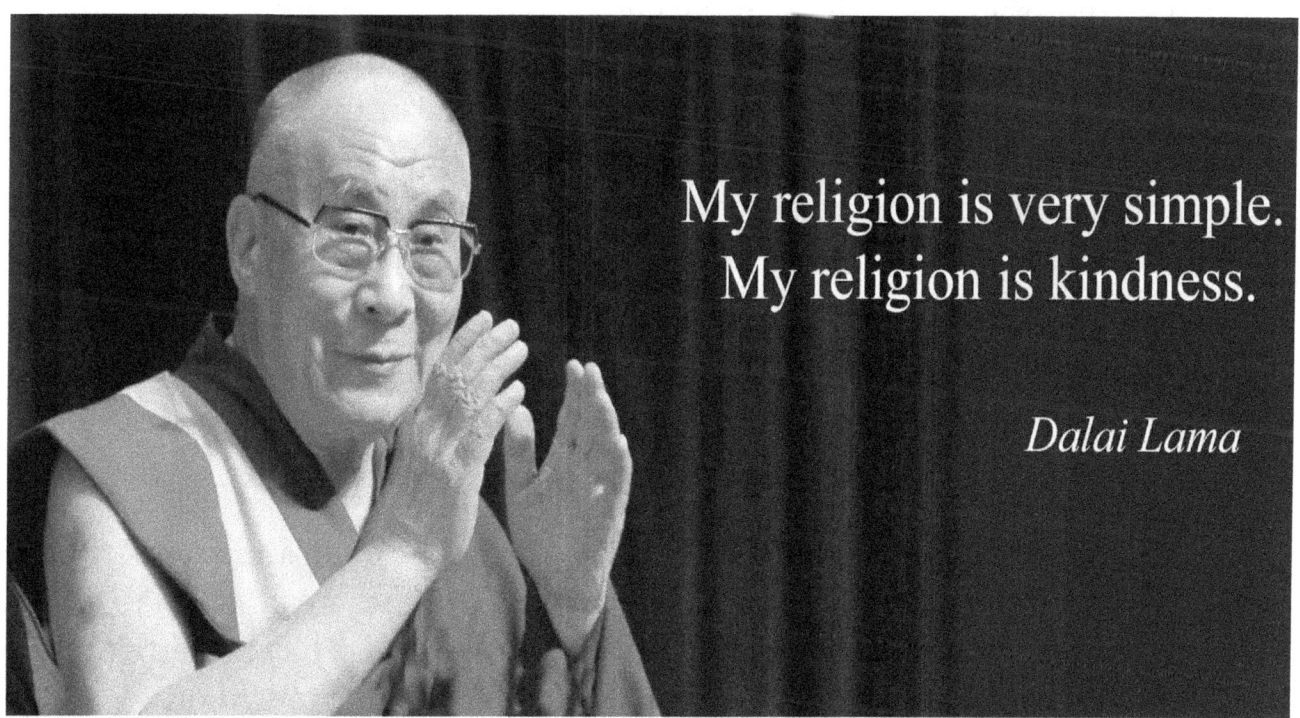

I'm not sure he honored this request, never found out his last name or saw him again. And within a few minutes I was back watching the pole dancers on the bar in front of me. And that's no coincidence. Anything to appease the gods of the Matrix.

THE MAN WHO KNEW TOO MUCH

You might think I am referring to myself in this instance, but I am not. Actually, you never know too much about this crazy, mixed up world regardless of our place in the space and time continuum. Though maybe the late Gray Barker, my first publisher, could be placed in that category, if for no other reason than he had written a bestselling book in 1956.

They Knew Too Much About Flying Saucers, was a real potboiler. It was the first place where the antics of the dreaded Men in Black were described in detail. The book revealed the astonishing events surrounding the mysterious silencing of a Bridgeport, Connecticut, man who stepped on the wrong shoes and evoked three men dressed in black, complete with dark hats and dark sunglasses, because he had apparently stumbled upon the true origins for the flying saucers and who was occupying them. Albert K. Bender was the founder of the International Flying Saucer Bureau, editor of Space Review, and presided over a worldwide organization consisting of several thousand members. The group had been very active with representatives in many foreign countries who reported directly to Bender, who in turn took the best reports and published them in his newsletter.

Suddenly, one day, he refused to talk about the subject any longer. He had alerted Gray Barker, who was one of the founding members, that he was closing the group down and threatened never to talk about the subject again. He said he had been WARNED, and he took the threats seriously.

At around the age of ten I got hold of a copy of the book and read it from cover to cover. I enjoyed reading; in fact, my mother read to me quite frequently and I got a hankering for the printed word that has not eroded to this very day. Fact is, I like reading more than I do watching television.

In the fourth grade we all had to do a book review. We could pick anything we were interested in, and so I selected **They Knew Too Much** as my book of choice.

I wrote the review in red pen and submitted it and actually got a B for a grade. That was pretty unusual for a kid whose average was a letter – or two – below that. Never really liked school all that much and frankly I figured in some cases I knew as much as the teachers. I remember one time I had labored doing a report on astronomy and had gotten a D minus because the teacher said I had copied it from somewhere. Utter nonsense. The word PRICK comes to mind.

Anyhow, the B was well received by me and I went on to struggle through middle school and high school till I was out, thank God, on my own and not under the yoke of some half-assed instructor. I began my writing career at a pretty early age. My first book was **Subterranean Worlds Inside Earth** followed by the **Book Of Space Brothers**. My publisher was (drum roll please) – GRAY BARKER! Gray was more or less my mentor. Got me started in the book trade. Showed me the ropes. He was a tall, lanky Southerner who made his home in Clarksburg, West Virginia. When he wasn't publishing UFO books under the Saucerian Press imprint, he was a booking agent for a number of small drive-ins. He was also a UFO trickster, somewhat of a prankster, but a gem of a fellow.

When Gray passed away I arranged with his estate to purchase the last fifty copies of the hardcover edition of **They Knew Too Much About Flying Saucers**. I still have a few copies on the shelf in the back room.

It can hardly be considered a "twist of fate" that my first book review at the age of ten was on Gray's bestselling book on the MIB and later I wrote several volumes for his small publishing firm, and eventually purchased the remaining copies of this very same title. It's synchronicity at its best. Hope your loving the attention Gray. I would love to give you a hardy handshake through the star-filled corridors of the cosmos. And say hello to the court jester of UFOlogy, Jim Moseley, for me, by the way!

UFO researcher Gray Barker was the first to tell the story of the Men In Black and their attempts to silence UFO witnesses.

It was more than a coincidence that made Tim Beckley select this book to do a review of in the fourth grade.

ENTERING THE REAL TWILIGHT ZONE

An ex of mine, Jean, introduced me to Rod Serling at a bar pretty close to the Plaza. I want to say Checkers but I can't find a bar with that name that was active in the 1970s. Rod was certainly an affable enough chap for someone who was at the zenith of his career. **Twilight Zone. Night Gallery**. I remember part of the conversation, not all now, was how he encouraged me in my writing. He explained that, before he had *Requiem for a Heavy Weight* produced, he would drive around with all sorts of manuscripts in the trunk of his car which he was having difficulty in placing. (He sold *Requiem* for $500). Yet when he finally "hit the jackpot," everyone in town started to call upon him to write for them. He opened the trunk of the car once again – and this time the same manuscripts were being bought up for thousands of dollars each. *Requiem for a Heavyweight* was a teleplay written by Serling and produced for the live television show Playhouse 90 on 11 October 1956. Six years later, it was adapted as a 1962 feature film starring Anthony Quinn, Jackie Gleason and Mickey Rooney.

Our mutual friend Jean eventually retired from being an agent in Manhattan – she did not represent Rod! – and moved to Florida. I think the rat race had done her in, as it will the best of us. Rod still stayed in touch with my ex. Apparently the subject of life after death came up between them and it would seem that Rod was skeptical that we pass through the heavenly gates to eternity and that life goes on somewhere else at its own pace and in its own way.

I guess Jean had a "thing" for Rod and I guess he had a "thing" for her as they ended up in a relationship that spanned several years; but I do not, admittedly, have all the details. Jean would sometimes have me telephone Rod's home in California and say I wanted to speak to him about some current project. I am willing to share what I do know. I put off telling the story for a long time because Sterling does have a daughter, but I am convinced that it can't be an issue any longer. There was some speculation that Rod was gay. Not a chance. He was small in stature, 5 foot 4 inches, and certainly wasn't known for pressing iron, but he seemed "all man" to me and I guess my ex, whom he was evidently seeing on the sly.

Without realizing it, Rod Serling invited Tim Beckley to become part of "The Twilight Zone."

Supposedly, and I know Jean would not lie, during the course of a conversation the subject of life after death came up and Rod reconfirmed the fact that he was far from being a believer. Kind of reminds me of the skeptical – somewhat harsh – attitude taken by Forest Ackerman that we described at length previously. When you're dead, you're dead, and that's all there is to it. Ain't nothing more to this holier than thou attitude!

But Rod did tell my friend that if there was such a thing as coming out on the other side, and it was possible to communicate, that he would visit her in the form of a butterfly.

OK, hold your hat here folks. If you recall, my ex had moved to the Sunshine State and opened a print shop. One day she told me she was driving home and a butterfly had gotten into the car even though she says the AC was on and there wasn't a window open. The butterfly fluttered around and didn't seem to want to leave, so my friend just let it be as it really wasn't bothering anything and maybe she was starting to put two and two together. She says the butterfly somehow got into the house and stayed there for some time before it just vanished. I'm sorry I can't supply you with any more details, but she did say she truly believed that this was the spirit of her amore.

In his final interview, Serling had gone so far as to question the notion of life after death, saying he believes death will be "a totally unconscious void in which you float through eternity with no particular consciousness of anything." This while also considering his own mortality: "I've begun to wonder about time running out. Is it sufficient unto itself that I don't plan? Because maybe next Thursday won't come one day. I'm concerned about that."

To many, the butterfly or the moth is the most-used symbol from those reaching out from the other side as it is proof of the soul's immortality. Art - Lovehaswon.org

Serling says he was often asked if he thought his writing career was preordained. That God had chosen him – intervened in his life – to become the creator of **The Twilight Zone** and so much more of importance in the world of literature. Rod thought about the question for a moment but he indicated that he wasn't able to go along with the concept of being preordained to do anything. "Why do I write? I don't know. I don't feel . . . God dictated that I should write. You know, thunder rents the sky and a bony finger comes down from the clouds and says, 'You. You write. You're the anointed.' I never felt that . . . I'm afraid that if I started to ponder who I am and what I am, I might not like what I find."

One quote I find most endearing –"It may be said with a degree of assurance that not everything that meets the eye is as it appears."

Well, at least he was being honest. I would have supposed, being the creator of some pretty farfetched TV dramas with a strong supernatural theme, he would have gone along with the hoopla and declared himself a diehard believer in anything remotely dealing with the macabre. Rod succumbed June 28 1975 from complications due to heart surgery. He was survived by his daughter. His wife passed the same year he did.

As it turns out, upon doing a bit of research, one of the signs that someone has returned to be with a loved one is that they will appear as a butterfly or a moth. Kind of in the same league as the pennies which befell our friend Nancy in a previous chapter, or Ackerman, who left an ink spot on a plain sheet of paper.

There is, in fact, a site on the internet www.butterflywebsite.com/ devoted to butterflies and moths, which states that this is the favorite symbol used by those on the other side who desire to communicate with their loved ones. "The butterfly is," they explain, "the most frequently mentioned ADC (after death communications) sign. It is a spiritual symbol for life after death because of its metamorphosis, or transformation, from a caterpillar that crawls on the ground to a beautiful, almost ethereal creature that flies through the air. It has also become a symbol for personal growth and spiritual rebirth."

To emphasize the value of this symbolism to the living, the same website points out that, "(The late) Elisabeth Kübler-Ross often spoke of the numerous drawings of butterflies she saw in the barracks at concentration camps in Europe. These lasting symbols of hope had been scratched into the wooden walls by courageous children and adults during the Holocaust. Today, pictures of butterflies can be found throughout almost every hospice. This symbol is also used extensively by many grief counselors, spiritual centers and support groups for the bereaved."

The butterfly site also gives us many touching examples of the continuing love and affection shown by those who can no longer be with us, regardless of what dimension or realm they might inhabit.

"Caroline is a secretary in Illinois. She had this informative experience after her 24-year-old daughter, Lindsey, was killed by a drunk driver while riding her bicycle: 'After my daughter's Catholic funeral service, we went out to the cemetery. While father was saying the final prayers, a big white butterfly landed on Lindsey's white casket and stayed there the whole time. When the service was over, Sister Therese hugged me and said, 'Oh, Caroline, did you see the white butterfly too? A butterfly is a symbol for the Resurrection!' I never knew that meaning before, and this put me at peace."

In another case, Margot, age 31, who is a clerk for an antique store in Washington had this lovely ADC after her uncle died of cancer: "We were at my Uncle Teddy's funeral in our Catholic church. I was praying during Mass and thinking of him. All of a sudden, this butterfly came fluttering down the aisle and stopped right by us. It was a real pretty orange and brown one. It fluttered around us, then turned and went up to where my sister was playing the piano. It did a twirl, then went over by the casket and up by the altar. Then the butterfly just flew off. It was wonderful! It was a miracle! As long as I have gone to that church that is the only time I've ever seen a butterfly inside. Of all the churches in the world, how many do you think had butterflies in them at that moment in time?"

One last story to illustrate this afterlife synchronization which was adapted by PKD, then we will continue on.

This story has to do with the magician and escape artist, Harry Houdini, who spent a good portion of his life exposing fraudulent mediums. Houdini went to extreme lengths to declare that when you die you are dead, and there is no place your soul will go. He did state that he would attempt to communicate with his wife of many years once he crossed over. And for ten years, Beatrice, with the help of Houdini's ghost writer/personal assistant Walter Gibson, attempted to reach out at midnight every Halloween to communicate with Houdini's spirit without apparent success. There is, it must be said, some controversy to this day as to whether or not the medium, Arthur Ford, once again as in the case of Bishop Pike, got through to the other side and broke a prearranged code which had been established with HH's wife before his death.

Master magician and escape artist Houdini spent years exposing fraudulent mediums, only to try and contact his wife after his passing.

What most people don't realize is that Houdini's able-bodied assistant, Walter Gibson, was a hardcore believer when his boss certainly was not. Gibson wrote several books on the occult. I am sure he saw and heard many things, because it was a known fact that in some instances Houdini actually "set up" the mediums to make it look like they were fraudulent when they were not pulling any shenanigans. Turns out, as far as Houdini is concerned, his biographer and friend WG was a "good man" and took Houdini's "flimflam" secrets to the grave.

But there is the incident regarding a moth which he relates which will have us all wondering once again.

Gibson says that there was a banquet being given in Houdini's honor by the Society of Magicians. All the members were given the opportunity to express their admiration to the man who had thrilled millions with his escape routines. At one point in the proceedings, a magician named Robinson attempted the feat of changing a rolled cigarette paper into a live moth. Unfortunately, the moth, when produced, was dead. But just as the metamorphosis was to occur, a living moth appeared from somewhere and circled his head. It vanished as it came, and a believer might have decided that it was the astral body of Houdini. "Of course," declared Gibson, "most of those in attendance thought it was a coincidence, but certainly a miraculous one. I myself was startled and so was everyone else, the performer possibly most of all. I have never seen anything like it in my experience with the art of conjuring."

SUGGESTED READING

REVEALING THE BIZARRE WORLD OF HARRY HOUDINI – PSYCHIC?

MEDIUM? PROPHET?

By Tim Beckley, Harry Houdini, Walter Gibson

ENTER ALEX JONES

Let it be known from the start that I don't think much of Mr. Info Wars. As far as I am concerned, Alex Jones is crazy on his best days and possibly a populist hatemonger the rest of the week. He is an opportunist who takes extreme positions just to attract an audience. His bullying and use of a bull horn when trying to attack an opponent on the street reminds me of someone who is close to the edge. In the beginning, I gave him the benefit of the doubt when he videotaped the proceedings at Bohemian Grove where international bigwigs seemed to be bowing down and worshiping a giant owl – said to represent Satan? – while nude under their black and purple robes. But since then he has gone off the deep end and falls deeper and deeper with each passing day until he has, in my opinion, been pulled as far out to sea as you can possibly go. His love of Donald Trump would seem contrary to his political views of exposing the New World Order, but that's neither here nor there – basically I can't stand him.

And even more so since he tried to suck me into one of his grand conspiracies with the added assistance of the very whacky David Icke, who thinks the Queen is a shape-shifter and the world is pretty much run by reptilians. Their scheming was responsible for my having to change the title of one of my movies. In the horror community I am known as Mr. Creepo, having produced a number of low budget R-rated horror films, one of which was originally titled **Sandy Hook Lingerie Party Massacre**. But, because of Icke and Jones, I ended up losing money due to their utterly scheming, conspiratorial nature, though there is a synchronicity tucked away in all this madness that warrants mentioning.

Says *USA Today* in a recent piece on the bombastic TV personality: "A self-proclaimed libertarian, Jones, 43, has built a steady audience the past two decades by trafficking conspiracy theories ranging from the U.S. government blew up the Alfred P. Murrah Federal Building in Oklahoma City in 1995 to the 9/11 terror attacks were an 'inside job' planned and carried out by the federal government. His flagship site, Infowars.com, draws more than six million unique global visitors a month and his YouTube channel has more than two million subscribers. More recently, Jones proliferated the theory that the 2012 Sandy Hook Elementary School shooting, which left twenty

"We had to change the name of the video from Sandy Hook to NJ Lingerie Party Massacre," notes Tim Beckley, *"because of Alex Jones and David Icke, who said they had discovered a sinister synchronicity where the name of the town Sandy Hook had showed up as a prediction or warning from the Illuminati."*

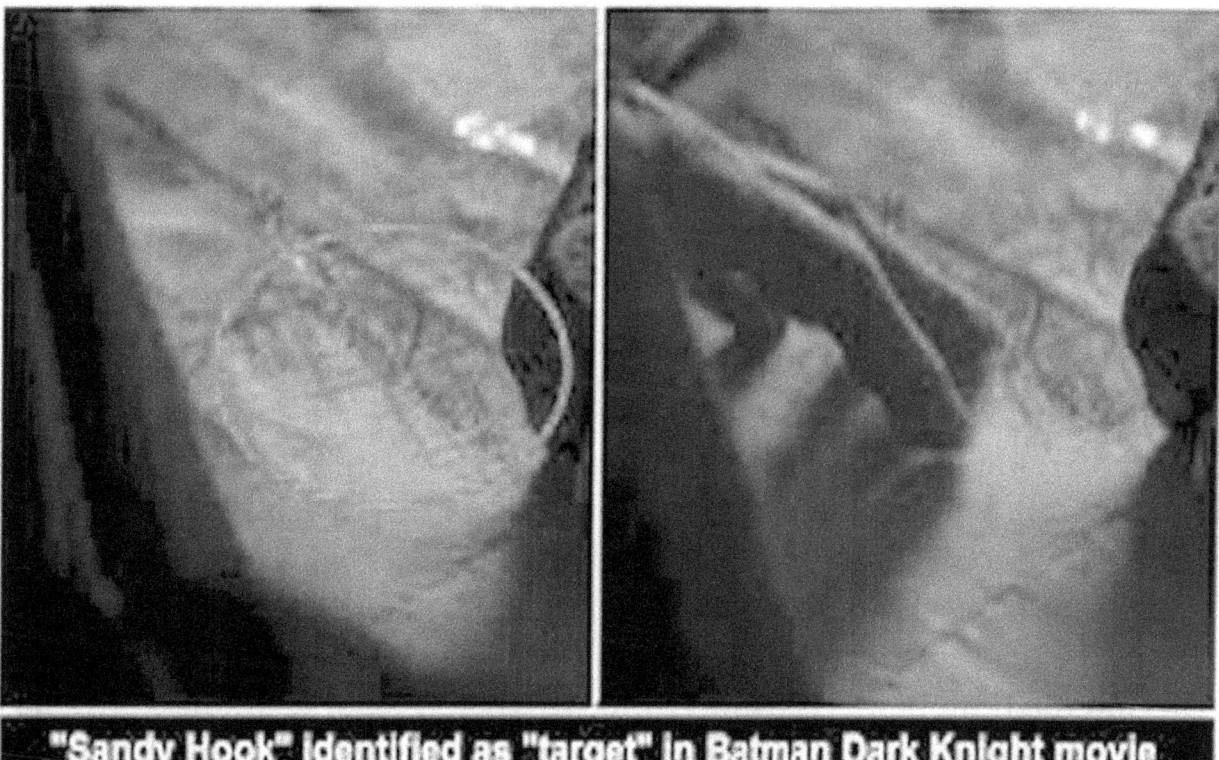

"Sandy Hook" identified as "target" in Batman Dark Knight movie

children and six adults dead, never happened and that child actors played the roles of the school-aged victims. In November, he clarified his stance, stating, 'I don't know what the truth is. All I know is that the official story of Sandy Hook has more holes in it than Swiss cheese.'"

As far as I am concerned, Mr. Jones has more holes than any five pounds of Swiss cheese.

I first got wind of the matter from Tracy Twyman, who has been writing about alternative history and the occult for going on twenty years. She is the author of several nonfiction books and is also the former editor of *Dagobert's Revenge Magazine*, a journal of esoterica published from 1996 to 2003. Tracy is also among the most knowledgeable individuals I know when it comes to the Illuminati. Back in 2008 we published a print version of her **Mind Controlled Sex Slaves of the CIA**, which has remained one of our most popular "counterculture" titles for over a decade.

Seems Twyman was the producer of the nightly *"Ground Zero"* syndicated radio show hosted by Clyde Lewis – the man whose voice was made for radio – when she contacted me about the most recent shenanigans of Alex Jones and company as relates to me.

The story goes that there was a man on a train crossing the UK who had gotten a hold of a copy, dubbed in Russian, of my "Sandy Hook" film. He had written up a review of the movie and had posted it on the Internet the very day that the **The Dark Knight Rises** (featuring the comic book hero Batman, and the ultra-sinister Joker) opened in Aurora, Colorado and a mass killing took place in the theater there.

In **The Dark Knight Rises** – dark cinema at its worst – there is a scene where the word "AURORA" supposedly shows in bright RED LETTERS on top of a tall building in the center of Gotham City. Then there is a second incident where the police have gathered around a map where a major crime is expected to happen. Someone points to the map where the expected crime is going to transpire and puts his fingers under the words "Sandy Hook." It is said that the Illuminati, the New World Order, and Skull and Bones have been known to telegraph their plans in advance, a smug and arrogant, mocking laugh at the pathetic sheep who are under the ruling thumb, reports Jeff Rense's web site.

Is this all just a coincidence or disinformation planted by the Masters of the Matrix? I can't say for certain, and I can't even tell you how I got caught in the middle of this dilemma. I did find out that there are no less than seven cities named Sandy Hook in North America.

From what I hear, the "responsibility" for this confusing matter lies with the film's property master, who would have inserted references to Aurora and Sandy Hook into the scenes as part of his job. You would think that we could go directly to Scott Getzinger and get the 411 on how he came about implanting these "warnings" in the final edited footage. Did he try to tell us we were in grave danger? Was this part of a predictive, programmable psy-ops? We cannot ask Scott, as he was killed in a head-on auto accident around the same time as **The Dark Knight Rises** was released. Was he murdered, by chance? Any speculation is only guesswork at this juncture.

Talk about Fake News, Debbie Rochon, the star of Sandy Hook Lingerie Party Massacre, has probably never been to the Sandy Hook in Connecticut where the elementary school shooting took place.

And then we have the production designer Nathan Crowley, who is said to be related to the British occultist, Aleister Crowley, who we are told was his grandfather's cousin. A long way removed from Sandy Hook but a possible coincidence nonetheless. There are too many synchronicities here to dismiss the entire issue, but I don't think I deserve to have had the squeeze placed on me by "madman" Jones, resulting in something less-than-the-expected profit for the DVD release.

And, by the way, Alex Jones, in good ole Info Wars fashion, refuses to back off, insisting, "We've sent reporters up there (in Sandy Hook), man, and that place is like 'Children of the Corn' or something. I mean, it is freaking weird." He concluded by saying, "All I know is something's going on and you don't like us looking at it. You don't like us questioning you."

Because of all this hoopla, the distributor made me change the title from **Sandy Hook** to **New Jersey Shore Lingerie Party Massacre**, but save your money. The video company selling the DVD is as big a rip-off as Alex Jones. Unlike Jones, the distributor may believe in the mass murders, but he certainly doesn't believe in paying any sort of royalties to the producer that he screwed over. A pox on you. Oh, if you want to be more confused: our Sandy Hook was in New Jersey, not Connecticut, where the murders of school children took place. There are seven Sandy Hooks in North America.

https://jonrappoport.wordpress.com/

www.tracytwyman.com

SYNCHRONISTIC SCANTIES

There is something about synchronicities and cab drivers in my life. Usually, if you leave something in the back seat of a taxi, the chances of you seeing that item again are 50/50 I would guess. One Saturday night I was out doing my usual weekend pub crawl. Somewhere along the line my key ring had fallen out of my pocket but I didn't realize this till I was about to head home feeling no pain (which would soon turn into a great deal of pain as any decent hangover is likely to do). There is hardly anything worse than being in this predicament, except maybe getting mugged. What the hell to do with ten bucks left in your pocket after buying drinks for the entire bar?

As luck (i.e. the man in the Matrix) would have it, as I began wandering the streets in a zigzag fashion, I heard the honking of a horn. A cab driver was half-hanging out the front window of his vehicle and dangling a set of keys at me.

The hack had left me off in a different part of town, maybe twenty blocks away, and was somehow bobbing and weaving in traffic just when the bars were emptying out and the streets would begin to become crowded. He sees me in his rearview mirror and realizes the keys he has found in the back seat belong to the fellow with the wild hair.

I thank the cab driver profusely and hit him up with a ten dollar tip. Without those keys I would have been up Shit Creek paddling backwards. He got me home in another fifteen minutes by putting the pedal to the metal. They were, in fact, my keys, so I got into the building OK and lived to tell the tale.

But I bet you would rather hear about the porn star's panties rather than my missing keys. Certainly can't say that I blame you.

I guess you know that in my freelance career that spans half a century I have had some pretty diversified ways of making ends meet – from being a wannabe music promoter, to being a stringer for the tabloids (*Enquirer, Globe, Tattler*), the movie review critic for *Hustler Magazine*, and the packager of some rather shoddy – and some downright seedy – magazines. I found out most publishers at the height of the pulp magazine craze did not read their own publications. They were pretty much accountants who knew how to kite advances so that the national distributors would end up paying for the printing and the small cost of the editorial and typesetting. These micro-publishers knew they could get my crew of writers for a song, while we often had to dance in order to get paid.

Can you believe I put together magazines like *Front Page Disasters, Moped Action, Soap Opera Today, Super Bowl Classics,* (never watched a football game), *Future Fantasy,* and "one shot" specials on Peter Frampton,

John Lennon, Elvis Presley and the band Kiss. Most didn't last more than a couple of issues, due mainly to lack of distribution and poor management. There was little color in the magazines; they were printed on cheap newsprint and looked it. I did package *UFO Universe* and its sister publications, *Unsolved UFO Sightings* and *UFO Files*, before the bottom fell out of the magazine business and the owner said we were closing shop after an eleven-year run. We put out a decent UFO magazine and made money – a concept in publishing that is unheard of today.

I could write a book on my career in the publishing business, but that's not our objective here. Go to BadMags.com for a mad historical treat!

In the mid-1980s, I found myself putting together an adult magazine (in the trade, porno magazines are given the classy title of "adult sophisticates" so as not to offend your local Seven Eleven dealer). *Adult Cinema Review* was aimed at an audience who were buying adult videos in increasing numbers and playing them at home, instead of sitting in some darkened theater with a rain coat over their laps. You might be surprised to learn that this group was made up of single men and women and lots of couples.

The magazine consisted mainly of stock photos from the latest XXX releases which I got for free, interviews I did with up-and-coming adult actresses, and at least one photo shoot of a porn "centerfold" which I happily took myself, being a fairly decent photographer and not having the funds to hire someone who had lights and a couple of cameras, while I shot with a flash. The budget was exceedingly low. The printing was so bad that the girls often complained that their skin appeared blue or yellow or some horrible shade of "skin tone" that doesn't exist on Earth.

One non-porn actress, whose nude pictures appeared, she says, without her permission, in another publication put out by the same publisher, was said to be doubly teed off because her skin was tinged purple or pink in the magazines pages. She still looked good to me, but I'm used to Martians more than most people would be. I was working for this mega publishing "empire" pretty much because I needed the money . . . when they paid without a hassle.

In order to enhance our respectability among our hardcore readers (take that anyway you wish), we decided to hold a contest. Win a porn star's panties. Exploitation at its weirdest. Got to have a chuckle over this. I know I did. But the contest was presented very seriously. The panties belonged to a long legged, brunette, Marlene Willoughby, who was not only stunning looking but had a most agreeable personality. She was always willing to aid an editor in need of some promotional assistance.

I think we paid for a particularly frilly pair of panties – nothing was too good for our readers – and Marlene went ahead and autographed them for the prospective winner of our contest. We received maybe two or three hundred entries and we had promised to present the scanties in person to the winner, but, since we had no budget, we had to pick someone from Manhattan or thereabouts.

In another space time continuum, Tim Beckley is in reality the horror film host Mr. Creepo, pictured with Carla to the left and an understudy to the right.

Our winner was a New York City hack. That's "cab driver" for you suburbanites unfamiliar with the term. He came to our Time Square office and we took photos of him and he took his newfound treasure home with him that afternoon. He vanished like dust in the wind.

Never figured I would have the opportunity to run into him again – why would I?

Some four years later I am roaming the city rather late at night in my persona as Mr. Creepo, looking for some big time excitement up around Times Square. Out of the blue and totally unexpectedly, I hear the honking of a horn and a yellow vehicle pulls over to the curb in front of me. It's a taxi, and it turns out that it's being driven by the winner of the contest and he is happy to see me.

With a beaming smile, he points to the rearview mirror and there, hanging where all his out-of-town passengers can see, are Marlene's most intimate apparel. Marlene was really touched when I told her about my meeting up with the lucky grand prize winner.

I guess you can say that some synchronicities are more personal than others. Sometimes the Matrix dares to share an intimate – or intimidating – moment with us all.

WHITLEY AND ME

One of the bestselling UFO books of all time is 1987's **Communion**, by Whitley Strieber. It made it to the number one slot on the New York Times bestseller list with two million copies sold of the hardcover and paperback editions. Before this first person account of an ongoing series of encounters with what Whitley refers to as "the Visitors," the stylish and trendy young writer was best known for his novels and not nonfiction. He penned such horror stories, now considered staples in this genre, as the **The Wolfen** and **The Hunger**, the big screen version of which starred our friend Mr. Pop Starman, David Bowie, as a gorgeous immortal vampire.

I think I first met Whitley at one of our New York Fortean Society meetings organized by John Keel. Whitley updated his abduction experiences and gave me a shout out in the audience, saying he was glad I was there to hear his men in black story. I have, since then, hooked up with Whitley a few other times. When he was part of a panel discussion at the large Fifth Avenue branch of Barnes and Noble with Velvet Underground front man Lou Reed, I was right there in the front row to pepper the panel with questions. In particular, I wanted to know if Lou Reed had undergone any meetings with aliens, to which he admitted he hadn't, but that he might later that night on the way home. As expected, the response got a chuckle from the audience.

Communion author Whitley Strieber (left) and Global Communications writer Sean Casteel at the Dark Delicacies bookstore in Burbank, California.

And I was a guest on Whitley's *Dreamland* podcast shortly after David Bowie died, talking about the celebrity's fixation with the cosmos, its perceived occupants, and my personal tracking of David's musical career. I also spoke about David's many occult- and UFO-related episodes, as well as his having to deal with the demons of drug abuse, both real and aberrational.

For the most part, Whitley lived in Manhattan while turning out one hit book after another before moving back to San Antonio. While on the East Coast, he produced a motion picture version of **Communion**, starring Christopher Walken. I thought it was a wonderful film, but Whitley was not happy with the revised dialogue and themes not traceable back to the book. Over the years, Strieber has repeatedly expressed frustration that his experiences have been taken as "alien contact" when he does not actually know what they were. Strieber has reported anomalous childhood experiences and suggested that he may have suffered some sort of early interference by intelligence or military agencies. He was extensively tested for temporal lobe epilepsy and other brain abnormalities at his own request, but his brain was found to be functioning normally. The results of these tests were reported in his book ***Transformation***.

I would have to say that while rightfully Whitley can be placed in the category of cult celebrity status, especially at the peak of his notoriety after appearing on the Johnny Carson Show, it is hard to rank him as a household name along with the Kardashians or rapper Jay Z. I can't honestly say if his name rings a bell with the "man on the street," though he is probably more recognizable than any other individual in UFOlogical circles.

One evening I was on my way to the Bitter End in the west side of Greenwich Village. The Bitter End is a historical musical landmark. In the early to mid-1960s, the club helped introduce to the world such folk music luminaries as Bob Dylan, Joan Baez, Ramblin' Jack Elliot and Roger McGuinn. I had hopped into a cab near the Empire State Building and told the driver I wanted to get off on Bleaker Street. As we rolled through the village just before midnight, the driver slows down before a high rise apartment building on LaGuardia Place, near NYU, and asks me kind of conceitedly if I know who lives there. Well, it's not like Judy Garland or Elvis lives there. It's not Trump Towers, by any means. Just a nice residential building. He thought he would stump me and I am sure he would just about anyone else who hopped into his taxi.

"Why, Whitley Strieber lives there. I know him!" The cab driver just about ran a red light, being so taken aback that I would recognize the moniker of one of America's literary icons. That will show him a thing or two – it will show everyone, I am convinced, except for those behind that computer simulation PKD was so familiar with. It would have been a hoot to be a fly on the wall if Philip and Strieber ever met and held a conversation.

And here again is a synchronicity that involves me being a passenger in a cab.

VISIT WHITLEY STRIEBER'S WEBSITE AT:

www.UnknownCountry.com

IT COULD BE A FRONT PAGE DISASTER – HELP RESCUE ME!

Of all the magazines I put together outside of *UFO Universe*, the one I liked doing the most, the one I felt I was personally getting something out of doing, was a publication dealing with personal tragedy and global catastrophes. Pretty rough stuff, hey? But educational overall. In *Front Page Disasters*, you could find articles on the Johnstown flood, the Hartford, Connecticut, circus fire, shark attacks, the Pan Am helicopter crash that decapitated several New Yorkers, a variety of air crashes, the massive explosion of a Galveston, Texas, grain elevator that killed 15, volcanic eruptions, plagues – well, I think you've gotten the gist by now, and it's not a very pleasurable one.

Being chief cook and bottle washer, I could do anything I wanted to with the magazine and it was fine with the publisher because his big concern was the bottom line, not the editorial content. I did come highly recommended and I knew how to chase a dying turkey around the yard. Every issue I would sneak in an article which at first didn't seem to belong in this type of magazine. I felt that nothing was out of bounds if it intrigued me and fit in, even though it may have required a broad stretch of the imagination.

With this in mind, I assigned my writers to put together features on mysterious disappearances inside the Bermuda Triangle, animals that predicted earthquakes, UFOs sighted around volcanoes while erupting. Most striking was one of my favorite stories, which concerned the battalion of New Zealand Expeditionary Forces that vanished upon marching into a thick cloud bank while fighting the Turks during the battle of 1915 on Gallipoli. A thousand of the best World War I fighting forces New Zealand had to offer were never heard from again. The clouds eventually lifted from the battlefield, joined another group of clouds and vanished by simply floating away.

I was disappointed when the publisher killed the magazine after three or four issues. It just hadn't sold even the mandatory twenty-five percent that would have kept it going. Most magazines are – I should say were – placed in specific sections at your local newsstand. All romances were in the same row of magazines. The car and boat magazines would have their own section. News magazines, crosswords puzzle books, you get the idea. If you didn't fit into a group, you probably wouldn't be put out at all and immediately sent back to the wholesaler for credit. Where in the hell do you put a magazine on disasters when there isn't a category that fits that bill? So I figured I would never see or hear of the magazine again; its demise was a personal bummer.

Then one night, let's say eight years after *Front Page Disasters* had become a disaster itself and was no more, I am watching TV with a couple of people who have come over to the apartment. I am showing them some of the magazines I have edited, mostly the rock and roll music zines, as this is what interests them the most. I remember there is a thriller on the TV. No one is really paying much attention to it, but it is blaring away regardless. I think the movie they were playing starred Richard Dreyfuss, but I am not really sure.

In fact, this is where you have to give me a hand at finding the name of the movie. It is a film that obviously had played in the theater; in other words, it was not a straight-to-video release. As I recall, it involved a series of murders that were taking place inside a Manhattan apartment building, but no one knows who is responsible for the ongoing homicides, even though the main character is doing his best to find out who the culprit is.

At some point a murder has just taken place and Dreyfuss – or whoever the main male character is – chases after a shadow form through the revolving front door of the apartment complex and out into the street, where he races down the block and turns the corner. But which way did he go? Dreyfuss stops in front of an outdoor newsstand, the type that sells your basic newspapers, gum, lottery tickets and maybe a few of the better selling magazines.

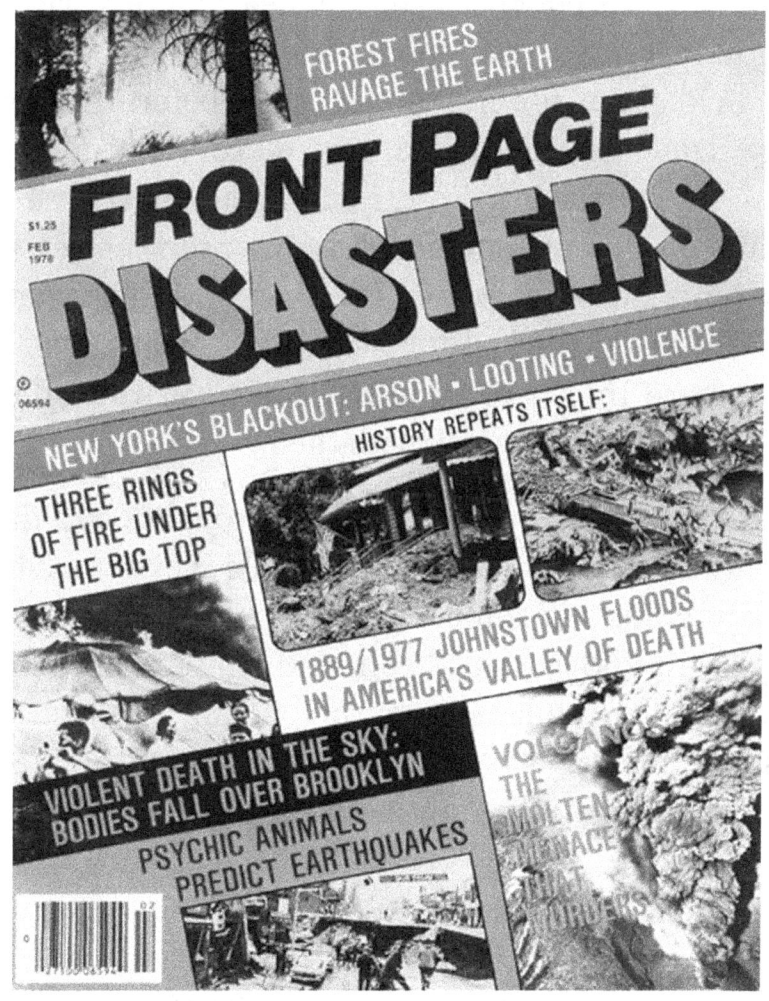

A row of copies of "Front Page Disasters" showed up in a murder mystery without rhyme or reason ten years after the magazine had suspended publication.

There is a fairly close-up shot of Dreyfuss and the newsstand and its dealer. But there isn't an issue of *Cosmo* or *Glamour* or *TV Guide* to be seen. Instead, strung up in various corners of the stand by clothespins are copies of – damn if this doesn't take the cake – my very own publication, *Front Page Disasters*. Nothing else can be seen behind the counter, just maybe ten nicely displayed copies of this hard-to-come-by magazine.

How is that possible? And why would I happen to see this particular scene in a film, which I've never seen again, showing a publication that had sold maybe a few thousand copies nationally? The unsold copies of all magazines are usually shredded or sold at flea markets without covers. Yet someone had gotten a hold of a good handful – maybe a carton – of the magazines and held them for nearly a decade before they showed up "by accident," I say, coughing loudly, in this murder mystery. It's a mystery alright. Unless I am suffering from the Mandela Effect (see the end of this chapter for details on this phenomenon), some prop master would have had to retain copies in his garage or warehouse. And how did he get a hold of them to begin with? Unless he worked for a magazine wholesaler. The publisher never even had more than two or three copies in the office, never mind enough to decorate an outdoor kiosk with them.

I know I am not losing my mind. I even brought out a dusty copy of the magazine from my files to show my friends while they were sitting around. So if any of you reading this remember the movie, who starred in it and so forth, drop me a note at mrufo8@hotmail.com and clue me in. Otherwise this just has to be considered a random synchronicity in a long list of perplexing synchronicities sent my way by the gleeful masters of the Matrix, who could be watching over you ready to pounce with a puzzling coincidence or two at any given moment.

ONLY IN THE MOVIES

She was absolutely striking. Very attractive. "Hot." I knew she would look sexy behind the camera and I was certainly looking for a sexy actress to star in an upcoming horror movie I was planning to shoot in the next month.

I had placed an ad in *Backstage*, looking for undiscovered talent, which is code for we are not union and can't afford to pay very much. Received lots of calls from gals who wanted to hear more about what we were doing. "Shooting a vampire movie," I explained to those who responded. And you know lady vampires have to be seductive. It's part of what draws an audience. There was, I went on, some nudity, but nothing outrageous, as I was going for an R-rating. Four or five gals showed up. I was not overwhelmed until this one starlet-in-waiting appeared and abruptly took my breath away.

Dark hair. Slender. Thin waste. Perky in all the right places. I would have hired her on the spot, but I wasn't running a casting couch. I actually interviewed those wanting to be in the movie. I knew most didn't have much, if any, experience, but you want your Scream Queens to be, outside of pretty, talented enough to deliver a line and shriek on cue. I had each of the actresses scream for two or three minutes in front of the camera, pull their hair and generally act like they were being attacked by some maniac. The screams were so piercing that I was certain someone in the building was going to call the cops, thinking that an actual murder was taking place.

Teresa did everything well enough to offer her a starring role, which she accepted without hesitation. We were both hoping this would be the start of a nice career in the performing arts for her, despite the low budget we were going to be making the film on.

As we sat chatting on the couch, I had an open notebook to scribble down whatever I needed to remember. There were a couple of pens in front of us and I noticed that Teresa was doodling in a sketch pad. It looked like a cross between graffiti art and some sort of cartoon character, but I was at a bad angle to get a very good look or otherwise I might have recognized the figure she was sketching.

Curiosity getting the better of me, I asked her what she was drawing. "Oh, it's an artist whose work I think is super cool." It was like she was channeling; she was so busy working on her doodle that I began to think she was deliberately ignoring our conversation. "There is this underground cartoonist," she explained. "He's deceased now. His name is Vaughn Bodē, and his principle character that everyone loves so much is called Cheech Wizard."

Turns out, the Wizard was once described, "as a pot-smoking, pot-inspired, hedonistic mystic with an earthy libido for voluptuous babes. It was a funny and sexy cartoon," wrote critic Mark Emery.

Turns out I had met Bodē years before when he was introduced to me through my witchy friend, Walli Elmlark, who had also introduced me to some of the legends of rock like David Bowie and Robert Fripp, guitarist for the British band King Crimson. Walli was known as the White Witch of New York and was a frequent speaker/teacher at my occult center.

Cheech Wizard was a pot smoking, hedonistic mystic with an earthy libido for voluptuous women.

Walli had a charisma and style about her that was appealing and had made friends with tons of counterculture people, Vaughn being one of them. In fact, Bodē was so counterculture that he stood out in a crowd as being counter to everyone else's style. Says cartoon archivist Craig Yow, "Vaughn stood out even in that hippie era and in New York, where you expect the unconventional. Vaughn Bodé looked like Jesus. Long white robe and hair like Jesus wore it. Hallelujah, I adored it! The robe and the hair were joined by long fingernails – bright blue in color."

In fact, the artist had once done a cartoon panel of Walli in the same style as Cheech, but, then again, they certainly were both wizards.

The White Witch of New York, Walli Elmlark, was a comrade of underground artist Vaughn Bode. He even caricatured her for one of his comics.

Bodē had created his own world of fantasy to make up for a disastrous childhood at the hands of abusive parents. Bodē's life unfortunately came to an untimely and premature end by his own hand, while experimenting with erotic asphyxiation He died, in July 1975, "coincidentally" at the age of 37, the same age that some believe Jesus had also died. Once again, Jesus becomes part of the synchronized equation, as if he too were created by those cloaked figures behind the Matrix.

Teresa was duly impressed that I knew who her favorite artist was. And I guess she should have been, as Bodē was not exactly in the same league as Peter Max, though they were contemporaries. Bodē's work was for a select clientele, a slightly more hip audience, as it was full of voluptuous women and one over-the-top wizard who was always in search of a party.

Bodē stood out in a crowd even in New York – where you expect the unconventional.

She was even more surprised that I had met her favorite artist, but our reflections on the cartoonist ended at that point, until it was bought up several months later through an unexpected turn of events.

One Friday or Saturday, they were showing independent, low budget movies in the back room of Max Fish's on Orchard Street in Greenwich

Village. The bar's Facebook page describes the place as "a legendary LES NYC bar/Art Gallery/Skater, Musician and Oddball Haunt opened in 1989." You will have to figure out what Skater (a form of music?) and LES (lesbian?) stand for, but I didn't see any of that in the back room where a projector was throwing a tiny micro-budget flick on the wall.

Eventually Teresa and I adjourned to a table near the bar for a drink. The place was fairly crowded and everyone was in a good mood, chatting among themselves and making new friends as one is apt to do in a Les/Skater watering hole in the Village. One young fellow took a seat across from us, and we engaged him in conversation. Somehow the subject of art came up, something I know little about, nor am I particularly interested in.

The young man said his father had been a relatively well-known artist and he was following in his dad's footsteps. His name was – hold onto your garter belts, ladies, and your suspenders, gentlemen – Mark Bodē! Apparently, Mark was in town, I think from Boston, to arrange the sale of some art, whether his or Vaughn's, I don't remember. From what I gather, Mark often produces works similar to the elder Bodē's style and is best known for his works *"Cobalt-60," "Miami Mice"* and *"The Lizard of Oz."*

Naturally, I told him I had met his dad, but he was skeptical until I said we were both mutual friends of the white witch of New York Walli Elmlark. "That's a name I haven't heard for a long, long time," Mark admitted. We chatted for a while and eventually said our goodbyes, though we had a more than passing synchronicity under our belt to refer to. I mean, Teresa, my stunning new actress, had been doodling in the style of the late artist the first night I met her, and here we run into his son out of the blue. I had never been to this bar before in my life (in this reality anyway). I don't think Mark had, not sure about Teresa.

So go figure, and have a good time at Max Fish's while you're doing it.

markbode.com

BEAM ME UP BRUCE

We have had Bruce Raphael on *Exploring The Bizarre* several times – direct from mainland China. Since first meeting him, he's become wrapped up in the UFO phenomena, in dragons, earth grids, lost pyramids and a host of other topics we've come to be fascinated with. Bruce has sojourned around the world exploring these mysteries. When I first met Bruce, he was living in New York and working at a travel agency near Penn Station and wasn't seeking out information on any of these subjects.

Bruce Raphael

I guess you could say I met Bruce under somewhat unusual circumstances – though nothing is unusual as we have come to learn.

I had purchased a round-trip plane ticket to San Diego to visit with my friend Diane Tessman and pay homage to a UFO "landmark" in the Mojave Desert. Giant Rock was the "Wailing Wall" of UFOlogy standing over seven stories tall. It was the largest standing rock in America until an earthquake lobbed off a huge chunk some years back. The rock was at the end of an airstrip where its owner, George Van Tassel, says he established face-to-face contact with the human-looking occupant of a spaceship in the early 1950s. Van Tassel had once worked for Howard Hughs and was an inventor in his own right. It's a great place to visit and soak up the unearthly energies, though the stifling heat can be a bit much when it reaches the hundred-degrees mark, which it does on almost a daily basis in the months between June and October.

On the way back, there was a mix-up in my airline ticket and I had to purchase another one at my own expense, even though I had originally paid for a coach seat from the travel agency that Bruce worked for. Now I should point out that I did not know Bruce, had never met him in my life. I had gotten the ticket on the phone before going on my merry way. It wasn't Bruce

I originally spoke with to make the reservation, just someone else at random depending upon who had picked up the phone.

In order to get a partial refund for the return passage which wasn't accepted, I went to visit the agency – a rather large one – in person to iron out the situation and to voice my complaint for sloppy service. At random the receptionist ushered me to Bruce's cubical. While we did the paper work to get my Amex credited, Bruce and I chatted. Nothing I can remember about the conversation after three decades or more. I do recall him asking me what I did and I told him about publishing a magazine on UFOs and he said something like, "Hmm, that's interesting." Nothing more.

Five or six years later I attended a birthday party for UFO contactee Marc Brinkerhoff, who has the uncanny ability to go outside in the daytime or at night, point a camera at the sky and have UFOs appear all over the film, usually a number of them frolicking about in formation. Remarkable! Check out our book **UFO Repeaters, The Camera Doesn't Lie**. Dozens of pictures taken by Brinkerhoff are printed in this volume, including the shadow of an alien inside the port of a ship..

At the party there were some interesting people. One of them turned out to be Bruce Raphael from the travel agency. Seems Bruce and Marc had been friends at this point for some time. I was perplexed regarding how they got to know each other. Turns out, following our meeting at the travel agency, Bruce went and read up on the subject. He found he was fascinated with UFOs and ended up becoming part of Marc's inner circle after hearing him give a lecture on his contact experiences.

Bruce got married to a Chinese lady and was living in China for a while. He is back in the states again. Have to hook up with him eventually—or maybe ECCO will do it for us once more!

www.newdawnmagazine.com/Articles/Megalithic%20Science.html

www.siloam.net/mossman/aussies/194403251839/ufopiece.html

SLICE OF PIZZA WITH A TOPPING OF COINCIDENCE

Its 8:50 AM, and I have been working on and off all night. So it looks like it's time to shut it down. Time to retire – for now – PKD's life in a computer simulation and my "there is no end to this" synchronicities and serendipitous events. I think you would have to agree that there is something totally "alien" afoot here. No one could possibly undergo so many experiences of such a provocative and unexplainable nature.

As for whatever – or whomever – is behind this phenomenon in my life, I don't see them as being particularly negative or sinister – a bit playful perhaps, but not threatening, except in the instances where there is tie-in with a person's death. Then we are likely on shaky ground.

It might be that, if this is all a computer simulation, it was set up at the beginning of time and there is no one at the helm. Or maybe they check into the "computer room" every century or so. Maybe "they" don't even know what effect they are having on us, or perhaps it's just an updated version of Pac Man we find ourselves maneuvering around in. Or, as I have suggested throughout this work, maybe we are being controlled and are like Charles Fort suggests, pieces on a chessboard to be moved about at someone's whim. Could be we are moving about from one reality to another, living in several time zones and "places" simultaneously, brushing against each other and transferring remembrances through this method.

This is part of a trending theory being touted by amateur physicists and conspiracy theorists. It is most often called the Mandela Effect, named after the South African anti-apartheid leader who many said they thought had died years before his real passing. They wonder how so many people can be "wrong" about an event in history that supposedly appeared in papers and on the news. Could be we are all wrapped up in different realities or timelines, if you consider there might be a massive interdimensional grid system existing all around us and drawing us into its spidery web.

Me, I think I have made friends with ECCO, so I'm not about to switch my allegiance just because something is trending. This isn't YouTube or Facebook now, is it? Look up the Mandala Effect and see what you think.

Would PKD have gone along with this theory developed by the generation of new millennials we hear so much about on CNN and MSNBC because of their voting patterns?

Another question is: are certain people more susceptible to synchronicities than other individuals, like I would seem to be?

Perhaps it has something to do with being at the right – or wrong – place at the right time, or a combination of all of the above.

I got an inkling of this maybe from the ECCO itself recently while having a slice of pizza across from the Empire State Building when I was out one night having a late night snack. Here is my latest – and last – experience.

This pizzeria is more or less a hole in the wall, but the Sicilian squares with mushroom are really good, hot and fresh, even at this hour. The large bay windows open onto the street and so there is usually a breeze even on the most humid of evenings. The place is still rather crowded with tourists coming down from the Empire State Building at the height of the summer season.

I was wedged in between quite a few people, minding my own business, chowing down and trying to read the latest edition of the *Fortean Times* (named after Charles Fort) from the UK. There was a young man across from me and his girlfriend next to me; we are almost rubbing elbows. As the girl gets up to leave, she turns to me and says: "Are YOU Timothy Beckley?" I thought, ah, a fan, and a pretty one at that. So I said, "Yup, I sure am," to which she replies, "Well I think it's strange. My boyfriend's name is Timothy and I'm Becky!"

She had gotten my name from an envelope that I had been carrying my reading material in so as not to get pizza sauce on it. At the time, I figured, well, this isn't all that much of a coincidence that her boyfriend's first name is the same as mine and that she is a Becky, which IS two letters off from Beckley. I would only give this a five or six on a sliding scale of synchronicities.

But then, the more I thought about it, the more I began to ponder the situation. Why would this gal in her late teens or early twenties even say something like this to a complete stranger? Who would look over at a beat-up old Fed Ex envelope and even notice what my name was? And why think there was something all so strange about this?

Then I realized it was either that I draw synchronicities like a magnet or that ECCO was up late (I assume they have no need to sleep) and thought they would twist things around a bit for the sake of entertaining me with another coincidence.

Maybe they figured it was time for me to go on Paul and Ben Eno's *Behind the Paranormal* show and talk about them – and the overall structure of the universe – once again.

Good night.

25.

Here we let Philip K. Dick speak for himself, in his missive from 1977, a few years after his breakthrough experience with the Christian medallion at his front door.

ONCE UPON A MAD LITTLE WORLD
By Philip K. Dick

MAY I tell you how much I appreciate your asking me to share some of my ideas with you? A novelist carries with him constantly what most women carry in large purses: much that is useless, a few absolutely essential items, and then, for good measure, a great number of things that fall in between. But the novelist does not transport them physically because his trove of possessions is mental. Now and then he adds a new and entirely useless idea; now and then he reluctantly cleans out the trash – the obviously worthless ideas – and with a few sentimental tears sheds them. Once in a great while, however, he happens by chance onto a thoroughly stunning idea new to him that he hopes will turn out to be new to everyone else. It is this final category that dignifies his existence. But such truly priceless ideas . . . perhaps during his entire lifetime he may, at best, acquire only a meager few. But that is enough; he has, through them, justified his existence to himself and to his God.

An odd aspect of these rare, extraordinary ideas that puzzles me is their mystifying cloak of – shall I say – the obvious. By that I mean, once the idea has emerged or appeared or been born – however it is that new ideas pass over into being – the novelist says to himself, "But of course. Why didn't I realize that years ago?" But note the word "realize." It is the key word. He has come across something new that at the same time was there, somewhere, all the time. In truth, it simply surfaced. It always was. He did not invent it or even find it; in a very real sense it found him. And – and this is a little frightening to contemplate – he has not invented it, but on the contrary, it invented him. It is as if the idea created him for its purposes. I think this is why we discover a startling phenomenon of great renown: that quite often in history a great new idea strikes a number of researchers or thinkers at exactly the same time, all of them oblivious to their compeers. "Its time had come," we say about the idea, and so dismiss, as if we had explained it, something I consider quite important: our recognition that in a certain literal sense ideas are alive.

Philip K. Dick at Metz France, 1977

What does this mean, to say that an idea or a thought is literally alive? And that it seizes on men here and there and makes use of them to actualize itself into the stream of human history? Perhaps the pre-Socratic philosophers were correct; the cosmos is one vast entity that thinks. It may in fact do nothing but think. In that case either what we call the universe is merely a form of disguise that it takes, or it somehow is the universe – some variation on this pantheistic view, my favorite being that it cunningly mimics the world that we experience daily, and we remain none the wiser. This is the view of the oldest religion of India, and to some extent it was the view of Spinoza and Alfred North Whitehead, the concept of an immanent God, God within the universe, not transcendent above it and therefore not part of it. The Sufi saying [by Rumi] "The workman is invisible within the workshop" applies here, with workshop as universe and workman as God. But this still expresses the theistic notion that the universe is something that God created; whereas I am saying, perhaps God created nothing but merely is. And we spend our lives within him or her or it, wondering constantly where he or she or it can be found.

I enjoyed thinking along these lines for several years. God is as near at hand as the trash in the gutter – God is the trash in the gutter, to speak more precisely. But then one day a wicked thought entered my mind – wicked because it undermined my marvelous pantheistic monism of which I was so proud. What if – and here you will see how at least this particular SF writer gets his plots – what if there exists a plurality of universes arranged along a sort of lateral axis, which is to say at right angles to the flow of linear time? I must admit that upon thinking this I found I had conjured up a terrific absurdity: ten thousand bodies of God arranged like so many suits hanging in some enormous closet, with God either wearing them all at once or going selectively back and forth among them, saying to himself, "I think today I'll wear the one in which Germany and Japan won World War II" and then adding, half to himself, "And tomorrow I'll wear that nice one in which Napoleon defeated the British; that's one of my best."

This does seem absurd, and it certainly seems to reveal the basic idea as nonsense. But suppose we recast this "closet full of different suits of clothes" just a little and say, "What if God tries out a suit of clothes and then, for reasons best known to him, changes his mind?" Decides, using this metaphor, that the suit of clothes that he possesses or wears is not the one he wants. . . in which case the aforementioned closet full of suits of clothes is a sort of progressive sequence of worlds, picked up, used for a time, and then discarded in favor of an improved one? We might ask at this point, "How would the suddenly discarded suit of clothes – the suddenly abandoned universe – feel? What would it experience?" And, for us even more importantly, what change, if any, would the life forms living in that universe experience? Because I have a secret hunch that this exact thing does indeed happen; and I have a keen additional insight that the endless trillions of life forms involved would suppose, incorrectly, that they had experienced nothing, that no change had taken place. They, as elements of the new suit of clothes, would incorrectly imagine that they had always been worn – always been as they now were, with complete memories by which to prove the correctness of their subjective impressions.

We are accustomed to supposing that all change takes place along the linear time axis: from past to present to future. The present is an accrual of the past and is different from it. The future will accrue from the present on and be different yet. That an orthogonal or right-angle time axis could exist, a lateral domain in which change takes place – processes occurring sideways in reality, so to speak – this is almost impossible to imagine. How would we perceive such lateral changes? What would we experience? What clues – if we are trying to test out this bizarre theory – should we be on the alert for? In other words, how can change take place outside of linear time at all, in any sense, to any degree?

Well, let us consider a favorite topic of Christian thinkers: the topic of eternity. This concept, historically speaking, was one great new idea brought by Christianity to the world. We are pretty sure that eternity exists, that the word "eternity" refers to something actual, in contrast, say, to the word "angels." Eternity is simply a state in which you are free from and somehow out of and above time. There is no past, present, and future; there is just pure ontological being. "Eternity" is not a word denoting merely a very long time; it is essentially timeless. Well, let me ask this: Are there any changes that take place there; i.e., take place outside of time? Because if you say, "Yes, eternity is not static; things happen," then I at once smile knowingly and point out that you have introduced time once more. The concept "time" simply denotes – or rather posits – a condition or state or stream – whatever – in which change occurs. No time, no change. Eternity is static. But if it is static, it is even less than long-enduring; it is more like a geometric point, an infinitude of which can be determined along any given line. Viewing my theory about orthogonal or lateral change, I defend myself by saying, "At least it is intellectually less nonsensical than the concept of eternity." And everyone talks about eternity, whether they intend to do anything about it or not.

Let me present you with a metaphor. Let us say that there exists this very rich patron of the arts. Every day on the wall of his living room above his fireplace his servants hang a new picture – each day a different masterpiece, day after day, month after month – each day the "used" one is removed and replaced by a different and new one. I will call this process change along the linear axis. But now let us suppose the servants temporarily running out of new, replacement pictures. What shall they do in the meantime? They can't just leave the present one hanging; their employer has decreed that perpetual replacement – i.e. changing the pictures – is to take place. So they neither allow the current one to remain nor do they replace it with a new one; instead, they do a very clever thing. When their employer is not looking, the servants cunningly alter the picture already on the wall. They paint out a tree here; they paint in a little girl there; they add this; they obliterate that; they make the same painting different and in a sense new, but as I'm sure you can see, not new in the sense of replacing it. The employer enters his living room after dinner, seats himself facing his fireplace, and contemplates what should be – according to his expectations – a new picture. What does he see? It certainly isn't what he saw previously. But also it is somehow . . . and here we must become very sympathetic with this perhaps somewhat stupid man, because we can virtually see his brain circuits striving to understand. His brain circuits are saying, "Yes, it is a new picture, it is not the same one as yesterday, but also it is the same one, I think, I feel on a very deep, intuitive basis . . . I feel that somehow I've seen it before. I seem to remember a tree, though, and there is no tree." Now, perhaps, if we extrapolate from this man's perceptual, mentational confusion to the theoretical point I was making about lateral change, you can get a better idea of what I mean; I mean, perhaps you can, to at least a degree, see that although what I'm talking about may not exist – my concept may be fictional – it could exist. It is not intellectually self-contradictory.

As a science fiction writer I gravitate toward such ideas as this; we in the field, of course, know this idea as the "alternate universe" theme. Some of you, I am sure, know that my novel, **The Man in the High Castle**, utilized this theme. There was in it an alternate world in which Germany and Japan and Italy won World War II. At one point in the novel, Mr. Tagomi, the protagonist, somehow is carried over to our world, in which the Axis powers lost. He remained in our world only a short time, and scuttled in fright back to his own universe as soon as he glimpsed or understood what had happened – and thought no more of it after that; it had been for him a thoroughly unpleasant experience, since, being Japanese, it was for him a worse universe than his customary one. For a Jew, however, it would have been infinitely better – for obvious reasons.

In **The Man in the High Castle**, I give no real explanation as to why or how Mr. Tagomi slid across into our universe; he simply sat in the park and scrutinized a piece of modern abstract handmade jewelry, sat and studied it on and on, and when he looked up, he was in another universe. I didn't explain how or why this happened because I don't know, and I would defy anyone, writer, reader, or critic, to give a so-called "explanation." There cannot be one because, of course, as we all know, such a concept is merely a fictional premise; none of us, in our right minds, entertains for even an instant the notion that such alternate universes exist in any actual sense.

But let us say, just for fun, that they do. Then, if they do, how are they linked to each other, if in fact they are (or would be) linked? If you drew a map of them, showing their locations, what would the map look like? For instance (and I think this is a very important question), are they absolutely separate one from another, or do they overlap? Because if they overlap, then such problems as "Where do they exist?" and "How do you get from one to the next?" admit to a possible solution. I am saying, simply, if they do indeed exist, and if they do indeed overlap, then we may in some literal, very real

The Matrix Control System of Philip K. Dick
And The Paranormal Synchronicities of Timothy Green Beckley

sense inhabit several of them to various degrees at any given time. And although we all see one another as living humans walking about and talking and acting, some of us may inhabit relatively greater amounts of, say, Universe One than the other people do; and some of us may inhabit relatively greater amounts of Universe Two, Track Two, instead, and so on.

It may not merely be that our subjective impressions of the world differ, but there may be an overlapping, a superimposition, of a number of worlds so that objectively, not subjectively, our worlds may differ. Our perceptions differ as a result of this. And I want to add this statement at this point, which I find to be a fascinating concept: It may be that some of these superimposed worlds are passing out of existence, along the lateral time line I spoke of, and some are in the process of moving toward greater, rather than lesser, actualization. These processes would occur simultaneously and not at all in linear time. The kind of process we are talking about here is a transformation, a kind of metamorphosis, invisibly achieved. But very real. And very important.

Contemplating this possibility of a lateral arrangement of worlds, a plurality of overlapping Earths along whose linking axis a person can somehow move – can travel in a mysterious way from worst to fair to good to excellent – contemplating this in theological terms, perhaps we could say that herewith we suddenly decipher the elliptical utterances that Christ expressed regarding the Kingdom of God, specifically where it is located. He seems to have given contradictory and puzzling answers. But suppose, just suppose for an instant, that the cause of the perplexity lay not in any desire on his part to baffle or to hide, but in the inadequacy of the question. "My Kingdom is not of this world," he is reported to have said. "The Kingdom is within you." Or possibly, "It is among you." I put before you now the notion, which I personally find exciting, that he may have had in mind that which I speak of as the lateral axis of overlapping realms that contain among them a spectrum of aspects ranging from the unspeakably malignant to the beautiful. And Christ was saying over and over again that there really are many objective realms, somehow related, and somehow bridgeable by living – not dead – men, and that the most wondrous of these worlds was a just kingdom in which either He Himself or God Himself or both of them ruled. And he did not merely speak of a variety of ways of subjectively viewing one world; the Kingdom was and is an actual different place, at the opposite end of continua starting with slavery and utter pain. It was his mission to teach his disciples the secret of crossing along this orthogonal path. He did not merely report what lay there; He taught the method of getting there. But, tragically, the secret was lost. The enemy, the Roman authority, crushed it. And so we do not have it. But perhaps we can re-find it, since we know that such a secret exists.

This would account for the apparent contradictions regarding the question as to whether the Just Kingdom is ever to be established here on Earth or whether it is a place or state we go to after death. I'm sure I don't have to tell you that this issue has been a fundamental one – and an unresolved one – throughout the history of Christianity. Christ and St. Paul both seem to say emphatically that an actual breaking through into time, into our world, by the hosts of God, will unexpectedly occur. Thereupon, after some exciting drama, a thousand-year paradise, a rightful Kingdom, will be established – at least for those who have done their homework and chores and generally paid attention. . . have not Gone To Sleep, as one parable puts it.

We are enjoined repeatedly in the New Testament to be vigilant, that for the Christian it is always day, there is always light, by which he can see this event when it comes. See this event. Does that imply that many persons who are somehow asleep or blind or not vigilant – that they will not see it, even though it occurs? Consider the significance that can be assigned to these notions. The Kingdom will come here, unexpectedly (this is always stressed); the rightful faithful shall see it, because for them it is always daytime, but for the others ... what seems expressed here is the paradoxical but enthralling thought that – and hear this and ponder – the Kingdom, were it established here, would not be visible to those outside it. I offer the idea that, in more modern terms, what is meant is that some of us will travel laterally to that best world and some will not; they will remain stuck along the lateral axis, which means that for them the Kingdom did not come, not in their alternate world. And yet meantime it did come in ours. So it comes and yet does not come. Amazing.

Parousia

Please ask yourself, What event signals the establishment or reestablishment of the Kingdom? Of course it is nothing other than the Second Advent, the return of the King Himself. Following my reasoning as to the existence of worlds along a lateral axis, one could reason, "Certainly the Second Coming has not taken place – at least not along this Track, in this universe." But then one could speculate, logically, "But perhaps it came exactly as stipulated in the New Testament: during the lifetime of those living then, back in the Apostolic Age." I enjoy – I find fascinating – this concept. What an idea for a novel, an alternate Earth in which the Parousia took place, say, around A.D. 70. Or, say, during the medieval period – say, at the time of the Catherist Crusades. . . how neat an idea for an alternate-world novel! The protagonist somehow is transported from this, our universe, in which the Second Coming did not take place or has not taken place – is transported to one in which it occurred centuries ago.

But if you have followed my conjectures about the overlapping of these alternate worlds, and you sense as I do the possibility that if there are three there may be thirty or three thousand of them – and that some of us live in this one, others of us in another one, others in others, and that events in one track cannot be perceived by persons not in that track – well, let me say what I want to say and be done with it. I think I once experienced a track in which the Savior returned. But I experienced it just very briefly. I am not there now. I am not sure I ever was. Certainly I may never be again. I grieve for that loss, but loss it is; somehow I moved laterally, but then fell back, and then it was gone. A vanished mountain and a stream. The sound of bells. All gone now for me; entirely gone.

I, in my stories and novels, often write about counterfeit worlds, semi-real worlds, as well as deranged private worlds inhabited, often, by just one person, while, meantime, the other characters either remain in their own worlds throughout or are somehow drawn into one of the peculiar ones. This theme occurs in the corpus of my twenty-seven years of writing. At no time did I have a theoretical or conscious explanation for my preoccupation with these pluri-form pseudo-worlds, but now I think I understand. What I was sensing was the manifold of partially actualized realities lying tangent to what evidently is the most actualized one, the one that the majority of us, by consensus gentium [general consent], agree on.

Although originally I presumed that the differences between these worlds was caused entirely by the subjectivity of the various human viewpoints, it did not take me long to open the question as to whether it might not be more than that – that in fact plural realities did exist superimposed onto one another like so many film transparencies. What I still do not grasp, however, is how one reality out of the many becomes actualized in contradistinction to the others. Perhaps none does. Or perhaps again it hangs on an agreement in viewpoint by a sufficiency of people. More likely the matrix world, the one with the true core of being, is determined by the Programmer. He or it articulates – prints out, so to speak – the matrix choice and fuses it with actual substance. The core or essence of reality, that which receives or attains it and to what degree, that is within the purview of the Programmer; this selection and reselection are part of general creativity, of world-building, which seems to be its or his task. A problem, perhaps, which he or it is running, which is to say in the process of solving.

This problem-solving by means of reprogramming variables along the linear time axis of our universe, thereby generating branched-off lateral worlds – I have the impression that the metaphor of the chessboard is especially useful in evaluating how this all can be – in fact must be. Across from the Programmer-Reprogrammer sits a counter-entity, whom Joseph Campbell calls the dark counter-player. God, the Programmer-Reprogrammer, is not making his moves of improvement against inert matter; he is dealing with a cunning opponent. Let us say that on the game board – our universe in space-time – the dark counter-player makes a move; he sets up a reality situation. Being the dark player, the outcome of his desires constitutes what we experience as evil: non-growth, the power of the lie, death and the decay of forms, the prison of immutable cause and effect. But the Programmer-Reprogrammer has already laid down his response; it has already happened, these moves on his part. The printout, which we undergo as historic events, passes through stages of a dialectical interaction, thesis and antithesis as the forces of the two players mingle. Evidently some syntheses fall to the dark counter-player, and yet they do not, by virtue of the fact that,

The Matrix Control System of Philip K. Dick
And The Paranormal Synchronicities of Timothy Green Beckley

in advance, our great Advocate selected variables, the alteration of which brings final victory to him. In winning each sequence in turn he claims some of us, we who participate in the sequence. This is why instinctively people pray, "Libera me Domine," which decodes to mean, "Extricate me, Programmer, as you achieve one victory after another; include me in that triumph. Move me along the lateral axis so that I am not left out." What we sense as "being left out" means remaining under the jurisdiction of, or falling prey to, the malignant power. But that malignant power, for all its guile, has already lost even as it wins, for in some way the counter-player is blind and so the Programmer-Reprogrammer possesses an advantage.

The great medieval Arabic philosopher, Avicenna, wrote that God does not see time as we do; i.e. for him there is no past nor present nor future. Now, supposing Avicenna is correct, let us imagine a situation in which God, from whatever vantage point he exists at, decides to intervene into our space-time world; i.e. break through from his timeless realm into human history. But if there is only omnipresent reality from his viewpoint, then he can as easily break through into what for us is the past as he can break through into what for us is the present or future. It is exactly like a chess player gazing down at the chessboard; he can move any of his pieces that he wishes. Following Avicenna's reasoning, we can say that God, in desiring, for example, to bring about the Second Advent, need not limit the event to our present or future; he can breach our past – in other words, change our past history; he can cause it to have happened already. And this would be true for any change he wished to make, large or small. For instance, suppose an event in our year A.D. 1970 does not meet with God's idea of how it all should go. He can obliterate it or tinker with it, improve it, whatever he wishes, even at a prior point in linear time. This is his advantage.

I submit to you that such alterations, the creation or selection of such so-called "alternate presents," is continually taking place. The very fact that we can conceptually deal with this notion – that is, entertain it as an idea – is a first step in discerning such processes themselves. But I doubt if we will ever be able in any real fashion to demonstrate, to scientifically prove, that such lateral change processes do occur. Probably all we would have to go on would be vestiges of memory, fleeting impressions, dreams, nebulous intuitions that somehow things had been different in some way – and not long ago but now. We might reflexively reach for a light switch in the bathroom only to discover that it was – always had been – in another place entirely. We might reach for the air vent in our car where there was no air vent, a reflex left over from a previous present, still active at a subcortical level. We might dream of people and places we had never seen as vividly as if we had seen them, actually known them.

But we would not know what to make of this, assuming we took time to ponder it at all. One very pronounced impression would probably occur to us, to many of us, again and again, and always without explanation: the acute, absolute sensation that we had done once before what we were just about to do now, that we so to speak lived a particular moment or situation previously. But in what sense could it be called "previously," since only the present, not the past, was evidently involved? We would have the overwhelming impression that we were reliving the present, perhaps in precisely the same way, hearing the same words, saying the same words. . . I submit that these impressions are valid and significant, and I will even say this: Such an impression is a clue that at some past time point a variable was changed, reprogrammed, as it were, and that, because of this, an alternate world branched off, became actualized instead of the prior one, and that in fact, in literal fact, we are once more living this particular segment of linear time. A breaching, a tinkering, a change had been made, but not in our present; it had been made in our past. Evidently such an alteration would have a peculiar effect on those persons involved; they would, so to speak, be moved back one square or several squares on the board game that constitutes our reality. Conceivably this could happen any number of times, affecting any number of people, as alternative variables were reprogrammed. We would have to go live out each reprogramming along the subsequent linear time axis, but to the Programmer, whom we call God – to him the results of the reprogramming would be apparent at once. We are within time and he is not. Thus, too, this might account for the sensation people get of having lived past lives. They may well have, but not in the past; previous lives, rather, in the present. In perhaps an unending repeated and repeated present, like a great clock dial in which grand clock hands sweep out the same circumference forever, with all of us carried along unknowingly, yet dimly suspecting.

Since at the resolution of every encounter of thesis and antithesis between the dark counter-player and the divine Programmer a new synthesis is struck off, and since it is possible that each time this happens a lateral world may be generated, and since I conceive that each synthesis or resolution is to some degree a victory by the Programmer, each struck-off world, in sequence, must be an improvement upon – not just the prior one – but an improvement over all the latent or merely possible outcomes. It is better but in no sense perfect – i.e. final. It is merely an improved stage within a process. What I envision clearly is that the Programmer is perpetually using the antecedent universe as a gigantic stockpile for each new synthesis, the antecedent universe then possessing the aspect of chaos or anomie in relation to an emerging new cosmos. Therefore the endless process of sequential struck-off alternate worlds, emerging and being infused with actualization, is negen-tropic in some way that we cannot see.

In my novel, **UBIK**, I present a motion along a retrograde entropic axis, in terms of Platonic forms rather than any decay or reversion we normally conceive. Perhaps the normal forward motion along this axis, away from entropy, accruing rather than divesting, is identical with the axis line that I characterize as lateral, which is to say, in orthogonal rather than linear time. If this is so, the novel **UBIK** inadvertently contains what could be called a scientific rather than a philosophical idea. But here I am only guessing. Still, the fiction writer may have written more than he consciously knew.

What blinds us to this hierarchy of evolving form in each new synthesis is that we are unaware of the lesser, un-actualized worlds. And this process of interaction, continually forming the new, obliterates at each stage that which came before. What, at any given present instant we possess of the past, is twofold but dubious: We possess external, objective traces of the past embedded in the present, and we possess inner memories. But both are subject to the rule of imperfection, since both are merely bits of reality and not the intact form. What we retain existentially and mentally are therefore inadequate guides. This is implied by the very emergence of true

The Matrix Control System of Philip K. Dick
And The Paranormal Synchronicities of Timothy Green Beckley

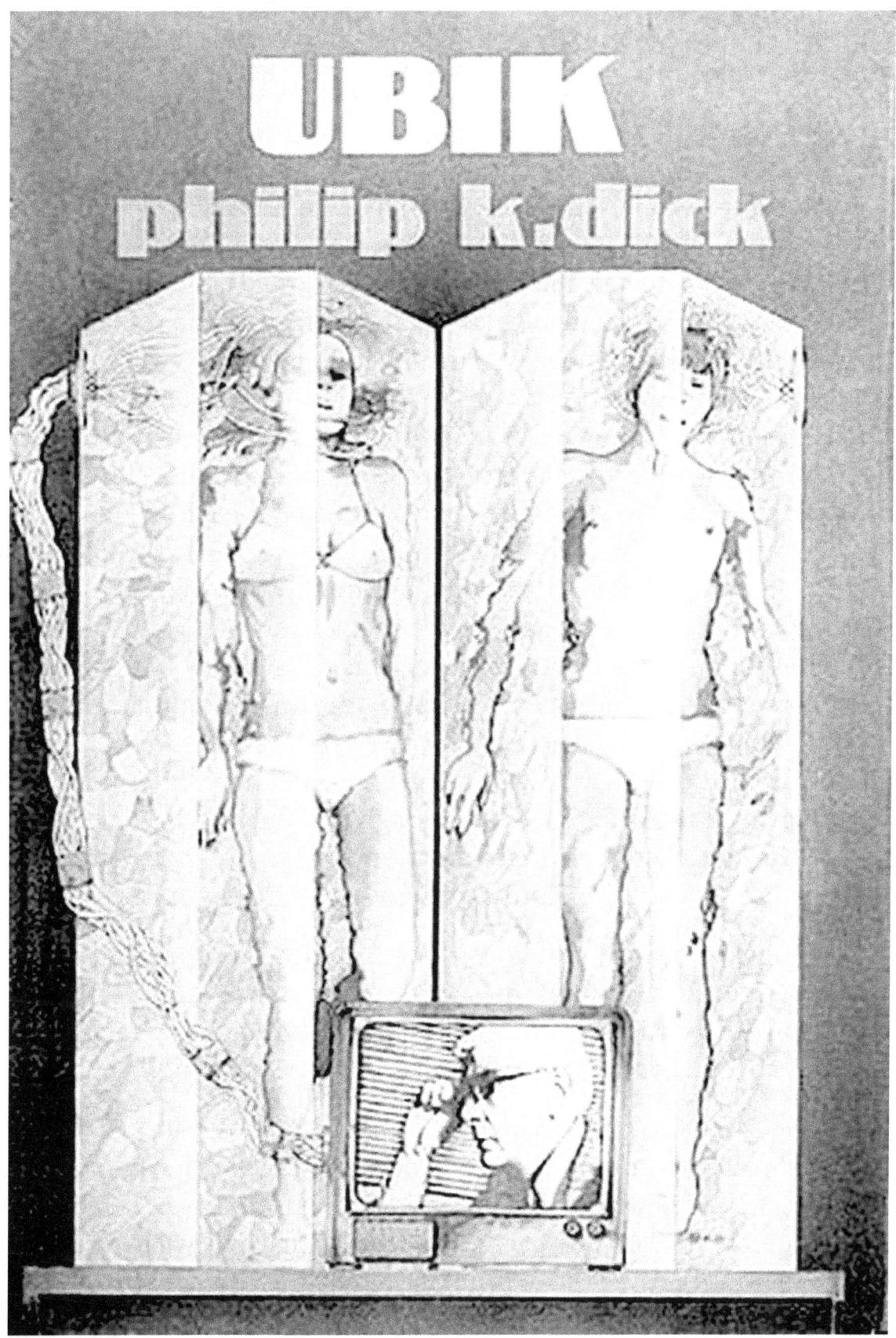

newness itself; if truly new, it must somehow kill the old, the that which was. And, especially, that which did not come to fully be.

What we need at this point is to locate, to bring forth as evidence, someone who has managed somehow – it doesn't matter how, really – to retain memories of a different present, latent alternate world impressions, different in some significant way from this, the one that is at this stage actualized. According to my theoretical view, it would almost certainly be memories of a worse world than this. For it is not reasonable that God the Programmer and Reprogrammer would substitute a worse world in terms of freedom or beauty or love or order or healthiness – by any standard that we know. When a mechanic works on your malfunctioning car, he does not damage it further; when a writer creates a second draft of a novel he does not debase it further but strives to improve it. I suppose it could be argued in a strictly theoretical way that God might be evil or insane and would in fact substitute a worse world for a better one, but frankly I cannot take that idea seriously. Let us then pass over it. So let us ask, does any one of us remember in any dim fashion a worse Earth circa 1977 than this? Have your young men seen visions and our old men dreamed dreams? Nightmare dreams specifically, about a world of enslavement and evil, of prisons and jailers and ubiquitous police? I have. I wrote out those dreams in novel after novel, story after story; to name two in which this prior ugly present obtained most clearly I cite **The Man in the High Castle** and my 1974 novel about the United States as a police state, called **Flow My Tears, the Policeman Said**.

I am going to be very candid with you: I wrote both novels based on fragmentary residual memories of such a horrid slave state world – or perhaps the term "world" is the wrong one, and I should say "United States," since in both novels I was writing about my own country.

In **The Man in the High Castle** there is a novelist, Hawthorne Abendsen, who has written an alternate-world novel in which Germany, Italy, and Japan lost World War II. At the conclusion of **The Man in the High Castle**, a woman appears at Abendsen's door to tell him what he does not know: that his novel is true; the Axis did indeed lose the war. The irony of this ending— Abendsen finding out that what he had supposed to be pure fiction spun out of his imagination was in fact true – the irony is this: that my own supposed imaginative work **The Man in the High Castle** is not fiction – or rather is fiction only now, thank God. But there was an alternate world, a previous present, in which that particular time track actualized – actualized and then was abolished due to intervention at some prior date. I am sure, as you hear me say this, you do not really believe me, or even believe that I believe it myself. But nevertheless it is true. I retain memories of that other world.

That is why you will find it again described in the later novel **Flow My Tears**. The world of **Flow My Tears** is an actual (or rather once actual) alternate world, and I remember it in detail. I do not know who else does. Maybe no one else does. Perhaps all of you were always – have always been – here. But I was not.

In March 1974 I began to remember consciously, rather than merely subconsciously, that black iron prison police state world. Upon consciously remembering it I did not need to write about it because I have always been writing about it. Nonetheless, my amazement was great, to remember consciously suddenly that it was once so, as I'm sure you can imagine. Put yourself in my place. In novel after novel, story after story, over a twenty-five-year period, I wrote repeatedly about a particular other landscape, a dreadful one. In March 1974 I understood why, in my writing, I continually reverted to an awareness, in intimation of, that one particular world. I had good reason to. My novels and stories were, without my realizing it consciously, autobiographical. It was – this return of memory – the most extraordinary experience of my life. Or rather I should say lives, since I had at least two: one there and subsequently one here, where we are now.

I can even tell you what caused me to remember. In late February 1974 I was given sodium pentothal for the extraction of impacted wisdom teeth. Later that day, back home again but still deeply under the influence of the sodium pentothal, I had a short, acute flash of recovered memory. In one instant I caught it all, but immediately rejected it – rejected it, however, with the realization that what I had retrieved in the way of buried memories was authentic. Then, in mid-March, the corpus of memories, whole, intact, began to return. You are free to believe me or free to disbelieve, but please take my word on it that I am not joking; this is very serious, a matter of importance. I am sure that at the very least you will agree that for me even to claim this is in itself amazing. Often people claim to remember past lives; I claim to remember a different, very different, present life. I know of no one who has ever made that claim before, but I rather suspect that my experience is not unique; what perhaps is unique is the fact that I am willing to talk about it.

If you have followed me this far, I would like you to be kindly enough disposed to go a little further with me. I would like to share with you something I knew – retrieved – along with the blocked-off memories. In March 1974 the reprogrammed variables, tinkered with back at some earlier date, probably in the late forties – in March 1974 the payoff, the results, of at least one and possibly more of the reprogrammed variables lying along the linear time line in our past, set in. What happened between March and August 1974 was the result of at least one reprogrammed variable laid down perhaps thirty years before, setting into motion a thread of change that culminated in what I am sure you will admit was a spectacularly important – and unique – historical event: the forced removal from office of a president of the United States, Richard Nixon, as well as all those associated with him. In the alternate world that I remembered, the civil rights movement, the antiwar movement of the sixties, had failed. And, evidently, in the mid-seventies Nixon was not removed from power. That which opposed him (if indeed anything existed that did or could) was inadequate.

Therefore one or more factors tending toward that destruction of the entrenched tyrannical power had retroactively, to us, come to be introduced. The scales, thirty years later, in 1977, got tipped. Examine the text of **Flow My Tears** and, keeping in mind that it was written in 1970 and published in February 1974, make an effort to construct the previous events that would have had to take place, or not take place, to account for the world depicted in the novel as lying slightly in the future. One small but critical theme is alluded to twice (I believe) in **Flow My Tears**. It has to do with Nixon. In the future world of **Flow My Tears**, in the dreadful slave state that exists and evidently has existed for decades, Richard Nixon is remembered as an exalted, heroic leader – referred to, in fact, as the "Second Only Begotten Son of God." It is evident from this and many other clues that ***Flow My Tears*** deals not with our future but the future of a present world alternate to our own. Blacks, by the time ***Flow My Tears*** takes place, have become an ecological rarity, protected "as are wild whooping cranes." In the novel one rarely sees blacks on the streets of the United States. But the year in which ***Flow My Tears*** takes place is only eleven years from now: October 1988. Obviously the fascist genocide against the blacks in the United States in my novel began long before 1977; a number of readers have pointed this out to me. One of them even pointed out that a careful reading of ***Flow My Tears*** not only indicates that the society depicted, the U.S. police state of 1988, had to be an alternate-world novel, but this reader pointed out that mysteriously, at the very end of the novel, the protagonist, Felix Buckman, appears somehow to have slipped over into a different world, one in which blacks were not exterminated.

Early in the novel it is stipulated that a black couple is allowed by law to bear only one single child; yet, at the end of the novel, the black man at the all-night gas station proudly gets out his wallet and shows Police General Buckman photographs of his three children. The open manner in which the black man shows the pictures to a perfect stranger indicates that for some weird and unexplained reason it is now no longer illegal for a black couple to have several children. Somehow, just as Mr. Togomi slipped over briefly into our alternate present, General Buckman in ***Flow My Tears*** did the same thing. It is even evident in the text of Flow My Tears when and where the police general slipped over. It was just before he landed his flying vehicle at the all-night gas station and encountered – hugged, in fact – the black man; the slipover, which is to say the moment in which the absolutely repressive world of the bulk of the novel faded out, took place during the interval in which General Buckman experienced a strange dream about a king-like old man with white wool-like beard, wearing robes and a helmet and leading a posse of similarly helmeted robed knights – this king and these helmeted knights appearing in the rural world of farmhouse and pastureland where General Buckman had lived as a boy. The dream, I think, was a graphic depiction in General Buckman's mind of the transformation taking place objectively; it was a kind of inner analog to what was happening outside him to his entire world.

The Matrix Control System of Philip K. Dick
And The Paranormal Synchronicities of Timothy Green Beckley

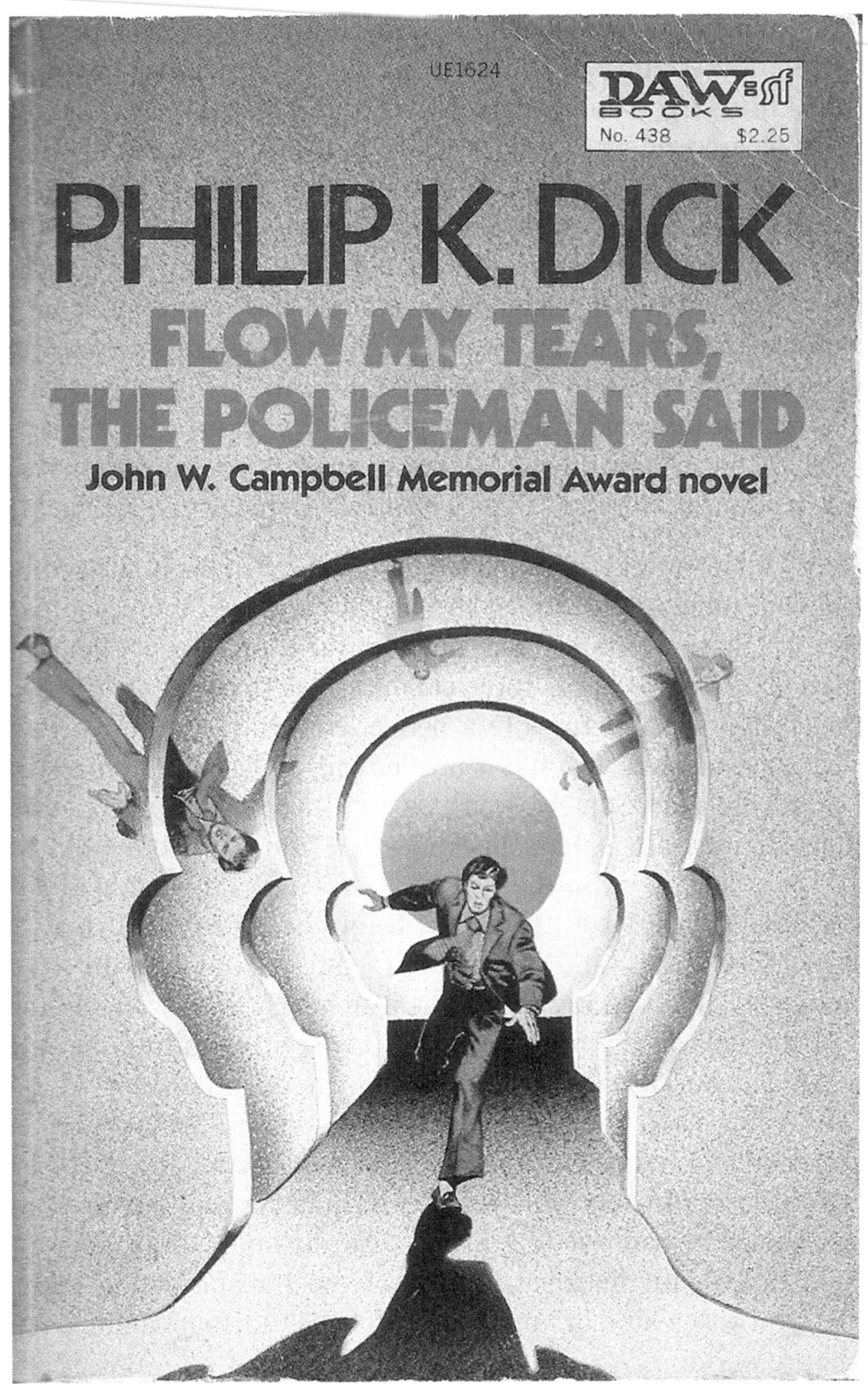

This accounts for the changed Buckman, the very different police general who lands at the all-night gas station and draws the heart with an arrow piercing it, giving the piece of paper with its drawing to the black man as a communication of love. Buckman at the gas station in encountering the black stranger is not the same Buckman who appeared earlier throughout the book: The transformation is complete. But he is unaware of it. Only Jason Taverner, the once-famous television personality who woke up one day to find himself in a world that had never heard of him – only Taverner, when his mysteriously taken-away popularity seeps back, understands that several alternate realities – two upon a cursory reading, but at least three if the ending is studied scrupulously – only Jason Taverner remembers.

This is the whole basic plot of the novel: One morning Jason Taverner, popular TV and recording star, wakes up in a fleabag dingy hotel room to find all his identification papers gone, and, worse yet, finds that no one has ever heard of him – the basic plot is that for some arcane reason the entire population of the United States has in one instant of linear time completely and collectively forgotten a man whose face on the cover of *Time Magazine* should be a face virtually every reader would identify without effort. In this novel I am saying, "The entire population of a large country, a continent-sized country, can wake up one morning having entirely forgotten something they all previously knew, and none of them is the wiser." In the novel it is a popular TV and recording star whom they have forgotten, which is of importance, really, only to that particular star or former star. But my hypothesis is presented here nonetheless in a disguised form, because (I am saying) if an entire country can overnight forget one thing they all know, they can forget other things, more important things; in fact, overwhelmingly important things. I am writing about amnesia on the part of millions of people, of, so to speak, fake memories laid down. This theme of faked memories is a constant thread in my writing over the years. It was also Van Vogt's. And yet, can one contemplate this as a serious possibility, something that could actually happen? Who of us has asked himself that? I did not ask myself that prior to March 1974; I include myself.

You will recall that I pointed out that after Police General Buckman slipped over into a better world he underwent an inner change appropriate to the qualities of the better world, the more just, the more loving, the warmer world in which the tyranny of the police apparatus was already beginning to fade away as would a dream upon the awakening of the dreamer. In March 1974, when I regained my buried memories (a process called in Greek anamnesis, which literally means the loss of forgetfulness rather than merely remembering) – upon those memories reentering consciousness I, like General Buckman, underwent a personality change. Like his, it was fundamental but at the same time subtle. It was me but yet it was not me. I noticed it mostly in small ways: things I should have remembered but did not; things I did remember (ah, what things!) but should not have. Evidently this had been my personality in what I call Track A.

You may be interested in one aspect of my restored memories that strikes me as most astonishing. In the previous alternate present, in Track A, Christianity was illegal, as it had been two thousand years ago at its inception. It was regarded as subversive and revolutionary – and, let me add, this appraisal by the police authorities was correct. It took me almost two weeks, after the return of my memories of my life in Track A, to rid myself of the overpowering impression that all references to Christ, all sacerdotal acts, had to be veiled in absolute secrecy. But historically this fits the pattern of a fascist takeover, especially those along Nazi lines. They did so regard Christianity. And, had they attained a victory in the war, this surely would have been their policy in that portion of the United States that they controlled. For example, Jehovah's Witnesses, under the Nazis, were gassed in the concentration camps along with the Jews and Gypsies; they were placed right up at the top of the list. And, in that other modern totalitarian state, for the same reason it is banned and its members persecuted; I mean, of course, the USSR. The three great tyrannical states in history that have murdered their domestic Christian populations – Rome, the Third Reich, and the USSR – are, from an objective standpoint, three manifestations of a single matrix. Your own personal beliefs about religion are not an issue here; what is an issue is a historic fact, and therefore I ask you to ponder objectively what the overwhelming fear I felt regarding Christian rites and protestations of faith signifies about the Track A society abruptly remembered. It is a decisive clue about Track A. It tells us how radically different it was. I would like you, if you have gone this far, to accept my statements about my other memories that, under the sodium pentothal, returned; it was a prison. It was dreadful; we overthrew it, just as we overthrew the Nixon tyranny, but it was far more cruel, incredibly so, and there was a great battle and loss of life. And, please, let me add one other fact, maybe objectively unimportant but to me interesting nonetheless. It was in February 1974 that my blocked-off memories of Track A returned, and it was in February 1974 that ***Flow My Tears*** was finally, after two years' delay, published. It was almost as if the release of the novel, which had been delayed so long, meant that in a certain sense it was all right for me to remember.

But until then it was better that I did not. Why that would be I do not know, but I have the impression that the memories were not to come to the surface until the material had been published very sincerely on the author's part as what he believed to be fiction. Perhaps, had I known, I would have been too frightened to write the novel. Or perhaps I would have shot my mouth off and somehow interfered with the effectiveness of these several books – whatever effectiveness that might be or was. I do not even claim there was an intended effectiveness; perhaps there was none at all. But if there was one – and I repeat the word "if" emphatically – it was almost certainly to stir subliminal memories in readers back to dim life – not a conscious life, not an entering consciousness as in my own case, but to recall to them on a deep and profound, albeit unconscious level, what a police tyranny is like, and how vital it is, now or then, at any time, along any track, to defeat it.

In March 1974 the really crucial moves to depose Nixon were beginning. In August, five months later, they proved successful, although these re-programmings, this intervention in our present, may have been designed more to affect a future continuum rather than our own. As I said at the beginning, ideas seem to have a life of their own; they appear to seize on people and make use of them. The idea that seized me twenty-seven years ago and never let go is this: Any society in which people meddle in other people's business is not a good society, and a state in which the government "knows more about you than you know about yourself," as it is expressed in ***Flow My Tears***, is a state that must be overthrown. It may be a theocracy, a fascist corporate state, or reactionary monopolistic capitalism or centralistic socialism – that aspect does not matter. And I am saying not merely, "It can happen here," meaning the United States, but rather, "It did happen here. I remember. I was one of the secret Christians who fought it and to at least some extent helped overthrow it."

And I am very proud of that: proud of myself in time Track A. But there is, unfortunately, a somber intimation that accompanies my pride as to my work there. I think that in that previous world I did not live past March 1974. I fell victim to a police trap, a net or mesh. However, in this one, which I will call Track B, I had better luck. But we fought here in this track a much lighter tyranny, a far stupider one. Or, perhaps, we had assistance: The anterior reprogramming of one or more historic variables came to our rescue. Sometimes I think (and this is, of course, pure speculation, a happy fantasy of my soul) that because of what we accomplished there – or anyhow attempted to, and very bravely – we who were directly involved were allowed to live on here, past the terminal point that brought us down in that other, worse world. It is a sort of miraculous kindness.

This gracious gift serves to delineate for us – for me at least – some aspects of the Programmer. It causes me to comprehend him after a fashion. I think we cannot know what he is, but we can experience this functioning and so can ask, "What does he resemble?" Not "What is he?" but rather "What is he like?"

First and foremost, he controls the objects, processes, and events in our space-time world. This is, for us, the primary aspect, although intrinsically he may possess aspects of vaster magnitude but of less applicability to us. I have spoken of myself as a reprogrammed variable, and I have spoken of him as the Programmer and Reprogrammer. During a short period of time in March 1974, at the moment in which I was resynthesized, I was aware perceptually – which is to say aware in an external way – of his presence. At that time I had no idea what I was seeing? [sic; this question mark appears, in context, to be a typo]. It resembled plasmic energy. It had colors. It moved fast, collecting and dispersing. But what it was, what he was – I am not sure even now, except I can tell you that he had simulated normal objects and their processes so as to copy them and in such an artful way as to make himself invisible within them. As the Vedantists put it, he was the fire within the flint, the razor within the razor case. Later research showed me that in terms of group cultural experience, the name Brahman has been given to this omnipresent immanent entity. I quote a fragment of an American poem ["Brahma"] by Emerson; it conveys what I experienced:

> *They reckon ill who leave me out;*
>
> *When me they fly I am the wings.*
>
> *I am the doubter and the doubt,*
>
> *And I the hymn the Brahman sings.*

By this I mean that during that short period – a matter of hours or perhaps a day – I was aware of nothing that was not the Programmer. All the things in our pluri-form world were segments or subsections of him. Some were at rest but many moved, and did so like portions of a breathing organism that inhaled, exhaled, grew, changed, evolved toward some final state that by its absolute wisdom it had chosen for itself. I mean to say, I experienced it as self-creating, dependent on nothing outside it because very simply there was nothing outside it.

As I saw this I felt keenly that through all the years of my life I had been literally blind; I remember saying over and over to my wife, "I've regained my sight! I can see again!" It seemed to me that up until that moment I had been merely guessing as to the nature of the reality around me. I understood that I had not acquired a new faculty of perception but had, rather, regained an old one. For a day or so I saw as we once all had, thousands of years ago. But how had we come to lose sight, this superior eye? The morphology must still be present in us, not only latent; otherwise I could not have reacquired it even briefly.

This puzzles me yet. How was it that for forty-six years I did not truly see but only guessed at the nature of the world, and then briefly did see, but soon after, lost that sight and became semi-blind again? The interval in which I actually saw was, evidently, the interval in which the Programmer was reworking me. He had moved forward as palpably sentient and alive, as set to ground; he had disclosed himself. Thus it is said that Christianity, Judaism, and Islam are revealed religions. Our God is the deus absconditus: the hidden god. But why? Why is it necessary that we be deceived regarding the nature of our reality? Why has he cloaked himself as a plurality of unrelated objects and his movements as a plurality of chance processes? All the changes, all the permutations of reality that we see are expressions of the purposeful growing and unfolding of this single entelechy; it is a plant, a flower, an opening rose. It is a humming hive of bees. It is music, a kind of singing. Obviously I saw the Programmer as he really is, as he really behaves, only because he had seized on me to reshape me, so I say, "I know why I saw him," but I cannot say, "I know why I do not see him now, nor why anyone else does not." Do we collectively dwell in a kind of laser hologram, real creatures in a manufactured quasi-world, a stage set within whose artifacts and creatures a mind moves that is determined to remain unknown?

A newspaper article about this speech could well be titled: AUTHOR CLAIMS TO HAVE SEEN GOD BUT CAN'T GIVE ACCOUNT OF WHAT HE SAW.

If I consider the term by which I designate him – the Programmer and Reprogrammer – perhaps I can extract from that a partial answer. I call him what I call him because that was what I witnessed him doing: He had previously programmed the lives here but now was altering one or more crucial factors, this in the service of completing a structure or plan. I reason along these lines: A human scientist who operates a computer does not bias nor warp, does not prejudice, the outcome of his calculations. A human ethnologist does not allow himself to contaminate his own findings by participating in the culture he studies. Which is to say, in certain kinds of endeavors it is essential that the observer remain occluded off from that which he observes. There is nothing malign in this, no sinister deception. It is merely necessary. If indeed we are, collectively, being moved along desired paths toward a desired outcome, the entity that sets us in motion along those lines, that entity which not only desires the particular outcome but that wills that outcome – he must not enter into it palpably or the outcome will be aborted. What, then, we must turn our attention to is – not the Programmer – but the events programmed. Concealed though the former is, the latter will confront us; we are involved in it – in fact, we are instruments by which it is accomplished.

There is no doubt in my mind as to the larger, historic purpose of the reprogramming that paid off so spectacularly and gloriously in 1974. Currently I am writing a novel about it; the novel is called ***V.A.L.I.S.***, the letters standing for "VAST ACTIVE LIVING INTELLIGENCE SYSTEM." In the novel a government researcher who is very gifted but a little crazy formulates a hypothesis that declares that, located somewhere in our world, there exists a mimicking organism of high intelligence; it so successfully mimics natural objects and processes that humans are routinely unaware of it. When, due to chance or exceptional circumstances, a human does perceive it, he simply calls it "God" and lets it go at that. In my novel, however, the government researcher is determined to treat this vast, intelligent, mimicking entity the way a scientist would treat anything under scrutiny. His problem is, however, that by his own hypothesis he cannot detect the entity – certainly a frustrating experience for him.

But also in my novel I write about another person, unknown to this government researcher; that person has been having unusual experiences for which he has no theory. He has in fact been encountering VALIS, who is in the process of reprogramming him. The two characters possess between them the whole truth: the correct but untestable hypothesis by one, the unexplained experiences by the other. And it is this other man, this nonscientific person, whom I identify with, because he, like me – he is beginning to retrieve blocked-off memories of another world, memories he cannot account for. But he has no theory. None at all.

In the novel I myself appear as a character, under my own name. I am a science fiction writer who has accepted a large advance payment for a yet unwritten novel and who must now come up with that novel before a deadline. I, in the book – I know both these men, Houston Paige, the government researcher with the theory, and Nicholas Brady, who is undergoing the unfathomable experiences. I begin to make use of material from both. My purpose is merely that of meeting my contractual deadline. But, as I continue to write about Houston Paige's theory and Nicholas Brady's experiences, I begin to see that everything fits together. I, in the novel, hold both key and lock, and no one else does.

You can see, I am sure, that it is inevitable, in my novel **VALIS**, that eventually Houston Paige and Nicholas Brady meet. But this meeting has an odd effect on Houston Paige, he with the theory. Paige undergoes a total psychotic breakdown as a result of getting confirmation of his theory. He could imagine it but he cannot believe it. In his head his ingenious theory is dissociated from reality. And this is an intuition which I feel: that many of us believe in VALIS or God or Brahman or the Programmer, but if we ever actually encountered it we could simply not handle it. It would be like a child driven mad by Christmas. He could sustain hoping and waiting, he could pray, he could wish, he could suppose and imagine and even believe; but the actual manifestation – that is too much for our small circuits. And yet the child grows up and there is the man. And those circuits – they grow, too. But to remember a different, discarded world? And to perceive the great planning mind that achieved that abolition, that unthreading of evil?

The Matrix Control System of Philip K. Dick
And The Paranormal Synchronicities of Timothy Green Beckley

One thing I really want you to know: I am aware that the claims I am making — claims of having retrieved buried memories of an alternate present and to have perceived the agency responsible for arranging that alteration — these claims can neither be proved nor can they even be made to sound rational in the usual sense of the word. It has taken me over three years to reach the point where I am willing to tell anyone but my closest friends about my experience beginning back at the vernal equinox of 1974. One of the reasons motivating me to speak about it publicly at last, to openly make this claim, is a recent encounter I have undergone, which, by the way, bears a resemblance to Hawthorne Abendsen's experience in **The Man in the High Castle** with the woman Juliana Frink. Juliana read Abendsen's book about a world in which Germany and Japan and Italy lost World War II and felt she should tell him what she comprehended about the book. This final scene in **The Man in the High Castle** has, I think, been the source for a similar scene in my later story **Faith of Our Fathers**, where the girl Tanya Lee shows up and acquaints the protagonist with the actual reality situation — which is to say, that much of his world is delusional, and purposefully so.

For several years I have had the feeling, a growing feeling, that one day a woman, who would be a complete stranger to me, would contact me, tell me that she had some information to impart to me, would then appear at my door, just as Juliana appeared at Abendsen's door, and would forthwith in the gravest possible way tell me exactly what Juliana told Abendsen — that my book, like his, was in a certain real, literal, and physical sense not fiction but the truth. Precisely that has recently happened to me. I am speaking of a woman who systematically read each and every novel of mine, more than thirty of them, as well as many of my stories. And she did appear; and she was a total stranger; and she did inform me of this fact.

At first she was curious to find out if I myself knew, or if not that, whether I suspected it. The probing between us, the cautious questioning, lasted three weeks. She did not inform me suddenly or immediately, but rather gradually, watching carefully each step of the way, each step along the path of communication and understanding, to see my reaction. It was a solemn matter, really, for her to drive four hundred miles to visit an author whose many books she had read, books of fiction, of the author's imagination, to tell him that there are superimposed worlds in which we live, not one world only, and that she had ascertained that the author in some way was involved with at least one of these worlds, one canceled out at some past time, rewoven and replaced, and – most of all – does the author consciously know this? It was a tense but joyful moment when she reached the point where she could speak candidly; that point did not arrive in our encounter until she was certain that I could handle it. But I had, three years earlier, posited theoretically that if my retrieved memories were authentic, it was only a matter of time before a contact, a cautious, guarded probing by someone would occur, initiated by a person who had read my books and for one reason or another deduced the actual situation – I mean, knew what the significant information was that the books and stories carried.

She knew, from my novels and stories, which world I had experienced, which of the many; what she could not determine until I told her was that, in February 1975, I had passed across into a third alternate present – Track C, we shall call it – and this one was a garden or park of peace and beauty, a world superior to ours, rising into existence. I could then speak to her of three rather than two worlds: the black iron prison world that had been; our intermediate world in which oppression and war exist but have to a great degree been cast down; and then a third alternate world that someday, when the correct variables in our past have been reprogrammed, will materialize as a superimposition onto this one. . . and within which, as we awaken to it, we shall suppose we had always lived there, the memory of this intermediate one, like that of the black iron prison world, eradicated mercifully from our memories.

There may be other persons like this woman who have deduced from evidence internal to my writing, as well as from their own vestigial memories, that the landscape I portray as fictional is or was somehow literally real, and that if a grimmer reality could have once occupied the space that our world occupies, it stands to reason that the process of reweaving need not end here; this is not the best of all possible worlds, just as it is not the worst. This woman told me nothing that I did not already know, except that by independently arriving at the same conclusion she gave me the courage to speak out, to tell this but at the same time knowing as I do so that in no way –

none that I know of, at least – can this presentation be verified. The best I can do, rather than that, is to play the role of prophet, of ancient prophets and such oracles as the sibyl at Delphi, and to talk of a wonderful garden world, much like that which once our ancestors are said to have inhabited – in fact, I sometimes imagine it to be exactly that same world restored, as if a false trajectory of our world will eventually be fully corrected and once more we will be where once, many thousands of years ago, we lived and were happy.

During the brief time I walked about in it I had the strong impression that it was our legitimate home that somehow we had lost. The time I spent there was short – about six hours of real elapsed time. But I remember it well. In the novel I wrote with Roger Zelazny, **Deus Irae**, I describe it toward the end, at the point where the curse is lifted from the world by the death and transfiguration of the God of Wrath. What was most amazing to me about this parklike world, this Track C, was the non-Christian elements forming the basis of it; it was not what my Christian training had prepared me for at all. Even when it began to phase out I still saw sky; I saw land and dark blue smooth water, and standing by the edge of the water a beautiful nude woman whom I recognized as Aphrodite.

At that point this other better world had diminished to a mere landscape beyond a Golden Rectangle doorway; the outline of the doorway pulsed with laser-like light and it all grew smaller and was at last alas gone from sight, the 3:5 doorway devouring itself into nothingness, sealing off what lay beyond. I have not seen it since, but I had the firm impression that this was the next world – not of the Christians – but the Arcady of the Greco-Roman pagan world, something older and more beautiful than that which my own religion can conjure up as a lure to keep us in a state of dutiful morality and faith. What I saw was very old and very lovely. Sky, sea, land, and the beautiful woman, and then nothing, for the door had shut and I was closed off back here.

It was with a bitter sense of loss that I saw it go – saw her go, really, since it all constellated about her. Aphrodite, I discovered when I looked in my Britannica to see what I could learn about her, was not only the goddess of erotic love and aesthetic beauty but also the embodiment of the generative force of life itself; nor was she originally Greek: In the beginning she had been a Semitic deity, later taken over by the Greeks, who knew a good thing when they saw it. During those treasured hours what I saw in her was a loveliness that our own religion, Christianity, at least by comparison, lacks: an incredible symmetry, the palintonos harmonie that Heraclitus wrote of: the perfect tension and balance of forces within the strung lyre that bowed by its stretched strings but that appears perfectly at rest, perfectly at peace. Yet, the strung lyre is a balanced dynamism, immobile only because the tensions within it are in absolute proportion.

This is the quality of the Greek formulation of beauty: perfection that is dynamic within yet at apparent rest without. Against this palintonos harmonie the universe plays out the other aesthetic principle incorporated in the Grecian lyre: the palintropos harmonie, which is the back-and-forth oscillation of the strings as they are played. I did not see her like this, and perhaps this, the continual oscillation back and forth, is the deeper, greater rhythm of the universe things coming into existence and then passing away; change rather than a static durability. But for a little while I had seen perfect peace, perfect rest, a past we have lost but a past returning to us as if by means of a long-term oscillation, to be available as our future, in which all lost things shall be restored.

There is a fascinating passage in the Old Testament in which God says, "For I am fashioning a new heaven and a new earth, and the memory of the former things will not enter the mind nor come up into the heart." When I read this I think to myself: I believe I know a great secret. When the work of restoration is completed, we will not even remember the tyrannies, the cruel barbarisms of the Earth we inhabited; "not entering the mind" means we will mercifully forget, and "not coming up into the heart" means that the vast body of pain and grief and loss and disappointment within us will be expunged as if it had never been. I believe that process is taking place now, has always been taking place now. And, mercifully, we are already being permitted to forget that which formerly was. And perhaps in my novels and stories I have done wrong to urge you to remember.

SANTA ANA, 1977 - CALIFORNIA, U.S.A.

26.

NOVELS BY PHILIP K. DICK
Compiled by Tim R. Swartz

Solar Lottery (1955)

The year is 2203, and the ruler of the Universe is chosen according to the random laws of a strange game under the control of Quizmaster Verrick. But when Ted Bentley, a research technician recently dismissed from his job, signs on to work for Verrick, he has no idea that Leon Cartwright is about to become the new Quizmaster. Nor does he know that he's about to play an integral part in the plot to assassinate Cartwright so that Verrick can resume leadership of a universe not nearly as random as it appears.

The Man Who Japed (1956)

Newer York is a post-holocaust city governed by the laws of an oppressively rigid morality. Highly mobile and miniature robots monitor the behavior of every citizen, and the slightest transgression can spell personal doom. This is a society so eager for order that it will sacrifice anything, including its freedom. Allen Purcell is one of the few people who have the capacity to literally change the way of the world, and once he's offered a high-profile job that acts as guardian of public ethics, he sets out to do precisely that. But first he must deal with the head in his closet.

The World Jones Made (1956)

Floyd Jones is sullen, ungainly and quite possibly mad, but he really can see exactly one year into the future. And this talent means that in a very short time he rises from being a disgruntled carnival fortune-teller to convulse an entire planet. Jones becomes a demagogue, whipping up the ideal-starved population into a frenzy against the threat of the "drifters," enormous single-cell protoplasms that may be landing on Earth soon. But, in a world of engineered mutants, hermaphrodite sex performers in drug-fuelled nightclubs, Jones is a tragic messiah. His limited precognition renders him helpless because he cannot bring himself to fight against what he knows will happen.

The Cosmic Puppets (1957)

As Ted Barton is driving through Baltimore, on vacation with his wife, he is seized with an irresistible urge to head into the Appalachian Mountains and visit the town where he was born. When Barton finds his way to Millgate, the town where he grew up, he is in for a deep shock. Street names and landmarks do not exist as he remembers them, and the inhabitants of the town are similarly oblivious to their contradictory past. His wife proves intolerant of her husband's interest and abandons him while he explores the town. Ted Barton discovers that Millgate has become the center of a supernatural war between two demigods and it is up to Ted, and the few remaining town members who remember their forgotten past, to restore order before it is too late.

Eye in the Sky (1957)

What begins as an ordinary laboratory visit turns into a bizarre and apocalyptic experience when a particle-light beam slices across the visitors' paths, plunging them into different worlds constructed from their innermost dreams and fears. In succession, the group moves through solipsistic personalized alternate realities related to their beliefs and opinions. As emergency works scramble to free them from the wreckage, their minds begin an incredible journey through one fantastic shared world after another.

Time Out of Joint (1959)

Ragle Gumm lives in a quiet little community where he is the world's long-standing champion of newspaper puzzle contests. It is only after a series of troubling hallucinations that he begins to suspect otherwise. It starts with what he thinks are hallucinations, a soft drink stand that disappears, leaving in its place a piece of paper labeled *SOFT DRINK STAND*. Then he hears pilots talking about him over the radio and he finds a phonebook from a place that doesn't seem to exist. And now, after his brother-in-law starts to notice the signs as well, they decide to skip town. However, it seems that the town doesn't want them to leave. There's always something in the way, a cop, a flat tire, a line at the bus depot that never ends. Ragle Gumm seems to be the center of the universe, a universe that is now going terribly awry.

Dr. Futurity (1960)

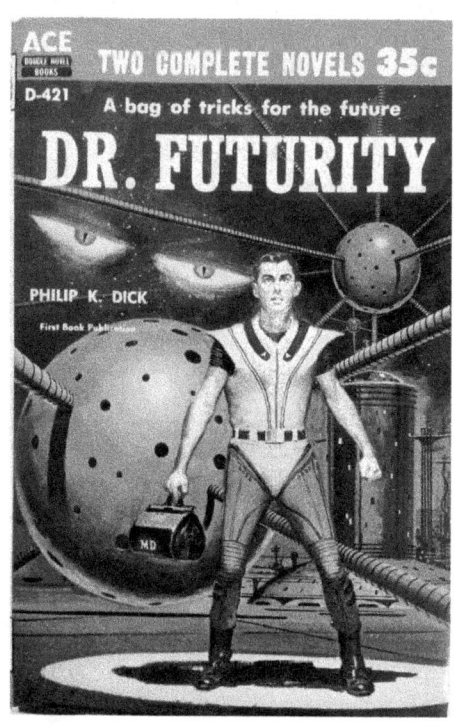

Jim Parsons is a talented doctor, skilled at the most advanced medical techniques and dedicated to saving lives. But after a bizarre road accident leaves him hundreds of years in the future, Parsons is horrified to discover an incredibly advanced civilization that zealously embraces death. Now, he is caught between his own instincts and training as a healer and a society where it is illegal to save lives. But Parsons is not the only one left who believes in prolonging life, and those who share his beliefs have desperate plans for Dr. Parsons' skills, and for the future of their society.

Vulcan's Hammer (1960)

In the year 2029, the world is run by the Unity organization. Humans are controlled from childhood education onwards through the Vulcan series of artificial intelligences. Objective, unbiased and hyperrational, the Vulcan 3 should have been the perfect ruler. The omnipotent computer dictates policy that is in the best interests of all citizens…or at least, that is the idea. But when the machine, whose rule evolved out of chaos and war, begins to lose control of the "Healer" movement of religious fanatics and the mysterious force behind their rebellion, all Hell breaks loose. William Barrios, the morally conflicted hero, may be the only person who can prevent the battle for control from destroying the world…if he can decide which side he's on.

The Man in the High Castle (1962)

It is 1962 and the Second World War has been over for seventeen years: people have now had a chance to adjust to the new order. But it's not been easy. The Mediterranean has been drained to make farmland, the population of Africa has virtually been wiped out and America has been divided between the Nazis and the Japanese. In the neutral buffer zone that divides the two superpowers lives the man in the high castle, the author of an underground bestseller, a work of fiction that offers an alternative theory of world history in which the Axis powers didn't win the war.

The Man in the High Castle has been made into a television series seen on Amazon Prime.

The Game-Players of Titan (1963)

Roaming the pristine landscape of Earth, cared for by machines and aliens, the few remaining humans alive since the war with Titan play Bluff, allowing them to win or lose property and also form new marriages in order to maximize the remote chance some pairings will produce a child. When Pete Garden, a particularly suicidal member of the Pretty Blue Fox game-playing group, loses his current wife and his deed to Berkeley, he stumbles upon a far bigger, more sinister version of the game. The telepathic, slug-like Vugs of Titan are the players and at stake is the Earth itself. The Game-Players of Titan is a brilliantly conceived vision of a future dystopia, full of imaginative detail, moments of pure humor and thought-provoking musings on the nature of perception, as the seemingly straightforward narrative soon turns into a tumultuous nightmare of delusion, precognition and conspiracy.

Clans of the Alphane Moon (1964)

When CIA agent Chuck Rittersdorf and his psychiatrist wife, Mary, file for divorce, they have no idea that in a few weeks they'll be shooting it out on Alpha III M2, the distant moon ruled by various psychotics liberated from a mental ward. Nor do they suspect that Chuck's new employer, the famous TV comedian Bunny Hentman, will also be there aiming his own laser gun. How things came to such a darkly hilarious pass is the subject of Clans of the Alphane Moon, an astutely shrewd and acerbic tale that blurs all conventional distinctions between sanity and madness.

Martian Time-Slip (1964)

On the arid colony of Mars the only thing more precious than water may be a ten-year-old schizophrenic boy named Manfred Steiner. For although the UN has slated "anomalous" children for deportation and destruction, other people...especially

Supreme Goodmember Arnie Kott of the Water Worker's union, suspect that Manfred's disorder may be a window into the future. Who would have thought that power politics, extraterrestrial real estate scams, adultery, and murder could come into play on Mars to penetrate the mysteries of time and reality?

The Penultimate Truth (1964)

World War III is raging - or so the millions of people crammed in their underground tanks believe. For fifteen years, subterranean humanity has been fed on daily broadcasts of a never-ending nuclear destruction, sustained by a belief in the all powerful Protector. But up on Earth's surface, a different kind of reality reigns. East and West are at peace. Across the planet, an elite corps of expert hoaxers preserves the lie.

The Simulacra (1964)

Set in the middle of the twenty-first century, The Simulacra is the story of an America where the whole government is a fraud and the President is an android. Against this backdrop Dr. Superb, the sole remaining psychotherapist, is struggling to practice in a world full of the maladjusted. Ian Duncan is desperately in love with the first lady, Nicole Thibideaux, who he has never met. Richard Kongrosian refuses to see anyone because he is convinced his body odor is lethal. And the fascistic Bertold Goltz is trying to overthrow the government. As the events play out, it seems as if there is always another layer of conspiracy beneath the ones that are seen.

Dr. Bloodmoney, or How We Got Along After the Bomb (1965)

Seven years after the day of the bombs, Point Reyes was luckier than most places. Its people were reasonably normal, except for the girl with her twin brother growing inside her, and talking to her. Their barter economy was working. Their resident genius could fix almost anything that broke down. However, they didn't know they were harboring the one man who almost everyone left alive wanted killed?

The Three Stigmata of Palmer Eldritch (1965)

On Mars, the harsh climate could make any colonist turn to drugs to escape a dead-end existence. Especially when the drug is Can-D, which transports its users into the idyllic world of a Barbie-esque character named Perky Pat. When the mysterious Palmer Eldritch arrives with a new drug called Chew-Z, he offers a more addictive experience, one that might bring the user closer to God. But in a world where everyone is tripping, no promises can be taken at face value.

The Crack in Space (1966)

It's the year 2080, and Earth's seemingly insurmountable overpopulation problem has been alleviated temporarily by placing millions of people in voluntary deep freeze. But in election year, the pressure is on to find a solution which will enable them to resume their lives. For Jim Briskin, Presidential candidate, it seems an insoluble problem until a flaw in the new instantaneous travel system opens up the possibility of finding whole new worlds to colonize.

Now Wait for Last Year (1966)

First, Gino Molinari was assassinated by a political Rival. Then he died of a heart attack. But now he is back, younger and more vigorous than ever, giving Earth new hope of survival in the war against the alien reegs. But is this really Molinari, or a robant masquerading as Earth's overlord? Whatever the truth, only he can save the Solar System, if he can stay alive long enough, or at least not stay dead for too long.

The Unteleported Man (1966)

Whale's Mouth was a planetary utopia for forty million Earth colonists - but none ever returned. It took only 15 minutes to get there by instant teleportation, but it was strictly a one-way journey. If you wanted to return, it was always possible to go the long way round, 18 years each way by conventional spacecraft. No one relished that, of course. Then one man decided to try it, and encountered some very powerful opposition. Originally published as a short story in 1964.

Counter-Clock World (1967)

The world has entered the Hobart Phase—a vast sidereal process in which time moves in reverse. As a result, libraries are busy eradicating books, copulation signifies the end of pregnancy, people greet with, "Good-bye," and part with, "Hello," and underneath the world's tombstones, the dead are coming back to life. One imminent old-born is Anarch Peak, a vibrant religious leader whose followers continued to flourish long after his death. His return from the dead has such awesome implications that those who apprehend him will very likely be those who control the fate of the world.

The Ganymede Takeover (with Ray Nelson) (1967)

In the 21st century Earth has been conquered by the Ganymedians, limbless, worm-like creatures whose physical needs are attended to by a slave-race of specialist "creeches." Mekkis is the leader of a Ganymedean faction that opposed the war when his Oracle (a creature capable of precognition) foresaw a "coming darkness." The apparent success of the invasion means he is now discredited. As a result, Mekkis is saddled with the Bale of Tennessee, home to the last remaining core of resistance on Earth. However, controlling Earth turns out to be more troublesome than the Ganymedians anticipated. Judging their proxy rule of Earth to be impractical, they decide to withdraw from the planet and destroy all life through a device that will block the sun's rays.

The Zap Gun (1967)

Lars Powderdry and Lilo Topchev are counterpart weapons fashion designers for a world divided into two factions—Wes-bloc and Peep-East. Since the Plowshare Protocols of 2002, their job has been to invent elaborate weapons that only seem massively lethal. But when alien satellites hostile to both sides appear in the sky, the two are brought together in the dire hope that they can create a weapon to save the world, a task made all the more difficult by Lars falling in love with Lilo even as he knows she's trying to kill him. The novel was expanded from his novella **Project Plowshare**, which was first published as a two-part serial in the November, 1965, and January, 1966, issues of *Worlds of Tomorrow* magazine.

Do Androids Dream of Electric Sheep? (1968)

By 2021, the World War had killed millions, driving entire species into extinction and sending mankind off-planet. Those who remained coveted any living creature, and for people who couldn't afford one, companies built incredibly realistic simulacrae: horses, birds, cats, sheep. . . . They even built humans. Emigrees to Mars received androids so sophisticated it was impossible to tell them from true men or women. Fearful of the havoc these artificial humans could wreak, the government banned them from Earth. But when androids didn't want to be identified, they just blended in. Rick Deckard was an officially sanctioned bounty hunter whose job was to find rogue androids and retire them. But cornered, androids tended to fight back, with deadly results.

Galactic Pot-Healer (1969)

The Glimmung wants Joe Fernwright. Fernwright is a pot-healer - a repairer of ceramics - in a drably utilitarian future where such skills have little value. The Glimmung is a being that looks something like a gyroscope, something like a teenage girl, and something like the contents of an ocean. What's more, it may be divine. And, like certain gods of old Earth, it has a bad temper. Why would an omnipotent entity want with a humble pot-healer? Or with the dozens of other odd creatures it has lured to Plowman's Planet?

Ubik (1969)

Glen Runciter is dead. Or is he? Someone died in the explosion orchestrated by his business rivals, but even as his funeral is scheduled, his mourning employees are receiving bewildering messages from their boss. Joe Chip and his colleagues start experiencing strange slips in time as the world around them seems to be decaying. With the help of others in the same dire straits, Joe Chip discovers Ubik, an aerosol spray that seems to counter the mystifying time-regression. The question remains though, is the world around Joe and his friends actual reality, or have they become imprisoned in a half-life where time is quickly running out?

A Maze of Death (1970)

Delmak-O is a dangerous planet. Though there are only fourteen citizens, no one can trust anyone else and death can strike at any moment. The planet is vast and largely unexplored, populated mostly by gelatinous cube-shaped beings that give cryptic advise in the form of anagrams. Deities can be spoken to directly via a series of prayer amplifiers and transmitters, but they may not be happy about it. And the mysterious building in the distance draws all the colonists to it, but when they get there each sees a different motto on the front. It seems as if on Delmak-O, God is either absent or intent on destroying His creations.

Our Friends from Frolix 8 (1970)

Nick Appleton is a menial laborer whose life is a series of endless frustrations. Willis Gram is the despotic oligarch of a planet ruled by big-brained elites. When they both fall in love with Charlotte Boyer, a feisty black marketer of revolutionary propaganda, Nick seems destined for doom. But everything takes a decidedly unpredictable turn when the revolution's leader, Thors Provoni, returns from ten years of intergalactic hiding with a ninety-ton protoplasmic slime that is bent on creating a new world order. Is this mysterious and intelligent slime friendly, or is its true purpose a terrifying doom for all of humanity?

We Can Build You (1972)

Louis Rosen and his partners sell people, ingeniously designed, historically authentic simulacra of personages such as Edwin M. Stanton and Abraham Lincoln. The problem is that the only prospective buyer is a rapacious billionaire whose plans for the simulacra could land Louis in jail. Then there's the added complication that someone...or something...like Abraham Lincoln may not want to be sold. Is an electronic Lincoln any less alive than his creators?

Flow My Tears, The Policeman Said (1974)

Jason Taverner is a Six, the result of top secret government experiments forty years before which produced a handful of unnaturally bright and beautiful people - and he's the prime-time idol of millions until, inexplicably, all record of him is wiped from the data banks of Earth. Suddenly he's a nobody in a police state where nobody is allowed to be a nobody. Will he ever be rich and famous again? Was he, in fact, ever rich and famous?

Confessions of a Crap Artist (1975)

Jack Isidore is a socially awkward, obsessive compulsive tire regroover who has been consumed with amateur scientific inquiry since his teens. He catalogs old science magazines, collects worthless objects, and believes disproved theories, such as the notions that the Earth is hollow or that sunlight has weight. Broke, Jack eventually moves in with his sister's family in a luxurious farm house in rural West Marin County, California. On the farm, Jack happily does housework and cares for livestock. He also joins a small apocalyptic religious group, which shares his belief in ESP, UFOs and believes the world will end on April 23, 1959. However, most of his time is dedicated to a meticulous "scientific journal" of life on the farm, including his sister's marital difficulties. Jack soon finds himself in the middle of a maelstrom of suburban angst from which he might not be able to escape.

Originally written in 1959, this is the only non-science fiction book of Dick's published during his lifetime.

Deus Irae (with Roger Zelazny) (1976)

In the years following World War III, a new and powerful faith has arisen from a scorched and poisoned Earth, a faith that embraces the architect of worldwide devastation. The Servants of Wrath have deified Carlton Lufteufel and re-christened him the Deus Irae. In the small community of Charlottesville, Utah, Tibor McMasters, born without arms or legs, has, through an array of prostheses, established a far-reaching reputation as an inspired painter. When the new church commissions a grand mural depicting the Deus Irae, it falls upon Tibor to make a treacherous journey to find the man, to find the god, and capture his terrible visage for posterity.

A Scanner Darkly (1977)

Substance D, otherwise known as Death, is the most dangerous drug ever to find its way on to the black market. It destroys the links between the brain's two hemispheres, leading first to disorientation and then to complete and irreversible brain damage. Bob Arctor, undercover narcotics agent, is trying to find a lead to the source of supply, but to pass as an addict he must become a user, and soon, without knowing what is happening to him, he is as dependent as any of the addicts he is monitoring.

VALIS (1981)

This disorienting book is about a schizophrenic hero named Horselover Fat; the hidden mysteries of Gnostic Christianity; and reality as revealed through a pink laser. Horselover Fat believes his visions expose hidden facts about the reality of life on Earth, and a group of others join him in researching these matters. One of their theories is that there is some kind of alien space probe in orbit around Earth, and that it is aiding them in their quest. It also aided the United States in disclosing the Watergate scandal and the resignation of Richard Nixon in 1974. There is a filmed account of an alternative universe Nixon, "Ferris Fremont" and his fall, engineered by a fictionalized Valis, which leads them to an estate owned by the Lamptons, popular musicians. Valis (the fictional film) contains obvious references to identical revelations to those that Horselover Fat has experienced. They decide the goal that they have been led toward is Sophia, who is two years old and the Messiah or incarnation of Holy Wisdom anticipated by some variants of Gnostic Christianity. She tells them that their conclusions are correct, but dies after a laser accident. Undeterred, Fat goes on a global search for the next incarnation of Sophia.

The Divine Invasion (1981)

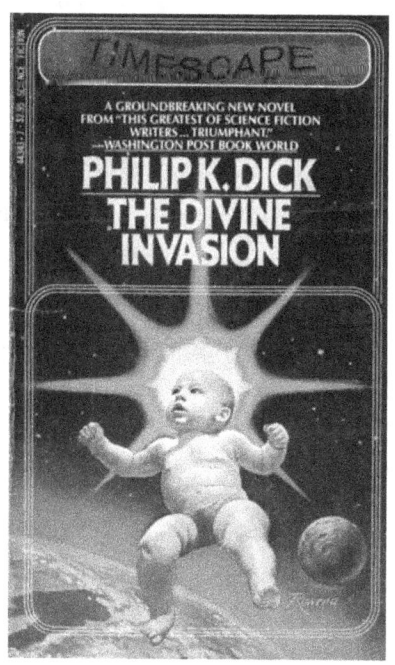

After the fall of Masada in 74 AD, God, or "Yah" is exiled from Earth and forced to take refuge in the CY30-CY30B star system. Meanwhile, the people of Earth are ruled by Belial, the spirit of darkness, but Yah is intent on reclaiming his creation. Rybys Romney and Herb Asher are two colonists inhabiting a planet in the CY30-CY30B star system. They live in separate domes and Herb is called upon by Yah to go help the ailing Rybys who is pregnant with Yah's child. The two must smuggle the unborn child back to Earth where it will confront the evil god Belial, who has corrupted the purity of the planet and its inhabitants. A few key figures in his reality know of the importance of this blessed child and they present to Herb piece by piece the nature of the eternal conflict.

This novel was originally conceived as a sequel to **VALIS** and was originally titled, **Valis Regained**.

The Transmigration of Timothy Archer (1982)

Loosely based on the story of Bishop James Pike, The Transmigration of Timothy Archer tells the story of Episcopal Bishop Timothy Archer, who must cope with the theological and philosophical implications of the newly discovered Gnostic Zadokite scroll fragments. This book has been included in several omnibus editions of the **Valis** trilogy as a stand-in for the unwritten final volume (**The Owl in Daylight**). Transmigration was not intended by Dick to be part of the trilogy; however, the book fits comfortably with the two finished volumes and Dick himself called the three novels a trilogy, saying "the three do form a trilogy constellating around a basic theme."

Written in 1981, this was Dick's final novel that was published shortly after his death in March 1982. The book was originally titled **Bishop Timothy Archer**.

The Owl in Daylight (Unfinished Book)

The Owl in Daylight was being written by Dick at the time of his death in 1982. He had already been paid an advance for the book by the publisher and was working against a deadline. After his death, the Philip K. Dick estate approached other writers about the possibility of someone completing the novel based on his notes, but this proved to be impossible as he had never formally outlined the story. The plot of the proposed book supposedly revolves around an amusement park owner who creates a super-intelligent computer, only to find himself trapped by the machine and forced to solve its puzzles in order to escape. In a letter to his agent, Dick cited other, more highbrow influences: **Dante's Commedia** and Goethe's **Faust**. And just weeks before his death, in an interview with Gwen Lee and Doris Elaine Sauter, Dick sketched out another plot for The **Owl in Daylight**, this one about a struggling music composer who gets a "bio-chip" implanted in his brain.

"The owl in daylight" is a phrase Dick heard on television. It means "not to understand", or "to be blind".

Books Published Posthumously

The Man Whose Teeth Were All Exactly Alike (1984)

Sometime between 1958 and 1962, Leo Runcible, a Liberal Jew, is working in the real estate field. On learning that Walt Dombrosio, Leo's neighbor, has had a Black visitor to his house in a "lily-white" suburb of Marin County, California, potential purchasers interrogate Runcible about the matter and ultimately incur his wrath over their narrow-minded bigotry. He thereby fails to close the deal and forfeits their friendship and a precious commission as well.

At the same time, Runcible has found what he believes to be Neanderthal remains in Carquinez, Marin County, and envisages rising property prices due to incipient archaeological interest and the avalanche of media coverage that naturally follows. As it turns out, however, Dombrosio is the culprit who modified and planted the modern human remains there to begin with. They are a legacy of the local 'chuppers' who developed facial, cranial and spinal deformations as a supposed result of the pollution of the local water supply.

The Man Whose Teeth Were All Exactly Alike was originally completed in 1960 and was initially rejected by potential publishers. It was posthumously published by a small press in 1984, two years after Dick's death.

Radio Free Albemuth (1985)

Written in 1976 and published posthumously in 1985. Originally titled **VALISystem A**, it was Dick's first attempt to deal in fiction with his strange experiences of early 1974. When his publishers at Bantam requested extensive rewrites he canned the project and reworked it into the **VALIS** trilogy. The book recounts the friendship of two California men, Nicholas Brady, a record store clerk and later a record company executive, and Philip K. Dick, a writer.

During the several decades spanned by the novel, America slides into fascism, particularly under the presidency of Ferris F. Fremont, who comes into office in 1969. Once entrenched, Fremont begins tossing dissidents into camps and in some cases executing them. Brady, meanwhile, has been receiving narrow-beam radio transmissions from a mysterious, alien, near-Earth satellite named VALIS. VALIS guides Brady in the secrets of the universe, in the conduct of his life, and in a plot to bring down the monstrous Fremont, a cause to which Brady is finally martyred.

In Milton Lumky Territory (1985)

Milton Lumky territory is both an area of the western USA and a psychic terrain: the world and world-view of the traveling salesman. The story takes place in Boise, Idaho, with some extraordinary long-distance driving sequences in which our hero (young Bruce Stevens) drives from Boise to San Francisco, to Reno, to Pocatello, to Seattle, and back to Boise in search of a good deal on some wholesale typewriters. He falls under the spell of an attractive older woman (who used to be his school teacher) and Milton Lumky, a middle-aged paper salesman whose territory is the Northwest. And then Bruce and the others slowly sink into the whirlpool of his immature personal obsessions and misperceptions.

Puttering About in a Small Land (1985)

Written sometime in 1957, this book remained unpublished until it was released posthumously in 1985.

Set in the 1950s, Roger and Virginia Lindahl are a generally unhappy couple living in Los Angeles. Roger, 30-ish, intense, very competent but also very insecure; he is married to Virginia, a cool, intelligent, distant woman. The Lindahls meet Chic and Liz Bonner, and as a friendship between the couples develops, Roger finds himself attracted to Liz. The two stumble into an absurd affair, and when Virginia discovers what has happened, she blackmails her husband out of his business and what is left of his self-respect.

Humpty Dumpty in Oakland (1986)

Set in the San Francisco Bay area in the late 1950s, Humpty Dumpty in Oakland is a tragicomedy of misunderstandings among used car dealers and real-estate salesmen. Jim Fergesson, an elderly garage owner with a heart condition, is about to sell up and retire; Al Miller is a somewhat feckless mechanic who sublets part of Jim's lot and finds his livelihood threatened by the decision to sell; Chris Harman is a record company owner who for years has relied on Fergesson to maintain his cars. When Harman hears of Fergesson's impending retirement he tips him off to what he says is a cast-iron business proposition: a development in nearby Marin County with an opening for a garage. Al Miller, though, is convinced that Harman is a crook, out to fleece Fergesson of his life's savings.
As much as he resents Fergesson, he can't bear to see that happen and, denying to himself all the time what he is doing, he sets out to thwart Harman.

Mary and the Giant (1987)

Twenty-year old Mary Anne Reynolds lives in Pacific Park, California, and is looking for love. The time is 1953. Seeking a "giant" of a man to make her life right, Mary has brief affairs with a black blues singer and the middle-aged owner of a classical music record store. Mary knows that she "wants out" of Pacific Park, but she doesn't know much more. This slice-of-life novel, a classic tale of 1950s frustration, has considerable literary merit both for characterization and the vividness of its setting.

The Broken Bubble (1988)

Set in mid-1950s San Francisco, this truly offbeat tale concerns disk jockey Jim Briskin, his ex-wife Pat, and married teenagers Art and Rachael. Briskin loves his ex-wife, classical music, and rock & roll. Pat loves no one. Art and Rachael idolize Jim because he is a disk jockey. Jim, in turn, sees himself as something of a father figure for Art and pregnant Rachael. After Pat seduces Art, it remains to Jim and Rachael to save both themselves and the other two.

Nick and the Glimmung (1988)

Nick has a problem. He has a cat named Horace, and cats are quite illegal on Earth. In fact all pets are illegal on Earth, and Horace has been reported to the anti-pet man. The only way for Nick and his family to keep Horace is to emigrate to Plowman's Planet. Little did they know that, rather than the pastoral paradise Nick's father envisioned, they would land in the middle of a planetwide war against an entity known as Glimmung, a conflict in which Nick and Horace would play a pivotal role.

Nick and the Glimmung is Philip K. Dick's sole surviving young adult novel.

Gather Yourselves Together (1994)

Three American workers are left behind in China by their employer, biding their time in an abandoned factory as the communists approach. As they while away the days, both the young and naive Carl Fitter and the older, worldly Verne Tildon vie for the affections of Barbara Mahler, a woman who may not be as tough as she acts. But Carl's innocence and Verne's boorishness might drive Barbara away from both of them.

Cantata 140 (2003)

It's the year 2080, and Earth's seemingly insurmountable overpopulation problem has been alleviated temporarily by placing millions of people in voluntary deep freeze. But in election year, the pressure is on to find a solution which will enable them to resume their lives. For Jim Briskin, Presidential candidate, it seems an insoluble problem until a flaw in the new instantaneous travel system opens up the possibility of finding whole new worlds to colonize.

Voices from the Street (2007)

Stuart Hadley is a young radio electronics salesman in early 1950s Oakland, California. He has what many would consider the ideal life; a nice house, a pretty wife, a decent job with prospects for advancement, but he still feels unfulfilled; something is missing from his life. Hadley is an angry young man, an artist, a dreamer, a screw-up. He tries to fill his void first with drinking, and sex, and then with religious fanaticism, but nothing seems to be working, and it is driving him crazy. He reacts to the love of his wife and the kindness of his employer with anxiety and fear.

The Exegesis of Philip K. Dick (2011)

Edited By Pamela Jackson

Based on thousands of pages of typed and handwritten notes, journal entries, letters, and story sketches, The Exegesis of Philip K. Dick is the magnificent and imaginative final work of an author who dedicated his life to questioning the nature of reality and perception, the malleability of space and time, and the relationship between the human and the divine. Edited and introduced by Pamela Jackson and Jonathan Lethem, this is the definitive presentation of Dick's brilliant, and epic, work.

In the Exegesis, Dick documents his eight-year attempt to fathom what he called "2-3-74," a postmodern visionary experience of the entire universe "transformed into information." In entries that sometimes ran to hundreds of pages, in a freewheeling voice that ranges through personal confession, esoteric scholarship, dream accounts, and fictional fugues, Dick tried to write his way into the heart of a cosmic mystery that tested his powers of imagination and invention to the limit. This book is a continuation from ***In Pursuit of Valis: Selections From the Exegesis***, which was published in 1991.

Movies Based on Philip K. Dick Books and Short Stories

Blade Runner (1982) Director: Ridley Scott. Starring Harrison Ford, Rutger Hauer — Based on *Do Androids Dream of Electric Sheep*?

Total Recall (1990, Remade in 2012) Director: Paul Verhoeven. Starring: Arnold Schwarzenegger, Sharon Stone, 2012-Director: Len Wiseman. Starring: Colin Farrell, Bokeem Woodbine — Based on *We Can Remember it for you Wholesale.*

Barjo (1992) Director: Jérôme Boivin. Starring: Richard Bohringer, Anne Brochet - Based on *Confessions Of A Crap Artist*.

Screamers (1996) Director: Christian Duguay. Starring: Peter Weller, Roy Dupuis — Based on *Second Variety.*

The Gospel According to Philip K. Dick (2001) Documentary, Director: Mark Steensland.

Minority Report (2002) Director: Steven Spielberg. Starring: Tom Cruise, Colin Farrell - Based on *The Minority Report*.

Imposter (2002) Director: Gary Fleder. Starring: Shane Brolly, Vincent D'Onofrio - Based on *The Imposter*.

Paycheck (2003) Director: John Woo. Starring: Ben Affleck, Aaron Eckhart - Based on *Paycheck*.

A Scanner Darkly (2006) Director: Richard Linklater. Starring: Keanu Reeves, Winona Ryder - Based on *A Scanner Darkly*.

Next (2007) Director: Lee Tamahori. Starring: Nicolas Cage, Julianne Moore - Based on *The Golden Man*.

Radio Free Albemuth (2010) Director: John Alan Simon. Starring: Shea Whigham, Jonathan Scarfe - Based on *Radio Free Albemuth*.

The Adjustment Bureau (2011) Director: George Nolfi. Starring: Matt Damon, Emily Blunt - Based on *Adjustment Team*.

The Man in the High Castle (Started 2015, Amazon Streaming) Director: Various. Starring: Alexa Davalos, Rupert Evans – Based on *The Man in the High Castle.*

IN PREPARATION – A PLAY BASED ON THE IMAGINARY THOUGHTS OF PHILIP K. DICK – *THE DULL ARE THE DAMNED*

By Joseph Green

A member of the Coalition on Political Assassinations for a number of years, and currently on the Board of Directors of the Hidden History Center, Joe Green has produced two full-length books with articles on JFK, MLK, Malcolm X, as well as 9/11, Richard Nixon, and films like **The Parallax View** and **Blade Runner**. *Dissenting Views II* also features interviews with people ranging from Peter Bogdanovich to Bobby Seale and John Judge.

Green also served as a co-writer and co-producer of the film **King Kill 63**, starring Oliver Stone, which debuted at the Dallas International Film Festival in 2015. He has made two appearances on the "Ancient of Days" program hosted by Tessa Dick. Mr. Green is the author of the plays *Clowntime is Over*, *The Barrett Variations*, *Einstein's Wrong about Everything*, and *The Dull are the Damned*, based upon the intellectual thoughts of Philip K. Dick, one of Green's literary heroes.

Joe Green and satirist and UFO believer Dick Gregory, who once took a photo of a UFO.

The following is a sampling of the dialogue from one of the scenes.

(Copyright Joseph Green)

PHIL:

I once wrote a story – once upon a time, I wrote a story – about a murder plot in which a scientist figures out that consciousness survives death. It survives death, however, not as a ghost or a celestial figure floating about but in that lump of grey inside the skull, and although the impulses stop, the brain remains alive, absorbing information but unable to direct action. The story was called "Hades" because the Greeks had this notion that death was an eternal nightmare, it wasn't comforting at all, completely defeating the alleged psychological purpose of generating after-death fantasies. Anyway, the only way to get rid of consciousness is to destroy the brain completely via cremation, so all those people are very wise, whereas everyone who gets buried is sentencing themselves to years and years of pointless torture in the grave until the brain rots sufficiently so as to no longer exist. Then, only then, comes peace. In the story the scientist decides to murder his enemy and, knowing what he knows about death, keeps his body around in a basement and torments him in various ways by showing him everything he's missing. Only the lack of response eventually drives him mad – he knows that the torture is working but he's unable to observe it – and, as we all know from physics, observation is what matters in this universe. We are nothing without the universe, but it needs us, too. (beat) There are times now that I get confused about whether I wrote the story, whether I am the scientist who made the discovery, or whether I am dead and my brain is generating all this content just to keep away the dirt in my box.

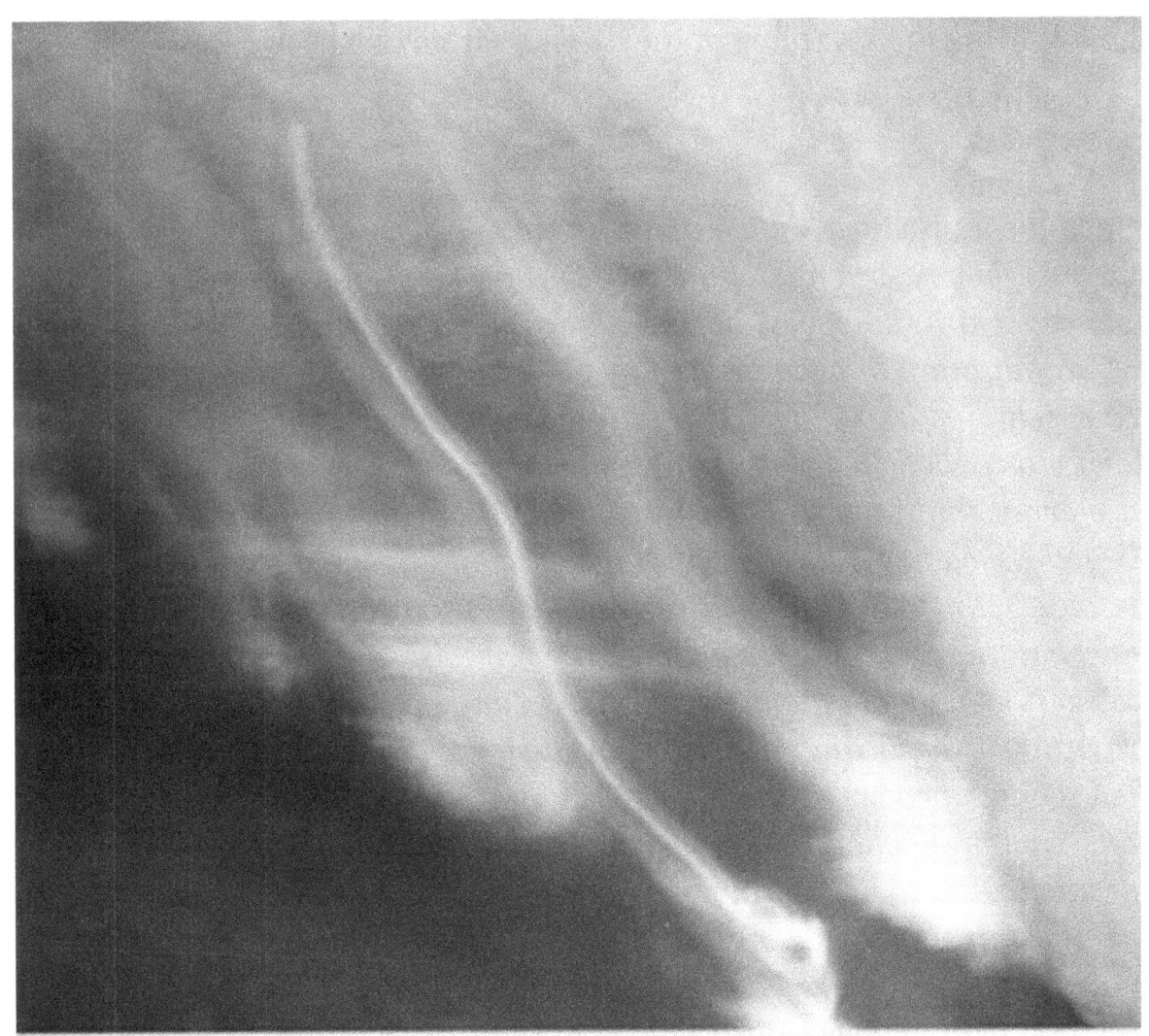

THE DULL ARE THE DAMNED

a play

Joseph E. Green

For our FREE catalog of books and other items of interest, send your name and mailing address to:

Global Communications
P.O. Box 753
New Brunswick, NJ 08903

Email: mrufo8@hotmail.com

www.conspiracyjournal.com

Mr UFOs Secret Files YouTube Channel
www.youtube.com/user/MRUFO1100

MOST BOOKS ARE PRINTED IN LARGE EASY TO READ FORMAT, AND FULLY ILLUSTRATED

FASTER THAN THE SPEED OF LIGHT!

THE TOP SECRET SCIENCE OF TOMORROW IS HERE TODAY!

Time Travel
Teleportation
Dimension Jumping
Invisibility

THESE TITLES AVAILABLE BASED UPON CONFIDENTIAL INFORMATION DERIVED FROM KGB, CIA AND CHINESE WHISTLEBLOWERS

❏ NAZI TIME TRAVELERS

Whistle blower indicates UFO that crashed outside Roswell might have been part of a secret Nazi space/time travel program covered up by CIA to make it look like an out of control space ship crashed. The top brass were looking to cover their tracks in regard to allowing Nazi engineers and rocket scientists into the US illegally under Project Paperclip. Evidence Nazis had been in contact with Aryan space beings who assisted in developing an advanced "flying disc" technology on advice from members of a German secret society the Vril. —$20.00

❏ TIME TRAVEL FACT NOT FICTION

Einstein had part of the equation correct but did not consider what has become known as the "string theory" of physics which says that everything in the universe exists simultaneously. In this work by Commander X and Tim Swartz a variety of topics are discussed, including: Spontaneous Cases of Time Travel. — Mystery of Time Slips. — Doorways in Time. — People, Buildings and Towns From Beyond Time. — The Restaurant At The Edge Of Time. — Flight Into The Future. — Is Death A Jump in Time? — Are UFOs Time Machines? — Working Time Machines — Nikola Tesla's Time Travel Experiments —$20.00

❏ TELEPORTATION – HOW-TO GUIDE FROM STAR TREK TO TESLA

Commander X says it is possible to master the art of teleportation. The well-known phrase, "Beam me up, Scotty" now has a rational application, the term Teleportation actually having been coined by the world famous researcher of unexplained mysteries, Charles Fort. The author says he worked on a secret teleportation project inside Area 51 in which a "beam ship" did a bit of "dimension jumping" while he was at the controls. Book contains experiences you can participate in.—$16.00

❏ Add $13 for OFFICIAL U.S.MANUAL ON TELEPORTATION released by Air Force Research Laboratories.

❏ TRAVEL TO OTHER DIMENSIONS

Discover how to: ** Become One With The Light — ** Discover The Reality Of Other Dimensions and Planes — ** What You Will Find On The Seven Planes Of Existence — ** Traveling In And Out Of Your Body At Will — ** Entering The Region Of The Disembodied, And The Sacred Resting Place Of The Soul — ** Life And Work On The Astral. –** Find Out The Entities You Are Likely To Encounter. –** What It Is Like To Mingle With Disembodied Souls, and learn to contact the spiritual teachers.—$18.00

❏ LEVITATION AND INVISIBILITY

This book is NOT to be used for unlawful or immoral purposes! Can we learn to fly through the air with the greatest of ease? Is it possible to walk through walls or other solid objects? Now thanks to Tim R. Swartz and retired military intelligence operative Commander X, working in tandem with various sages, shamans and adapts, we are prepared to proclaim the secrets to fulfilling these mystical "dreams" are at hand. Contents Include: ++ The Quest For Instant Invisibility. ++ What Is In The Mysterious Mist? ++ The Realm of Invulnerability. ++ Prayers and Spells For Invisibility. ++ Spiritualists And Mystics Who Have Proven They Possess Incredible Talents.—$21/95

❏ **SUPER SPECIAL**
Everything listed on this page PLUS A FREE Audio CD just $89.00 + $8 S/H

TIMOTHY G BECKLEY, BOX 753 NEW BRUNSWICK, NJ. 08903

WE ACCEPT MONEY ORDERS · CHECKS · PAYPAL (mrufo8@hotmail.com) Credit Cards: 732-602-3407

REVEALED FOR THE FIRST TIME: THE TRUE IDENTITY OF THE MYSTERIOUS WHISTLE BLOWER KNOWN AS. . .
COMMANDER X

WILL THE REAL COMMANDER X PLEASE STAND UP!

NEW! – COMMANDER X FILES UPDATED

For more than a decade the mysterious Commander X has caused dissension among conspiracy theorists, Area 51 aficionados and UFO believers. Some accept his hair-raising accounts of working behind the scenes with the CIA, the NSA and other government and quasi-federal agencies at face value, while others scratch their heads in bewilderment and wonder if his first-hand chronicles cannot be linked to a disinformation program.

For the first time, here is the complete dossier on Commander X's many exploits both with various groups of highly aggressive ultra-terrestrials, as well as his battle with our own earthly authorities hell-bent on keeping these matters TOP SECRET! –

Included among the many shocking – and surprising – revelations in this book:

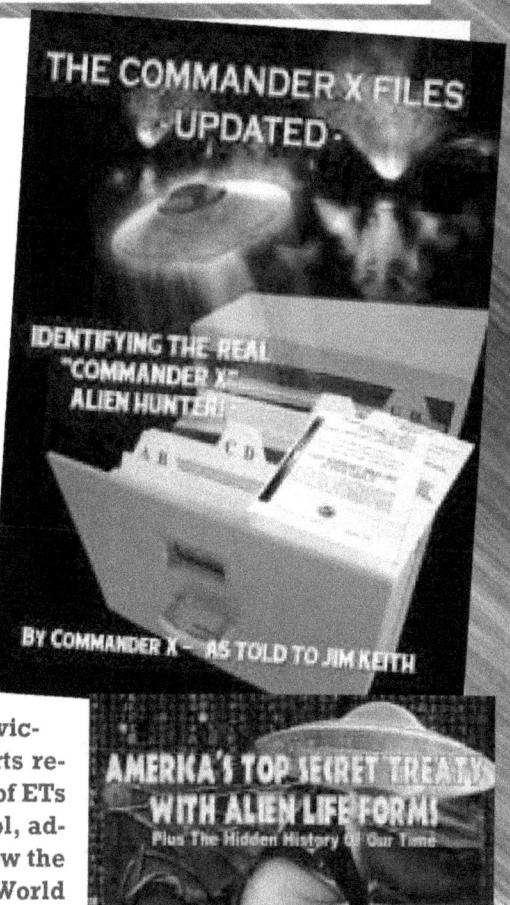

** The Alien Dinosaur Connection. – ** Who inhabits the Subterranean Regions of Earth? – ** Evidence suggests human victims were still alive, when their blood was drained and body parts removed in underground UFO bases. – ** The many special powers of ETs – including levitation, dematerialization, invisibility, mind control, advanced light beam technology. **A Nazi – Alien collaboration. How the Occult inner circle of the Third Reich contacted grey aliens before World War II using ritual magic. – ** Evidence Hitler shipped equipment and slave laborers to the Antarctic to construct a fleet of flying saucers. – ** Proof that the Nazis transferred into the midst of the American spy and space agencies.

AND MOST IMPORTANT OF ALL – ARE HUMAN CLONES GOING TO BE USED TO REPLACE ASSASSINATED POLITICIANS?

Only Commander X can dare answer these questions.
❏ Order THE COMMANDER X FILES - Large Format. 200+ Pages – $24.00.

❏ NEW! – AMERICA'S TOP SECRET TREATY WITH ALIEN LIFE FORMS – PLUS THE HIDDEN HISTORY OF OUR TIME!

Is The "Treaty" A "False Flag?" – Or Some CIA Sponsored "Smoke Screen?" They arrived without our knowledge or consent and told our military leaders they came in peace for the benefit of humankind, and would gladly start an exchange program with the people of the planet earth which could lead to a "Golden Age." We wholeheartedly believed them and agreed to the "Treaty" almost without any sort of protest. Then they began to abduct our women! Then they returned for our children! Soon after they began to rape the earth's resources! And it became apparent they ultimately wanted to control our minds and capture our souls for their selfish reasons, some too horrific to comprehend.

And because they are too embarrassed to admit they went along with this Treaty, the U.S. government and the military industrial complex refuse to let the public know what has been going on for nearly half a century, keeping a tight lid on this Treaty and its various "exchange programs." But now there might be a ray of hope thanks to the whistle blower known as Commander X. This is your opportunity to find out about the"Treaty," and protect yourself and your loved ones from a possible "enemy attack" that could come out of the sky, as predicted by Nostradamus, as detailed in the Book of Revelations.

Find Out The Truth For Yourself by ordering SECRET TREATY WITH ALIENS.
❏ Large Format – 186 Pages – $20.00.
❏ **SPECIAL: BOTH NEW BOOKS BY COMMANDER X - $39.00 + $5 S/H**
TIMOTHY G. BECKLEY, BOX 753, NEW BRUNSWICK, NJ 08903

www.ingramcontent.com/pod-product-compliance
Lightning Source LLC
Chambersburg PA
CBHW080357170426
43193CB00016B/2741